YEAR OF THE RAT

BOOK 1

Lunar New Years

Christian Adams

Disclaimer

This work is based on real events that occurred in real locations between real people. The author wishes the reader to know that certain names, dates, locations, and genders have been obscured or altered in a way that is not unrecognizable but, more accurately, not-accurate. Therefore, all characters in this work are technically fictitious; any resemblance to real persons, living or dead, is arguably coincidental. Some events in this work were referenced from the author's journals, diaries, and the best recollection, knowledge, and photographic evidence of said events, i.e., completely unreliable but not entirely the product of the narrator's imagination. Meanwhile, certain products, trade, and/or brand names appear in the narrative, mentioned without malice. Any statistical claims without a gratuitous reference can be considered subjective and a result of the author's speculation and/or bias toward (or against) statistics in general. Please do not encourage digital piracy and copyright infringement by copying or reproducing this work.

Dedication

For every living creature who is part of this story, whether they like it or not.

For my dearest mother, who would have been thrilled to read this book but horrified by half of what's in it.

For my wife and son.

Table Of Contents

In the Chinese zodiac, the Year of the Rat symbolizes prosperity and new beginnings.

1

You're Not Getting Any Younger

Going strictly by the book, an expatriate (expat) is a person voluntarily away from their home or country of origin. Likewise, the verb, to expatriate, is to establish and adopt a residence abroad. In both cases, the word has neutral connotations. One final definition refers to people who have been forcefully expelled from a country, and that is not what I'm talking about here.

One of the more common stereotypes about expats is we're losers who couldn't make it in our home countries, so we left for a place with a welcome mat for washouts. A place that values certain inherent individual skills such as language ability. A place where a pulse and a college degree are all you need to make the nut, where washouts are a necessary but not entirely beneficial part of the machine. It's a misinformed stereotype because one size does not fit all in the expatriate spectrum. There are just as many upstanding characters overseas as surly, drunken savages. Plus, a lot depends on the location of the expats in question, and that's where the *sexpat* angle comes in. Expats may visit Pattaya, Thailand, to engage in sex tourism, but only sexpats live there. These are two totally different things.

Anyway, it's unfortunate that yours truly, Charlie Birch, fits the expat "washout" stereotype to an arguably important degree, except it's not that I couldn't make it at home. I just didn't want to *stay* home. And in some respects, I was making it at home—in a soul-crushing, responsible adult, paying-the-rent sort of way. "Making it" was never enough for me.

We shouldn't be giving out awards for surviving unless you've beaten cancer or faced and conquered other insurmountable obstacles.

Above all, I left because I had the means and motivation, a U.S. passport, and a sense of nothing to lose.

According to the geographic trajectory of my life, I've mostly been heading west. Conceived in New York State, I was born and raised in Chicago, Illinois, where I bounced around for 30 years. Following my first "big move," I spent the next decade in San Francisco, California. At 40 years old, I moved to Southeast Asia, where I have been ever since. Once I established a home base in Taipei, Taiwan, the westward movement continued, with frequent travels to China, Thailand, and the Philippines. Technically, my last move from Taipei to Metro Manila, was the first time I'd ever moved significantly in a southeasterly direction.

Growing up in the sheltered and comfortable suburbs of Chicago, I was primarily driven by the idea of "getting out." Some people were content to stay in the bubble, but I couldn't spend the entirety of my existence within a 15-mile radius of Darien, Illinois. At the same time, I wasn't completely sure where I wanted to go, just...somewhere else. Many of my peers had a similar compulsion to leave, and there were several ways to achieve freedom. Some kids went to college and got jobs in other cities. I dropped out of college and started a rock band.

Traveling is a wondrous and life-changing experience, but children don't have a lot of say in the deal. For the most part, your parents decide where you're going, when you're going, and how you're gonna get there. My father worked for "The Railroad"–Atchison, Topeka & Santa Fe Railway–which gave him certain travel privileges that allowed our family to traverse the country by train several times before I was old enough to remember the trips.

Meanwhile, family vacations are mandatory unless indicated otherwise, aren't they? I've never met *anybody* whose family vacations were optional. It wasn't my idea to pack the whole crew into a Pontiac station wagon and drive 24 hours from Chicago to Oklahoma City, stopping overnight at a Motel 6 just off Interstate 80 in Lincoln, Nebraska. But there I was in the backseat, bitching, "Explain to me, again, why we couldn't have taken the train?"

There wasn't much of a choice when it came to semi-independent travel, either. My folks said, "You're going to summer camp in Burlington, Wisconsin, for two weeks in July. Deal with it." Et cetera.

Of course, I was happy to get out of town—for any reason. Even if Camp McLean was gonna suck, nothing but mosquitos, sunburns, and bed-wetters on the top bunk, I was kinda looking forward to summer camp. *I needed to travel*, that's all that mattered. The childhood and adolescent travel gauntlets are full of regrettable trips. Did I enjoy spending two weeks at my uncle's house in Boulder, Colorado? Not really. Would my life be complete without riding a donkey in the Grand Canyon? I think so. But I realized that any travel was good travel, and autonomous travel decisions would be mine to make very soon.

This is the story of how I became an expat and where it led me. This is also the story that fought me every step of the journey. Uncountable false starts and half-written drafts languish in the file directories of over a dozen USB flash drives in my possession. And I kept asking myself, why is it so hard to write this story? The self-doubting devil whispered, "Maybe there isn't a story here."

During my first return visit to the States, I realized that my friends weren't very interested in hearing about my life overseas. They were far more interested in discussing their lives and the comings and goings of home. They'd pepper me with a few questions before steering the conversation to something in the here and now. Anytime I started talking unprompted about my travels, I could see my friends mentally "switch off." They tuned out.

Somewhat of a sensitive soul and slightly ego-bruised by their disinterest in my travels, I kept most of my stories to myself for many years. Today, I see things from my friends' perspective. No matter your circumstances, you're involved in your singular little world and consumed with your life story. You don't need some joker like me to spike your snow globe with foreign elements. Aside from the general details, what use does *anybody* have for my stories? The novelty wears off quickly. Even if I could entertain my friends with tales of expat experience, it wasn't like they were gonna visit me anytime soon.

Some people are naturally curious about life, and others develop curiosity as they get older. Many people are indifferent to the origins and conditions of other people from faraway locations. Without curiosity, the indifferent don't strike up conversations with strangers in airport bars. They don't venture too far out of their comfort zones, not because they're cowardly or timid, but because they don't see any material value in taking abstract and ephemeral risks. It's much easier and safer to nurture and protect life at home and be a strict gatekeeper about what comes in and goes out.

The second-most critical moment of this story came in the timeline vicinity of my 39th year on the planet. I'm not happy about having to lay it all out like counterfeit merchandise at a flea market, but none of this happens unless you understand my circumstances before I left San Francisco for Taipei.

From the age of 19 to roughly 39 years old, I was first and foremost a musician who formed a series of independent rock bands that achieved little in the way of record sales, popularity, or critical acclaim—in a word, success. All those bands were good at what we did, but we were crippled by a litany of faults and failures that just about anybody who's ever been in a band can relate to. For one example, we were abject hobos when it came to self-promotion. We'd print 500 flyers for a gig and halfheartedly post 50 in places nobody would bother looking. That kind of bullshit. We thought our music was so good that people would appear at our shows by miraculous word of mouth. Suffice it to say, the word never spread.

Twenty years is a fair amount of time chasing the proverbial brass ring without success. In the meantime, I supported myself (and sometimes the band's activities) by working a prolific series of jobs in a diverse range of industries, including but not limited to:

Barback, barista, bartender, busboy, carpenter's apprentice, delivery driver (pizza, office supplies), doorman, dishwasher, entertainer, ESL teacher, file clerk, food runner, fry cook at McDonald's, general construction laborer, general manager of small Italian bistro, grocery clerk, guitar teacher, hardware salesman, janitor, landscape designer, landscaper, maintenance man, manager of a coffee shop, mover, office temp (multiple positions), parking lot attendant, personal assistant, phone clerk at a brokerage company, prep cook at a country club, psychic adviser, publisher's intern, retail clerk at K-Mart, runner at the Chicago

Board of Trade, quasi-sommelier, sound engineer, substitute high school English teacher, telemarketing job recruiter, tour guide, valet, waiter/server, warehouse order picker, window washer

I'm reluctant to introduce this information, but here it comes. Starting in adolescence and continuing with a vengeance throughout adulthood, I've been an avid consumer of drugs and alcohol. Let's not waste time parsing the degrees of abuse and addiction. For most of my adult life, I've been a highly functional alcoholic and drug abuser. Granted, I lost one or two menial jobs because I was too hungover to show up for work. And I failed a few pre-hiring drug tests. But no matter how the booze and dope may have hurt me, they helped me in uncountable ways. I wouldn't be where I am without them.

At the time of my 39th birthday, I was living alone in the Sunset District of San Francisco, working as a server in a swanky downtown restaurant and making decent money for not a lot of work. Director and comedian Woody Allen once said that 80 percent of life is simply showing up, i.e., a big part of success is starting something, be it a conversation or a new job. Ostensibly, the remaining 20 percent is how you behave once you get there. Showing up was *90 percent* of that restaurant gig.

Never married, no kids. I shuffled through a series of relationships and remained happily single. My last band folded a year earlier, but I converted my apartment into a home recording studio and continued to make music. And drink myself blind and take stupid combinations of drugs to the point that waking up naked on the sidewalk in front of my house at four o'clock in the morning was just another Thursday.

I started to feel something like a mid-life crisis kicking in. I didn't know it was a mid-life crisis, but I was certainly having an extended period of *intentional self-introspection.* Nudge, wink. My drug use and experimentation had escalated, but it wasn't alleviating the pervasive sense of emptiness in my life. It's a clichéd sort of theme, but there was a moment when I stopped and said, "What the fuck am I doing?"

Sadly, I looked back on the years. *Man, what a pathetic waste. I've achieved exactly nothing. I'm camped out here at the beach, getting wasted every night, staying high at work, making music that nobody is ever going to hear. I'm sucking up oxygen and nutrients, making zero positive or negative contributions to society at large. A black hole of human existence. No good to anybody. Is this how it's going to be? Is this what I want to do for the rest of my life?*

For whatever reason, I couldn't talk openly about depression with my friends. They were about the same age and dealing with their own demons and struggles. I didn't respond to previous attempts for professional help, and frankly, I couldn't afford it. And I realized, thankfully, that I'd have to wrangle this "crisis" on my own.

On the morning of my 39th birthday, I promised myself that I would not be 40 years old, selling lamb chops and marked-up bottles of wine to rich people, living in a ground-level flat near the beach in San Francisco, doing pointless drugs and drinking myself slowly to death. I typed, printed, and signed the promise, and taped it to the top half of the refrigerator—the freezer section—not ironically, where I kept my stash of marijuana, opiates, psychedelics, and a bottle of Stolichnaya vodka. The promise stood as a nagging reminder: the clock is ticking.

✳

There's no getting around the fact that some of this is going to make me look good, and some of it's going to make me look really, really bad. You might see both happen simultaneously. I hope my ever-present self-awareness will convince you to reserve judgment until you've heard the whole story.

It's safe to say that I'm an independent thinker who makes choices and lives with the consequences. Yet, prompting from external forces informed many of the important decisions in my life. In most cases, somebody said the right thing at the right time or exactly what I needed (or didn't need) to hear at a crucial moment of indecision or vulnerability.

At 31 years old, shortly before I moved from Chicago to San Francisco in the late 1990s, my grandmother gifted me a modest, five-figure sum of money. No strings attached. This windfall arrived at the tail end of an era. After a decade of trying and failing to scrape together a professional music career, I finally reached the point where I didn't want to do it anymore. Now, you must separate making music from the process of forging a career—they're not even remotely compatible. Music was my first true passion, but the ridiculously improbable dream of becoming a rock star was dead. I didn't even want to be a "rock star." I just wanted to be *somebody*. There were a hundred reasons why shit didn't work out, but to be justly harsh on myself, it was time to grow up and embrace some version of adulthood.

While discussing the money and my future, my mother said, "Before you spend anything, tell me something. What's your biggest regret?"

"Dropping out of college." *No doubt, nothing else even came close.*

"And why is that, dear?" My mother was fond of the smug, I-told-you-so approach.

I don't know what planet you're on, Mom, but down here on Earth, dropping out of college at 19 to start a rock band is generally considered a terrible idea.

"Because I want a college degree," I replied, "so maybe I can go overseas and find a job somewhere. See the world. Maybe I'll write a book about it." This was prophetic and true. Aside from music, traveling and writing were the only other things I wanted to do and the only other things I knew *how* to do. The previous decade was a constant cycle of moving from place to place. I started a rock band at 19 because I thought it was my fastest ticket to seeing the world. College seemed like a slow boat out of town.

Meanwhile, my mother said, "Uh-huh. Yes, of course," and the discussion flowed to a speedy conclusion.

Mom: You should go back to school. Get your degree.
Me: But it probably wouldn't be wise for me to stay in Chicago.
Mom: No...it probably wouldn't. Where do you want to go?
Me: California.
Mom: That sounds like a wonderful idea!

The next step was calling my good friend, Chet Monroe, who'd lived in San Francisco since the early 1990s. Chet hosted my first two visits to S.F. in 1997 and '98. We'd been friends for a long time, and I trusted him more than anybody. He understood the California bug. San Francisco was a magical place where anything was possible, and everything was fair game. All I needed was a slight but meaningful bump from someone whose opinion mattered to me.

I said to Chet, "Dude, I'm thinking about moving out there to finish my degree."

Chet said, "You should definitely do that."

It may sound improbable, but my exposure to substance abuse started as a toddler. My Opa (German for grandpa) was a robust Old World soldier who served in two world wars, left Germany after World War I, and carved out a life for himself and his family in the New World of America. Like many immigrants of his generation, Opa was a proud man who didn't suffer fools or insubordination.

By the time my older sister and I came around, Opa was in his late 60s. The heartless grind of his life had caught up with him. Now in retirement, Opa basically sat around the house drinking Old Style beer and barking at Oma, his long-suffering farm girl from Schneidemühle, and probably the only saint I've ever known.

This is what my parents told me. I was maybe two years old when it started. Once a month, my parents would send us to Oma and Opa's house in Cicero (IL) for a Friday night or the weekend. Oma went to Koehl's Delicatessen on Austin Boulevard for daily rations every morning except Sundays. My sister Anne was old enough to ambulate on her own, so Oma would take her along for the walk, leaving me, a mercurial toddler, in the care of Opa, who was a super good guy—nothing untoward about him—but he had zero experience handling a toddler. When I started crying inconsolably, Opa turned to the Old World remedy. He spoon-fed me beer until I calmed down and fell asleep.

One Sunday afternoon, I was roughly four years old, everybody was at our house in Clarendon Hills for dinner. My sister accidentally pushed me down the stairs. Uncle Fred saw the whole thing. "Poor kid took a header on that bottom step!" While the women tried to squash my crying, Opa said, "Just give the kid some beer. It works, trust me."

In the language of the times, my mother was a "spitfire" and a "pistol." She wasn't afraid of *anybody*. "You've been giving beer to the kid? Are you fucking kidding me?" There was a massive blowup. Opa stormed out and told my father that he would never set foot in our house again. Or, as my father recalled, in German, "never rest his legs under your table"—if my mother was still in the picture, and my mother wasn't going anywhere, for now. Of course, there was far more history, but this was the final breaking point in the relationship. It was several years before Opa returned to our house, shortly before he died of leukemia in 1977.

Around the ages of eight and five years old, respectively, Anne and I were out in the garage, perusing a second refrigerator used mostly for beer, soda, jugs of wine, and leftovers. Anne grabbed a beer from the shelf, cracked it open, handed it to me, and said, "Drink this." Like a good little dummy who usually followed the older sibling, I pounded the beer like a champ. And 20 minutes later, they found me face down in the backyard. My mother was beside herself. Even though it was my sister's doing, Mom blamed Opa, who wasn't anywhere in sight. Regardless, I learned something important about beer: I enjoyed the warm sensation in my tummy and the soft feeling in my brain. It tasted pretty good, too.

Generally, the above incidents notwithstanding, my parents partied as hard as the 1970s and 80s weekend warriors could manage—within reason. Rolling with a sizeable social crew from the neighborhood, there was a party or a "get-together" (as my mother loved to say), every weekend. And if you've ever seen a 1970s American television sitcom with "cool" and "hip" cats lounging around in corduroy and polyester jumpsuits, listening to disco, Tupperware transactions, drinking goddamn sangria, and using "jive slang" to discuss politics—that was it. Even though my parents didn't smoke, other people smoked in our crib at will. We had a bookshelf dedicated to artsy ceramic ashtrays that my mother couldn't wait to bust out for her friends.

Several uneventful years went by. Anne was 13 years old when she got caught smoking pot. She smoked cigarettes at age 10—we had free and easy access to cigs back then—and graduated to marijuana at 12. The girl was ahead of her time, or advanced or mature for her age. Getting busted only boosted her determination to do as she pleased. I was 11 when we first got high together. I can't say I "got high" the first few times we smoked weed, but I know I got light-headed.

I don't blame my older sister because I could have said no, but it was her idea to start raiding the beer in the garage refrigerator (and stashing the empties in the basement). We got away with it for a while, maybe a month, until one night, my father had some friends over for Monday

Night Football. He went out to the fridge, thinking he had cases of Old Style and Stroh's on hand, only to find a couple of stray cans on the top shelf. And once again, hell rained down from above. But while my sister denied it, I confessed to drinking my share of the beer, and my father was so proud of me for telling the truth that he suspended my punishment until further notice.

Meanwhile, my mother got sucked into a hardcore Jesus freak mindset around 1978-79. The spell lasted for just under a year before she tired of all the Bible study and volunteer work at church. "Her heart wasn't in it," my father deadpanned.

Everything got weird and Republican in the Eighties. Unfortunately for us, my mother developed a newfound intolerance for her children and their antics. Along with some other "concerned parents" in town, my mother formed a watchdog-type anti-drug group that might as well have been a terrorist organization. Without any religious affiliation, they were just plain mean people. Going around to school functions, passing out brochures like "What to Do If Your Child is on Drugs" and "How to Spot a Drug User in Your House." That lasted another year or two before Mom got bored with it. Either that, or she realized she was only making a bad situation worse. She embarrassed us, which canceled out all the cool stuff she did when she wasn't being a tyrant. Bless her soul, my mother tried so hard to be a good person.

My sister got her driver's license in 1981, and that's when our home life spun out of control. My mom and sister had a violent, messed-up relationship, and I spent most of my energy trying to stay out of their way. At the same time, I couldn't avoid Anne's influence. She turned me on to weed (and later became my first drug dealer). She gave me my first "upper" (speed). She gave me flasks of Southern Comfort to drink at school. Most kids had peer pressure—I had sibling pressure.

So, we're talking 1982-83, my sister is 17 now, and she's a train wreck. Hypocrisy and mixed signals were on the family menu. We could drink one glass of wine every Sunday with dinner, but my sister would get grounded for a month if she came home with alcohol on her breath, which she did, all the time. Grounding didn't work with Anne because she would walk out the front door and disappear for two days. She didn't give a single fuck. Two months before her 18th birthday and a quarter's worth of credits shy of graduating from high school, Anne left home for good. I didn't see her again for nearly two years, and when I did, she offered me an eighth of pot for $25.

It's nonchalant to say, "This is how it all started," but this is how it started. With my sister out of the family portrait for the time being, my parents gave me a wide berth. No more pressure about drinking and doing drugs. It was almost like they didn't care. At the same time, I was a decent athlete for a few years, so I couldn't be partying all the time anyway. Oh, and believe it or not, in the middle of all this, I joined the Boy Scouts and made the rank of Eagle Scout. There were all kinds of drug and alcohol-related sidebars we could get into. As a junior in high school, I was smoking pot every day. And *smoking* was never a problem. *Getting* weed was the problem.

Recreational drugs were moderately available in the western suburbs of Chicago. We had access to marijuana, cocaine, acid (LSD), speed, and sometimes, mushrooms. Now and then, somebody would score some hash or brown crystal meth. My friends and I had a partying ethos, and we all came from relatively comparable socio-economic backgrounds. We took risks and accepted the consequences. Occasionally, someone would get pinched with a quarter pound of weed or something, but overall, it was part and parcel of growing up. Everybody was doing it. Most parents said, "Oh, those kids are just experimenting."

My problems—and I hate to think of them as problems because they were fun and unusual circumstances—started in my senior year of high school when my friends and I started taking LSD and doing coke on weekends. When we were tripping during weekdays, I stopped going to school altogether. Part of "my problem" was wanting to impress people with my unpredictable wild card-type character. Like an intellectual burnout, not giving a fuck was a big part of my reputation. High school was a big joke to me, and academically speaking, vice versa. I was admitted to Illinois State University only by the grace of respectable ACT and SAT scores. Otherwise, I graduated 456 out of 468 in my class.

College was a foregone conclusion from different perspectives. For my parents, it was a given that I would attend college for four years and get a degree. For me, it was only a matter of time until I dropped out. So, in the meantime, it was a paid vacation. And what do you do on vacation? You party. Hard.

My freshman year of college would have been a complete waste of time if I hadn't gone completely off the fuckin' rails, which I did, with aplomb. If I was "experimenting" with drugs and booze in high school, I was producing scientific results in college. If it weren't for my parents' profound disappointment, I'd say it was one of the most fun years of my life. *Why stop now?* I thought. *How can I keep this party train rolling?*

Drop out and start a band!

⋆✶⋆

I learned to play drums in the junior high jazz band and taught myself to play guitar and piano as a teen. At the age of 19, I was a budding songwriter. Several of my friends had also dropped out of college. We were kicking around the suburbs, talking about forming a band. Eventually, we got a group together and started playing shows. It was ugly. We were awful in the beginning. But by the time we were legal age (21) to play the big clubs in Chicago, just before the Seattle grunge movement, we'd been together for nearly three years, playing all original material. We started attracting attention from music business types. We were going places we'd never imagined, even if those places sucked. That meant *everything* to me.

As the scenery changed, so did the landscape of our social lives. Drugs—mainly weed—were a daily and necessary part of the experience. We lived hand-to-mouth, practicing five nights a week, working shitty part-time jobs, and leaving a trail of destruction in our path. In 1992, we were invited to play a music festival in New York City under the guise of signing a dubious record deal. During the trip, there was a drug-fueled fight between me and the bass player, Jimmy Roseland, my best friend since freshman year of high school. The record deal didn't materialize, and the animosity between me and Jimmy got worse. The band folded in 1994. I never spoke to Jimmy again.

With the other two band members, Tom Taylor and Jason Weisman, I started a new band and relocated to the north side of Chicago. Once removed from the suburbs, we found new connections and friends. We developed some notoriety. People *knew who we were*; they just didn't come to our shows. We put out our records, had songs appear on compilations, and played some high-profile gigs. Another five years passed, and our collective and individual substance abuse reached professional levels. In late 1998, we released a record that we thought was going to be a big deal. It wasn't.

That was the end of life in Chicago for me. I had been in the game for over a decade with nothing to show for it—except, of course, a bunch of records nobody heard or bought and a drug and alcohol problem.

The situation with Tom and Jason is a story for another time. Those guys are still my brothers, and I love them to death. But they knew the score. They had demons to wrestle with, too. Our ship was sinking, and the captain—yours truly—was ordering everybody into the lifeboats.

My grandmother gave me the money in early 1999, and I left town. Tom was smart. A few months later, he followed me to San Francisco. Jason stayed in Chicago. I didn't look back.

★ ✱ ★

Moving to S.F. was the smartest thing I'd ever done. Most importantly, it took me three years, but I got a college degree at 34. Think about that for a second. I'm on the campus of San Francisco State University every day, like a proper goddamn student. Three years of bouncing from statistics to psychology on Mondays and Wednesdays. Tuesday and Thursday mornings in a lecture hall for astronomy. Friday afternoons in a theater watching films about art history. Working nights in a fancy restaurant and banging out homework during pre-dawn bong sessions.

And this is one of the parts where I'm going to look bad.

When I went back for a degree in creative writing, my career path was heading toward teaching, which is not something I ever wanted to do. Honest. My friend Chet Monroe was a special education teacher, and I reluctantly jumped on the teaching train during my undergraduate studies, which included school observations and education courses. My initial goal was to get the most painless degree possible, and I asked myself, what straight job could I be good at? And the answer was writing. Creative writing, to make it even easier. While teaching was one of the few viable career paths for a creative writer, I hoped to find something more fulfilling. I guess. I dunno.

I grew up thinking of myself as a musician, which involves a few axiomatic statements and situations, one of which is courtesy of George Bernard Shaw:

"Those who can, do; those who can't, teach."

By pursuing the teaching profession, I had to admit that I couldn't make it as a musician—a semi-conscious confession of failure. Consequently, I didn't go into teaching with a proper mindset, which should have been helping kids learn.

After graduating, I passed the CBEST (California Basic Educational Skills Test) and worked as a substitute English teacher for two summer school sessions in Half Moon Bay, California, an experience that all but ended my teaching career. Aside from one troubling incident with a suicidal student, nothing genuinely bad happened. I was simply a poor teacher who realized that teaching might not be for me. In turn, I dropped out of the teaching credential program at San Francisco State and applied to a handful of graduate writing programs. I was unceremoniously rejected by all three. In one of my worst and most embarrassing displays of foolishness, I showed up hammered—half drunk and high on heroin—to an interview for the Master of Fine Arts program at the University of San Francisco. The irresponsible and dysfunctional execution of the incident haunts me today.

I worked at the restaurant throughout my studies, but the part-time gig was merely an enjoyable utility. Suddenly, waiting tables seemed like a viable career path—for now—while I...continued to write? I'm not sure what I was thinking. So, I went to the general manager of the restaurant and asked, "Hey, can you start scheduling me full-time?" And he said, "Sure, dude."

A couple of years went by. I'm now 36 years old, college-educated, working four dinner shifts and one lunch shift at the restaurant during any given week, meaning I rarely spent more than 40 hours per week in the joint, and I was high for nearly every minute on the clock. I'd do a couple of bong hits before leaving for work, arrive high, and step out the back door every 90 minutes to take a quick one-hit of weed. And it was an open secret among my managers and co-workers. Nobody cared. Do the job, high or not-high. One night, I was getting salty with a regular barfly when the on-duty manager pulled me aside and said, "The fuck is wrong with you? Go get high and chill out already."

Meanwhile, working in a restaurant with a full bar is pretty much an open bar if you got in good with the bartenders, half of whom were drinking through the shift. To get on the good side of a bartender, follow these three simple rules:

Rule 1: Always be nice unless the bartender says otherwise. Don't be a dick unless you're asked to match the energy. Keep in mind that one bartender's "hello" is another bartender's "go fuck yourself." Tread carefully but be ready to swing when called upon.

Rule 2: Figure out which staff members the bartender in question doesn't like and don't like them, either.

Rule 3: Don't be greedy. Wait for the bartender to offer the first drink of the night unless your hands are visibly shaking, even when you're trying to keep them still. Then, and only then, can you go to the bartender and plead, "Help me out, brother!" Likewise, if the shots aren't flowing on a particular evening, don't push it. They'll explain later.

By 10:30 p.m. on any given night, I would be rocking a solid buzz on the dining room floor—a 4.2 on the 10-point spectrum of inebriation.

When my last table cleared out, I'd pop over to the tavern around the corner, joining my fellow restaurant drones for obligatory post-shift beverages. I'd throw down a couple of cans of Pabst Blue Ribbon—just a little something for the ride home—and either pick up a 12-pack of beer at the 7-Eleven near my house or open a bottle of wine upon returning to my crib. The night would be just getting started.

From there, I'd continue drinking and break out the dope. I mainly stuck to marijuana-based products, but I occasionally browsed the delightful selection of mind-altering substances on the menu in San Francisco. Let's put it this way: I've tried everything within a reasonable scope of the modern "classic" substances—and I've abused a handful of those substances on a consistently random basis.

Sometimes, I just felt like smoking heroin. Nothing topped a solid LSD trip if the set and setting were right. Psilocybin mushrooms were fun. You could microdose that shit for a week, and nobody would notice. And then there was the grab bag of pills available from the dealer at my local pub. There wasn't a problem in the world that couldn't be ground to sawdust by 20 mg of OxyContin. Have you ever mixed Xanex with champagne? You shouldn't.

Alcohol, amphetamines, cannabis, hallucinogens, opiates, and opioids were always within reach. Other than crystal methamphetamine, which I tried once and once was enough, there were only two drugs that I consistently refused to do: cocaine and ecstasy (MDMA). Having tried both many times, I had practical qualms rather than ethical dilemmas. Coke was expensive, and the high was short-lived. Plus, I hated the "jonesing" effect of coke—that relentless need to do more. Conversely, the only effects I felt from MDMA were cottonmouth and an unsavory urge to do some coke. Most of all, I never had a single instance of a good time on either substance, so I avoided them, which, to be honest, wasn't that hard. Otherwise, my philosophy on chemical recreation was: What you got? I'll take it.

Come 1:00 a.m., the buzz would be roaring like a fire, and it was time to hit "my local" for last call. Pittsburgh's Pub was 187 steps from my apartment. Back in those days, my body could handle hard liquor, so I'd order a shot of tequila and a bottle of Budweiser. Then I'd move to the Theater of Magic pinball machine and try to beat the high score. On some nights, depending on the bartender, they'd close the joint at 2:00 a.m. per municipal code but let a few of the regulars stay for after-hours. Anybody left standing at 3:00 a.m. would head to somebody's crib—usually mine—to keep drinking and smoking until sunrise.

The nutshell summary: I was consuming the alcoholic equivalent of *at least* a 12-pack every night, in addition to pumping my system full of whatever toxins were on hand. I repeat: *Every night.* And those were the "normal" nights. Things got way out of hand at least once a month.

Three more years passed. At the age of 39 and the end of my rope in San Francisco, I believed if I didn't leave town very soon, I'd go in a body bag, for sure. Nine months since making that promise to myself that I wouldn't be 40 years old, waiting tables and blowing dogs for beer money, I'd made zero—scratch that—*negative* progress toward keeping the promise.

San Francisco used to be Disneyland for crackheads. If you couldn't figure out how to enjoy yourself in S.F., you didn't deserve to live there. So far into my residency, life had become exceedingly carefree, disturbingly kaleidoscopic, and essentially meaningless. Again, no dependents. Stupid-easy job. Girlfriends came and went. *Laisse-faire, c'est la vie, avec moi.* Drugs falling from the trees. Kinky hook-ups on speed dial. Freaks next door, clowns down the street, and junkies crashing on my couch tonight. Abundant sunshine. Nobody in his right mind wants to leave San Francisco unless it all gets to be a little too much.

For some folks, working in the restaurant racket is one of those "I could never do that" type of gigs. For others, it's fun, interesting, and somehow related to one of their passions. My theory is people who couldn't or wouldn't be willing and able to wait tables are inherently flawed, insecure, and deeply anti-social. The reciprocal nature of the cycle—you need food, we have it, let's make this deal—is one of the most primal cooperative elements of humanity. Meanwhile, the same people who don't know how to make a sandwich are oftentimes the same people who can't change a flat tire.

Whenever someone said, "Oh, you're a server at Mykonia? That must be a tough gig, huh?" I'd say no, it's very easy. Anybody could do it. Aside from having a shitload of knowledge about the food and beverages we serve, it's as simple as having this conversation.

And it's true. If you can walk up to a stranger and say, "Hi, my name is Charlie. What's happening tonight?" you can wait tables in any restaurant in America. But again, not that you'd ever want to do that.

Every profession has its pros and cons, and being a server has its own set of conditions. First, the good stuff: You get to meet and interact with a never-ending gauntlet of (sometimes) interesting people. You're on your feet for most of the shift, so you're not parked on a chair in some cubicle. And there's a full buffet of food and drink at your disposal. For expediency, I'll spare you random details about what goes on in the back of the house.

Next, the bad stuff. You have to greet and service an infinite stream of entitled adult-children who think they matter. You're on your feet for the length of the shift, so you're probably gonna have back problems in your future. And there's an industrial kitchen full of food you're theoretically not supposed to eat. And again, I'll spare you random details about the auto-fellatio of management.

By far, the best part of the server gig was flexibility. You could usually take as much time off as you wanted if you found someone to cover your shift(s). The Christmas holiday season was the only time of the year when management cracked down on shift-swapping. Only servers with rank and seniority got time off to spend with family. That was fine with me since I didn't give a shit about Christmas or holidays in general. Those were "easy money days." I worked New Year's Eve—the most lucrative night of the year—for seven years straight. Come January, I would submit a proper vacation request. Meanwhile, my gig was fully staffed with a couple of hustlers on the roster: newer part-time cats, always hungry for shifts. When I didn't feel like working, *I didn't.*

Unfortunately, waiting tables for a living weighed heavily on me, especially considering a failed music career. With no disrespect to the lifetime restaurant servers who love their jobs, waiting tables seemed like an egregious waste of my talents. The sad part is few people in my life seemed to agree.

Enter Wilson, my landlord-slash-neighbor-slash-buddy.

Sometimes, given the right circumstances, people can be so brutally honest that your life is changed forever. It's usually unintentional, too. And, as I said before, sometimes it's just what you need. Sometimes, a relatively harmless comment can pierce the fog of mental and emotional warfare in your head. And sometimes, that shit *hurts your soul.* But it's a powerful motivational force.

Wilson and I co-inhabited the low-rise house two blocks from Ocean Beach on 46th Avenue in the Sunset District. The house was owned by Wilson's parents, who visited from Taiwan once a year. They were lovely people. Wilson lived upstairs in the main two-bedroom flat, while I inhabited the ground-floor in-law studio apartment behind the garage, affectionately called The Cave. My rent was extremely reasonable by S.F. standards, and Wilson always corrected me when I called him my "landlord." He introduced me to his friends as his "neighbor" or "buddy."

The night in question, Wilson and I stood by the back door getting high and talking shit, like we'd done dozens of times before. Wilson returned from a two-month trip to China, and sharing a joint was his way of thanking me for keeping an eye on the place. And he had every right to say what he did. Wilson was born in Taiwan but went to boarding school and college in California. He is a naturalized U.S. citizen but ethnically Taiwanese (or Chinese, whatever you want to call it) and a certified world traveler. I couldn't keep track of all the places Wilson had been.

More facts. When Wilson came downstairs and said what he did, I'd been living in San Francisco for nine years. I occupied the in-law apartment on 46th Avenue for five years. And I loved that place. There were some wild times down in The Cave, as you might imagine. The night Wilson came downstairs and said what he said, I was two months shy of my 40th birthday. Thanks to Wilson's travels, I was ruminating that I had never traveled outside of North America. I'd been to 32 of 50 states but never west of Eureka, CA, or east of Boston, MA. The furthest north was Ely, MN, and the furthest south was Puerto Vallarta, Mexico, for a week in 1992. I saw Niagara Falls from the Canadian side in 1997, the very same day Princess Diana and Dodi Fayed were killed in Paris. I'd been from Hilton Head, SC to Medford, OR and infinite places in between. I spent significant amounts of time in Colorado and Arizona. However, all in all, it was a ho-hum travel resume.

Wilson talked about celebrating the Lunar New Year (Year of the Rat) in Nanjing and Shanghai, and I was hanging on every word.

"Dude, it sounds like paradise!" I gushed.

"So, Charlie, when are you going to check it [Asia] out?"

"Oh, I don't know," I said. "Someday..."

"Someday," Wilson said, choking on an over-toke from the joint. "You've been saying that since you moved in here, Charlie, you know?" He was forcibly laughing like you do when you've heard somebody make the same excuse for five years. Wilson's facial expression said, "I understand, buddy," but his body language said, "Well, what the fuck?"

"I know," I said sheepishly. "I'll get there, man. For sure. I'll get there."

Wilson passed me the joint and looked me square in the glazed, bloodshot eyes. "You're not getting any younger, Charlie."

You're not getting any younger, Charlie.

Could Wilson have been any more on the money? Immediately, I remembered the promise that I would not be 40 years old, doing the same thing in the same place.

In hindsight, it should have been an easy promise to keep. In the grand scheme of things, I wasn't a total loser. I simply wasn't very successful at anything other than getting by–keeping my head above water. I was a natural restaurant server with a knack for spontaneous bullshit. I was a decent musician with talent and creativity. However, when it came to promoting myself as an artist or musician, I just couldn't do it. If people didn't like the music, recognize my genius, or come to the gigs, there was nothing I, nor 500 flyers on Sullivan Street, could do about it. Therefore, I sold thousands more lamb chops than I ever did records.

A year or two earlier, during one of our occasional long-distance phone calls, my mother, once again, made a poignant observation. We were talking about the fact that a mere three months after arriving in San Francisco, I formed another new band despite proclaiming that I wouldn't. This band tried and failed more respectably but failed, nevertheless. I told my mother how bad I felt about dissolving the group after seven years, feeling like I'd let everybody down. Those guys (in the band) weren't just my friends; they were my brothers. Tom Taylor was the drummer, and Chet Monroe was the bass player, too. And those cats weren't happy about my decision to quit.

"It just occurred to me," my mother said, "that you have been in one band or another since you were nine. Maybe that's what's been holding you back. *You need to do something completely on your own.*"

I needed to get back in touch with my inner survivalist. I needed to get back in touch with the spirit of the journey, not the destination. Thoughts are mundane or negligible when you're riding the safe and orderly metro train to work every morning. *What will the sexy new secretary be wearing today? What should I have for lunch today?* Lunch is the last thing on your mind when you're riding a rickety bus over a mountain range in Guangdong Province.

I needed to get back to genuine *survival*. Not just paying the rent and having pocket money for drugs, but going into strange and foreign places, getting from A to B to Z and back to B again, in one piece. To feel utterly vulnerable in my surroundings. To learn to trust my instincts again. To overcome the prevailing mediocrity of my existence. To be honest with myself, for a change. And if you can't be true to yourself, you'll never be worth a shit to anyone else. In the end, it was simply a matter of facing the facts and saying, "Fuck it. Wilson is right. I'm not getting any younger."

With absolutely nothing to lose and everything to gain, I didn't think about what would happen if I flamed out in Asia. I was tired of telling my friends and co-workers that someday I would "just get up and go" to Asia. I was finished with fooling myself. The fatigue of self-deception had become overwhelming, forming the kernel of truth in my decision. Wilson nailed the truth to a cross. Time was running out.

At the lowest points of depression, consumed by failure and self-doubt, I felt like a washout, and I hardly bothered to look at the dissipated face in the mirror anymore. I'd catch a glimpse of my reflection in a storefront window and say, "That's not me. I don't know that guy. He's an impostor." And honestly, I never considered suicide, but I wouldn't have been disappointed to die in a plane crash or some other act of God.

That's how it feels when you're living a life that's not what you wanted, not what you dreamed about, and not what you expected. But that last one is the rub—and I caught it. I figured it out. *Expectations.*

Expectations make cowards of us all, I think. The worst part was facing the fact that I fucked it up—nobody helped me. I couldn't blame my parents, my sister, or my friends.

Once I got over the acceptance of my faults, I felt like I was standing at the foot of a mountain, looking up. Whatever anybody might be searching for may or may not be at the top. But I had to find out for myself. And to start climbing, I knew I had to leave my expectations behind because that's such a heavy goddamn weight to be dragging up the face of a mountain you're not even sure is worth climbing.

Later that evening, I went online and checked the airfares to various cities in East Asia. Finding a reasonably priced, round-trip ticket to Taipei on China Airlines (departing on my 40th birthday), I clicked **Purchase This Fare**, and that was that. I continued to drink and eventually passed out on the couch. I woke up late the next morning and had no recollection of buying the ticket. I cruised up to Judah Street for coffee at Java Beach, read the paper, had a couple of smokes, and stopped at 7-Eleven to buy a turkey sandwich. It wasn't until I checked my email and saw the flight confirmation details from China Airlines that I realized what I had done. *Fuck it*, I thought. *If I decide not to go, it wouldn't be the first time I flushed $1,000 down the toilet.*

I went to work that Tuesday evening but didn't tell my managers or co-workers that I bought a ticket to Taipei—a precaution against making myself look foolish if I bailed out on the trip. Instead, I quietly unloaded the rest of my shifts for the week and skipped the post-work booze and drug routine. I went straight home and fell into a deep sleep that lasted well into Wednesday morning. I spent the rest of the day puttering in the garden, smoking weed, and staring into space with hardly a thought or concern.

Thursday afternoon, I made a beeline for the bookstore at Stonestown Galleria and bought the only two books they had about Taiwan. I spent the next four days in solitude, contemplating the contingencies and reading up on Taiwan. I made no phone calls, sent no emails, and didn't speak a word to another human being. I stayed in my apartment, getting high and talking to my cat. By the end of the weekend, I felt reasonably confident in my ability to make the trip. The next step was to tell my friends and inform management at the restaurant, which presented another set of contingencies. After that, I needed to apply for a Taiwan tourist visa. I started counting the days to my departure.

✱

Out of my depression and desperation, I came to a place of ambiguity and potential. It was a bumbling success despite myself. Echoing David Foster Wallace, most of the important things that occur in our lives happen without our engineering it. Good things can and will happen if you let them. Be at the right place at the right time, which is often hard to predict. Though innately curious, I wasn't a true "seeker." I still hadn't found what I was looking for because I hadn't been looking for *anything*. I'd just been looking.

Have you ever dreamed of a place, and you know where you are, but you're not sure where you are? The dream looks and feels and sounds like Milan, but you've never been to Milan, and you wake up wondering if maybe you lived in Milan during a previous life. How else could you have remembered it so vividly? Some people dream of France, others of Africa. For as long as I can remember, I always dreamed of Asia. These were dynamic dreams of substance in places I had never conceived. Were they real? I had to find out. And most importantly, I would take responsibility for the dream.

On Monday morning, I caught up with Wilson in the garage as he was leaving for work.

"Hey, buddy," Wilson said. "Can't talk now. I'm running late. Supposed to be in a meeting." He laughed.

"I just wanted to tell you that I'm going to Taipei in April."

"You're kidding me!" Wilson gasped.

"No, man. I bought the ticket. It's done."

"That's crazy! But dude, let me call you from the road."

"We can talk later."

"Are you working tonight?"

"No."

From the start, Wilson was wary of my plan to use Taipei as a home base to explore Southeast Asia. He wasn't concerned that I'd be overwhelmed by culture shock. He was worried I would run out of money before the 60-day visa expired. He knew me well, and he knew my habits.

"Dude," Wilson said, "Taipei is not San Francisco. If you want to get high, it's super expensive."

In the meantime, Wilson hooked me up with the email addresses of his old friends. He also said, "Don't count on them for anything unless it's an emergency." At some point, Wilson filled me in on the generalities of Taipei's geography and demographics. Despite the obvious flaws and oversights in my travel plan—not knowing shit about Taiwan or speaking a word of Mandarin, for starters—the momentum was undeniable and unstoppable. I was going.

Within days of making the grand announcement, it became clear that I had to answer the same trio of questions. The first question was: "Why Taiwan?" That was followed by: "What are you going to do in Taiwan?" And finally: "How long are you planning to stay in Taiwan?" Therefore, I quickly learned the awkward gymnastics of explaining and rationalizing this decision, not that I owed anybody an explanation.

We have a relatively strong—if not defensive—answer for the first question. **Why Taiwan?** Why *not* Taiwan? Why not Madagascar? Why not Estonia? Does it really matter where I go? I'm going to check it out, man. More to the point, I'm getting out of San Francisco while I'm still alive. Consider it a self-imposed form of detox mixed with adventure and challenge. It's sort of like the question: "Why do you masturbate?" *Because I can.*

The funny thing (to me) is that practically nobody knows anything about Taiwan. Half of the people in my life couldn't point to Taiwan on a map, and the other half thought I was talking about Thailand, so that group raised its eyebrows and said, "Thailand? Gonna get yourself some boom-boom, love-me-long-time, huh?"

Let's get this one thing straight. Sex was not the last thing on my mind, but it wasn't a motivating factor. I had a few Asian girlfriends over the years, but I didn't have Yellow Fever. I liked *some* Asian women.

However—I'm taking a deep breath here—like everything else related to this journey, I reckoned that sex would come as it may. Was I aware of prostitution in Southeast Asia? *Of course.* Did I have ethical or moral qualms with prostitution? *Yes and no.* Was I planning to engage in prostitution? *Not really.* I mean, again, let's check it out, and if it's something that seems attractive, then I'm probably going to pick up a hooker or two or seven. I didn't give it a lot of thought before buying the ticket. The following were my basic instincts.

Geographically, Taipei is strategically located at the gates of East Asia. Hong Kong and Manila are one and two-hour flights, respectively. Tokyo, Beijing, and Bangkok are three hours away. Since the plan was to visit as many places as possible, Taipei made the perfect launch pad or home base.

Taiwan had a reputation as one of the most "foreigner friendly" of all Asian countries, especially toward Americans, with all the ambiguous generality the phrase 'foreigner friendly' entails. At the same time, the guidebooks described Taipei as modern and cosmopolitan, which appealed to my sense of urban exploration.

Meanwhile, what I planned to do in Taiwan...was...an open question. Such an endeavor required zero expectations. For starters, I wasn't sure if I would look for a job. According to my research, if you had a white face and a bachelor's degree from an accredited Western university, you could easily find a gig teaching English in Taiwan. The job might even find you. Now, torturing Taiwanese kids with vocabulary flashcards was just about the last thing I ever wanted to do, but if that's all it took to make the nut, well, again, let's see what's happening over there.

Finally, I planned to stay in Taiwan for at least 60 days—the length of my multiple-entry tourist visa. Above all, as the sense of adventure unfolded, I couldn't let my imagination run wild. I didn't know if I'd even like Taiwan, or Asia, for that matter. But the answer would determine the future of my residency in The Cave, so it was one of the first things Wilson and I talked about.

Wilson said if I planned on returning to San Francisco at the end of two months, he was cool with me keeping the apartment and suspending my rent during that time. After all, I earned it by being a good tenant, in addition to making a few cosmetic and structural repairs around the house, free of charge. When I moved in all those years ago, the backyard was a disaster—full of weeds and junk. Within a few months, I transformed the space into a vegetable garden and recreation area—which pleased his parents the next time they came to visit.

Despite Wilson's concerns that I would run out of money, my financial report told me I had at least 180 days of cash to keep me afloat. Plus, a couple of credit cards with zero balances. The longer I looked at the calendar, the more I realized that 60 days was not enough time to visit a bunch of cities and still get a good idea of what's cooking in Taipei.

So, I didn't have to worry about paying rent on the apartment. The only problem was, who would take care of my cat? Wilson was a great guy and everything, but I had no intention of asking him to foster my beloved eight-year-old cat, Mao-mao.

Animal lovers are going to have a deeply empathetic response to the story I'm about to tell, and the rest of you are probably going to say, "For chrissakes, he's talking about a cat." I wouldn't blame anybody for skipping over this part. Nevertheless, at this stage of my life, on the verge of 40 years old, there was no living creature or thing for which I had anything remotely close to pure, unconditional love as I did for my cat, Mao-mao. He was the closest thing I ever had to a kindred spirit. After eight years together, we'd become an inseparable duo—the Pancho and Cisco of the Outer Sunset. Everybody in the neighborhood knew us, and they always said hello when we crossed paths.

Tom Taylor and I were roommates in Chicago and the first three years in S.F., sharing a flat on 21st Avenue in the Richmond District from 1999–2002. In June 2000, Tom brought a male kitten home without consulting me or the other roommate. Within days, I became the cat's primary caretaker. Coincidentally, I was dating a Chinese American woman, Sandy Chiu, who came over after the cat arrived. We still hadn't named him yet—we called him Dude or Cat. He was a noisy little fellow, too. Always meow-meow-meow. Sandy said, "It sounds like he's saying his name in Chinese." And I asked, "How do you say 'cat' in Chinese? She said, "Mao-mao." The name stuck.

I didn't object when Tommy showed up with Mao. I'm a cat lover who's had feline pets in the past, so having a cat around the house was not a problem—as long as the landlord didn't find out. We had a "no pets" clause in the lease.

Mao-mao was born to a litter of strays under a porch in Oakland and came into our lives as a tiny ball of black fur with vibrant green eyes. In time, he grew to a 16-pound behemoth of mostly muscle and bones. He was about a year old when we started letting him out the back door of the flat on 21st Avenue, and for a couple of weeks, he was having a good time exploring the back stairs and yard. One day, he got into a scrap with what we can only assume to be one of the badass neighborhood tomcats. Mao got fucked up. He could barely walk.

I was in the kitchen when Mao crawled through the back door, crying, clearly in pain. As soon as he saw me, Mao crashed on the kitchen floor. I scooped him up, brought him to my bedroom, and laid him on the bed. After an hour of scrambling to get out of work, I took Mao to the ASPCA, where the vet said Mao was badly bruised, but fortunately, nothing was broken or seriously damaged. "Keep the cat indoors for the next two weeks and monitor his progress," the vet said. "When he starts eating again, you know he'll be OK."

Mao didn't leave my bed for three consecutive days, not even to use the litter box. Worried about his condition, I took the weekend off, kept him company, and slept with him at night. On the fourth morning, Mao went to the kitchen to find an empty food bowl and woke me up by rubbing against my face. From that moment forward, there was no question or discussion that I would take Mao wherever I might happen to move next. While he was "our" cat, Mao-mao was intrinsically my cat. I was his father and Tommy was his uncle, more or less.

In 2002, I moved out to Oceanview with Mao-mao to be closer to SFSU, while Tom moved into a studio in Nob Hill. In the meantime, Tom and I continued to make music and hang out regularly. In early 2003, I moved to The Cave in the Outer Sunset. It was 2008 when I decided to visit Taiwan.

I never quite understood why Tom stayed in Nob Hill. He'd been talking about leaving his studio on Bush Street for a couple of years. In the face of this Taiwan gambit, part of me thought Mao should stay with Tommy in Nob Hill. But Mao was a dedicated indoor/outdoor cat—he couldn't handle staying in Tom's apartment for two months. It would have been torture for any cat. Still, I felt like Tom was at least partially on the hook for Mao's well-being.

Over the years, Mao spent two-thirds of the time outdoors. As a pair of swinging bachelors, we didn't have any rules at The Cave. Mao came and went as he pleased but curled up with me in bed every night. The back door was rigged to give him 24/7 access, so I rarely had to call for him—or get up to let him out. Most nights when I returned from work, he'd see the lights come on and hear me moving around, and he'd come bolting in, all meow-meow this and meow-meow that. He had grown into a big boy and could take care of himself against the raccoons, too. He was living the dream out there. Mao was the happiest cat you ever saw.

During my time in the Sunset, I took occasional trips out of town, and I had a pair of friends—one from the neighborhood and one from work—who would come and housesit-slash-catsit while I was gone. So I pitched the proposition of living rent-free in The Cave for two months while I was in Taiwan. Neither was interested in the gig, primarily because of the apartment's naturally dark and subdued environment. My neighborhood pal said, "A week is manageable, but two months is just too long down there. I'd go nuts!"

When I told Tommy about booking the trip to Taiwan, he asked, "What are you going to do about Mao-mao?" And pausing incredulously, "Don't tell me Wilson's gonna take care of the cat!"

"No, I wouldn't even think of asking him."

"What did he say about the apartment?"

"He said I can keep it. No rent for two months. After that, I gotta find somebody to sublet."

Over the next few days, and a lot of talking about the situation, I finally came up with a plan.

"Look, Tom. You want out of Nob Hill, and here's a perfect chance. You can come stay in The Cave for two months—there's plenty of space for your stuff—you don't even have that much stuff to begin with—and you can stay rent-free while you look for a new place to live."

"And I'll have to be out by the time you get back?"

"Theoretically, yes."

"What do you mean 'theoretically'?"

"Well, there is an outside chance that I won't come back after two months. Could be six months. I dunno."

Tommy thought it over for a few days before returning with his demands. "First, I want to choose what stuff of yours stays in the apartment and what goes into storage."

"Not a problem."

"If you come back and I'm not ready to leave, you gotta figure something else out."

"OK…"

"I'm probably going to buy a car, so you need to work something out with Wilson about letting me park in the driveway sometimes."

"I don't see that being a problem."

Tommy paused. "And this one…you're not gonna like."

"What is it? Spit it out."

"Six months minimum stay. I'll start paying rent in June."

I took a deep breath and said, "I can live with that."

Once Tom agreed to move and Mao-mao would be cared for properly, the deal looked to be a win-win for everybody. Tommy was happy to leave Nob Hill and live near the beach. Plus, he would get to be with Mao again. Mao was a winner because he got to keep his backyard kingdom and reconnect with his old pal, Tommy. I was looking forward to my Asian adventure with the peace of mind that Mao would be in good hands.

In mid-March, I was simultaneously preparing for my trip and making room for Tommy to move in. Wilson let me use the garage as storage, so it wasn't a massive ordeal, but I had nine years' worth of junk stuffed into a two-year box, and way more "stuff" than I realized. There were several late-night "drops" of unwanted furniture at the corner of 48th Avenue and Moraga Street.

Cats like routine as much as the next guy, and Mao took notice of the activity at the crib. Stuff was disappearing, things were getting moved around. Mao wasn't thrilled, but he rolled with the changes in the past. Every now and then, he'd disappear for a night but always reappear in the morning.

On the evening of March 19, I returned home from my resto shift around midnight and went about my routine. While in the shower, I thought it was strange that Mao hadn't come home yet. He usually came in to greet me within a minute or two of arrival. On the nights he came in late, he was always really talkative after those excursions. Anyway, Mao didn't come home that night. It wasn't the first time he stayed out all night, and I wasn't freaked out. It was just a little odd.

The next morning, I was concerned that Mao still hadn't come home. Something wasn't right.

For at least a week after Mao's disappearance, I was nearly unable to sleep without being heavily medicated. Every night, I would get home from work and circle the block, calling Mao's name. Every morning, I would get up and canvas the neighborhood, knocking on doors. "Have you seen this cat?" I put up fliers, jumped over fences, and followed every trail he might have been on. Actually, Mao was a lot more popular than I thought. He was notorious in the backyards of the block. Everybody had seen Mao—many times—they just hadn't seen him in a while.

Two weeks passed without a sign of Mao. Heartbroken beyond anything I'd ever experienced, I mourned Mao in private on a nightly basis. He was gone, and I would probably never know what happened to him. And it was too late to back out of the trip. It was hopeless. Tommy moved in on March 31, and we both acknowledged the irony. The main reason he moved in was Mao, and now Mao was gone.

It was whatever is beyond bittersweet. I was shattered. However, the wheel of destiny was in motion, and there was no turning back.

* * *

"So, you've never been on a 13-hour flight?" Wilson asked.

"No."

"What's the longest flight you've ever been on?"

"Chicago to Puerto Vallarta. One time, I flew from Oakland to Minneapolis, and the flight got diverted to Houston, where we sat on the tarmac for three hours. The whole thing took, I dunno, eight, maybe ten hours. Something like that."

"Yeah," he replied, nodding and blinking, "you're gonna wanna be knocked out for most of the flight to Taipei. Trust me."

* * *

California was good to me for the first eight years. It gave me a college degree and many interesting and often enlightening work experiences. The quality of my life improved dramatically. San Francisco was a magical place, and I feel lucky that I got to live there before the Google occupation. I loved California. I used to say that I never worked a day in San Francisco because every day was a vacation from my previous existence. There was no substitute for a beautiful blue-sky day with a light breeze off the Pacific. For many years, I scoffed at the idea of living anywhere else. Why would I?

It was only that ninth and final year that shit started to get out of control. Somewhere along the way, California turned on me. Or maybe I unknowingly violated one of the unspoken rules. The wondrous journey became something of a nightmare. The magical feeling had disappeared. The love had turned to something else. And losing Mao-mao was the finishing touch.

2

Now Is Not the Time to Panic

The panic attacks started well before the security checkpoint at San Francisco International Airport (IATA code: SFO) and, technically, didn't end until three weeks after I'd been in Taipei. In the hours leading up to my departure, the game plan was to ingest as many divergent yet not-incompatible chemicals as possible and still breathe without a respirator for all or most of the 13-hour trans-Pacific flight. If I'd *really* had it my way, I would have closed my eyes on take-off and opened them on landing, no worse for the narcotic wear. An intravenous morphine drip would have been nice. Earlier in the evening, I ate a double dose of medicinal marijuana chocolate and swallowed 10 mg of OxyContin. I took 100 mg of Trazadone and wrapped another 100 mg plus a pair of Ambien CR in a Post-it note, and stuffed the packet into the corner hip pocket of my jeans. Then I drank a bottle of red wine and popped another 10 mg of Oxy. By the time Wilson and I were cruising down I-280 toward SFO, you could have sliced me in half with a chainsaw and I wouldn't have felt a thing. Wilson dropped me at the departure level and wished me good luck.

Standing alone in the cavernous international terminal, I started to feel something: waves of panic. The heart-seizing stabs of terror only increased once I boarded the plane. I wanted to do something drastic, and the plane hadn't even left the gate. On the verge of tears, I was starting to dehydrate. I pressed the service button and shakily asked a flight attendant for a cup of water, which I used to wash down one of the Ambien.

The 747-400 was the biggest plane I'd ever been on. Felt like it was wide enough to host a four-lane highway. Full flight. Three hundred and seventy-nine people on that flight. Not an empty seat. I was jammed into a middle seat on the left side of the plane, just over the wing, one row back from the emergency door, which is a stupid place to sit unless you want to be the first to die in a crash, and come to think of it, I would. Eagle Scout or not, I have never imagined myself wanting to survive an emergency water landing in the middle of the Pacific Ocean. However, I wasn't given an option at check-in, and, especially unfortunate for the fat guy sitting on the aisle seat, I generally make a lot of trips to the bathroom no matter how long the flight.

The chemical cocktail in my bloodstream had a marginally sedative effect, meaning I was in a mid-theta cycle brain wave stupor for approximately five hours of the 13-hour flight. The remaining eight hours were spent in a low-beta cycle punctuated by expulsive flashes of pure, knee-weakening, stomach-turning panic. Somewhere over Tokyo I began experiencing what I can only describe as Lights at the End of the Tunnel.

The plane touched down at Taoyuan International Airport (IATA code: TPE) around 5:30 a.m. I went stoically through the formalities, cleared immigration and customs, collected my luggage, and got in a taxi for a 30-minute ride from Taoyuan to Taipei City, where I booked a hotel room in an area called Ximendeng. I wasn't *disappointed* with my first impression of Taiwan, but it might as well have been the west side of Chicago with a mountain backdrop. The architecture was ugly, and the sky was industrial gray. But I was mostly disappointed in myself for embarking on the journey of a lifetime and losing my mind at the same time.

My Taiwanese visa was good for 60 days, which (I thought) was plenty of time to travel around *and* get established, e.g., find a job, an apartment, and some friends. But that's getting ahead of myself. I wasn't specifically worried about making it in Taipei. If I could make it in San Francisco, I could make it anywhere. I believed my bullshit. I did my research. I arrived with a virtual understanding of Taiwan, meaning I thought guidebooks and websites could prepare me for culture shock. The only glaring omission from my packing list was the prescriptive ability to speak even a little bit of Mandarin. I knew how to say *ni hao* (hello) and *xie xie* (thank you). That was it, and therein laid the root of my anxiety and panic attacks. I knew well in advance that my lack of Mandarin was going to fall on the negative side of the Culture Shock Survival Scale. My only attempt to learn the language was buying the *Lonely Planet Mandarin* phrasebook, which I perused in the bathroom during the increasingly frequent bouts of diarrhea in the days leading up to my departure.

Enduring a panic-stricken 13-hour flight was merely the *amuse bouche* of the existential growing pains that followed. My main concerns revolved around **How...?** and **What If...?** e.g., *How* will I order food if they don't speak English? *What if* the hotel lost my reservation, there's a plastics convention in town, and all the hotel rooms in Taipei are booked solid? I could've continued these internal contingencies forever, but the biggest What If? was: *What if this was a big mistake?*

More than anything else, I was terrified by the mere idea of going back to S.F. with my tail between my legs and waiting tables again, which would have been a slow suicide. Traveling to Taiwan sounded like a rock-solid genius plan up until I left for the airport. Those first 48 hours would tear the soul out of many people. So what? The hotel in Ximendeng didn't lose my reservation, but it looked much better on the website than in person.

Wilson gave me a lot of general advice about Taipei, like, "Zhongxiao Fuxing Sogo Department Store is where all the hot chicks go shopping," and "Tianmu in the Shilin District is where all the rich foreigners live." I mean, he was spot-on, for the most part, but he didn't give me any solid, on-the-ground advice except, "Stay out of trouble." A pair of travel guidebooks and the phrasebook informed most of my decisions and movements, and most importantly, choosing to stay in Ximending for simple geography and proximity to public transportation, i.e., the MRT station.

Based on the travel guides, Ximending was Taipei's answer to Tokyo's Harajuku—a place where the trendy kids hang out—home to the Red House Theater, an arts center with avant-garde exhibitions, bars and restaurants, live music, and LGBT events. The hub of fashion, subculture, and in-your-face commercialism. It sounded like a lot of fun for everybody involved.

Arriving in Ximen, I quickly noticed the rainbow flags everywhere. *Oh, it's kind of like the Castro District in San Francisco: the gayest place in town.* It was comforting and familiar amid the otherwise alien landscape. But since I didn't know if I'd be happy staying in Ximending—which is a lot different than posting up on a random Saturday night—I only booked a hotel for the first two nights. This turned out to be a smart move.

The Good Ground Hotel was one step above a youth hostel with a café in the lobby, tucked into a tight lane off Chengdu Road about 50 meters from Ximen MRT exit 6. I think I paid US$45 per night. The first room didn't even have a window. Dropping my bags—one roller suitcase full of clothes that were inappropriate for the climate, and a backpack with a laptop—I sat on the edge of the bed, rapt in shock, flush with adrenaline, pockets full of cash. *Oh no. This won't do. I'm moving to a decent hotel.* After complaining at the front desk—I booked a deluxe room on the website—they begrudgingly moved me to a room with a tiny window that looked out into the back alley.

The jet lag hit hard. Sleep was out of the question. I was barely able to communicate with the people at the front desk. The wireless internet only worked in the lobby. The hotel seemed to be popular with chain-smoking Japanese tourist girls. The acrid smell of cigarette smoke permeated my room, making me nauseous. I couldn't imagine smoking in that little box. But instead of feeling sorry for myself, I decided to cruise around and find another hotel. Strolling out into the lane, I realized it was only 8:30 a.m. in Taipei City.

Around 9:30 a.m., walking south on Kunming Street, I passed a couple of dudes sitting outside a coffee shop. Seemed like everything spilled out onto the sidewalks. The city was far more claustrophobic than any part of San Francisco, which was cramped as far as U.S. cities are concerned. Anyway, no sooner than I passed the coffee shop, one dude wearing a backward L.A. Dodgers baseball cap said, "Hey, man!" and so I circled back, warily.

"Where are you from?" he asked.

"California."

"Oh, Yankee boy! What are you doing in Taipei, Yankee boy?"

"That's a good question."

"My name is Johnny Wong."

"Charlie Birch. Nice to meet you."

Johnny offered to buy me a coffee, which I reluctantly accepted—not because he was creepy, but I didn't think caffeine was going to do me any good. I sat down and had a smoke and a cup of coffee with Johnny. He told me that he went to school at the University of Miami—which explained his decent English. I told him it was my first day in Taipei. He said, "Hey, listen. I can help you. What do you need? You got a cell phone? You got a hotel room? I'm your guy. I can help."

"Thanks, Johnny. That's very kind of you. What I'd like are some pharmaceutical-grade sedatives. But any kind of sleeping pill will do."

Johnny took me to a pharmacy, got me some worthless over-the-counter pills, and gave me his phone number. I downed twice the recommended dosage of pills with some grape juice.

Parting ways with Johnny for the time being, I wandered around the immediate vicinity looking for a different hotel. After checking over a dozen joints, I finally found one where the staff spoke English, what I thought was a boutique joint called the YS Hotel. The desk clerks and manager were very accommodating, but I could only get a three-night stay. They said I could rebook if there was availability.

Hunger was non-existent, and the thought of eating was repulsive. The convenience store around the corner had a nice selection of Japanese beers, so I got a few tallboys and threw down a couple more of the "sleeping pills." Unfortunately, sleep remained elusive, so I walked around the Ximending Pedestrian Area and took frequent cold-water showers while pounding tallboys of Kirin Beer until sunset. Taiwan doesn't have any open container liquor laws, so it's completely acceptable to drink in public a huge bonus (as far as I was concerned). The insomnia persisted while the flashes of panic subsided to occasional bolts of terror.

After sundown, I got in a taxi and headed for a bar called Carnegie's—the first paddle on the foreigner booze gauntlet in Taipei. Carnegie's was Taipei's unofficial answer to the Hard Rock Café, but it felt more like Omaha's Lame Duck. The walls and ceiling were plastered with classic rock memorabilia. My first impression was lackluster. However, in less than an hour, I managed to engage a surly fellow from New Zealand who reeked of body odor, an amusingly opinionated guy from South Africa who strongly encouraged me to "get the fuck out of Taipei as soon as possible," and a couple of dead-eyed female service staff who couldn't have been unhappier with their gig.

I barely made it into a taxi and back to the hotel before passing out cold. I was down for ten hours, waking up late the next morning, relieved that I hadn't embarrassed myself on the first night, especially at a place like Carnegie's. Later that afternoon, I checked out of the Good Ground and into the YS Hotel.

On my second night in Taipei, I simply walked around, drinking beer, sampling the public transportation system, snapping photos on my digital camera, sucking it all in—the lights, the sounds, the smells, the faces, the movements, the traffic. The city seemed like several copies of Detroit stacked on top of each other and dressed in 1,000-megawatt LED Christmas lighting. Much of the public signage was in Chinese and English, but that didn't help my general sense of disorientation. At some point, I took the last of the Trazadone and Ambien I'd smuggled in the Post-it Note. I still wasn't hungry, but I'd located a nearby McDonald's, so I considered that a victory. I returned to the hotel, took a long, hot shower, and crawled into bed. The slumber was welcome.

Everything was new and mind-blowing, but two distinct aspects of the journey materialized early in the trip. There were people, and there were places. At the start, I was much more interested in meeting people than seeing new places. The guidebooks were great for getting me around town, but even the simplest tasks—getting a cup of coffee—involved people. As for places, I reckoned Taipei 101, the main tourist attraction in town, would be there in a year. Worse came to worst, I could buy a postcard and say I'd been there. So, I cued in on meeting people—foreign or local, it didn't matter.

Mid-morning of the third day, I walked by the coffee shop on Kunming Street where Johnny Wong was sitting and smoking. "Hey, Yankee boy!" Johnny called out. "Did you get some sleep?"

"Yeah, man, I did. But those sleeping pills are rubbish. They didn't help."

"You need a prescription in Taiwan if you want the good stuff."

"That's...unlikely."

Johnny and I were about the same age. He had a large frame for a Taiwanese guy, which matched his gregarious nature. And he turned out to be something of a godsend.

"Why didn't you call me yesterday?" Johnny asked, vaguely interested in my reply.

"Well, I haven't got a SIM card for my phone yet. I'm...having a bit of difficulty with that. They keep telling me I need an ARC. That's like a Green Card, right? To get a SIM card?"

"Yeah, that's the alien resident certificate," Johnny confirmed, "but you don't need one of those to get a SIM card."

"I don't?"

"No," he said, getting up from the chair. "They're just saying that because they don't want to deal with foreigners. Come on, I'll take you to a place. I know the girl. Do you have your passport?"

"Not on me. But I can cut back to the hotel and grab it."

After getting my phone squared away, Johnny asked, "What are you doing for lunch?"

It was maybe 10:30 a.m. "Nothing," I replied.

"Have lunch with me. I'll take you to one of my favorite spots."

Johnny led me through the Ximending Pedestrian Area to a TGI Friday's, which hadn't even opened for lunch service yet. "Let's sit at the bar," he said. Over the next week, Johnny took me to four different TGI Friday's locations in the Taipei area. I had no idea TGI Friday's was so popular in Asia, let alone Taiwan. Johnny was well-known among the staff at every stop, too. They greeted him by name at all four branches. I wouldn't say I was impressed, but I was very pleased to be out and about with a local. He introduced me to shitloads of people—few of whom I remember—and took me to a bunch of must-see sites.

Now that I had a phone, Johnny called every morning. I'd tell him what I wanted to see. We spent a lot of time together during those first ten days, mostly during the daytime because he worked the night shift at a hotel in Xindian. He took me all over the city on the back of his scooter. At one point, I asked him why he was so generous with his time, and he said, well, I miss hanging out with my American friends from college. And you're an American, so it's the next best thing.

On the third night, I took the MRT from my hotel to a bar on Heping East Road called 45. The bar was near a couple of universities, so the whole area was crawling with students, some of whom happened to be foreigners studying Chinese. It was somewhere around 7:30 p.m. when I climbed the stairs to the second floor. The bar was empty except for a middle-aged female bartender and a bored-looking waitress. I belly-upped to the bar, ordered a bottle of Budweiser, and had a change of heart.

"Wait. Make it a bottle of Taiwan Beer." I smiled like I'd somehow said something witty.

"Whatever," the bartender said. She brought the beer and deadpanned, "A hundred and twenty, for your '*Taiwan Beer*.'"

I produced a $1,000 Taiwan dollar note (US$30). "Here you go, ma'am."

"This all you got? Nothing smaller?"

"Sorry."

The bartender groaned, said something to the waitress in Mandarin, and disappeared to a room in the back of the bar.

I drank my beer and looked around the joint. *Not bad*, I thought. *Lots of Americana, very homey. I can see why foreigners might like this place. It demands a bartender with a surly attitude.* Five minutes later, the bartender returned and slapped my change on the bartop with a thud.

The first beer went down quickly, and I motioned to the bartender for another. This transaction went a bit smoother. She brought the beer and subtracted money from the change on the bar. No words exchanged.

Two white guys entered the bar in mid-conversation. They had distinctly North American accents, but I couldn't be sure if they were from the U.S. or Canada. They sat a few stools down the bar, locked in a heated discussion about a bachelor party that went awry. I heard "strippers didn't get paid." And "Jackson...detained in Macau," and a lot of "it's not my fault." I felt guilty for eavesdropping and started peeling the label off the beer bottle.

A minute later, one of the guys dropped an "a-boot" which clearly indicated he was Canadian. I waited for an opportunity to engage them. Finally, they stopped bickering, and I managed to say, "Hey, guys." They looked in my direction, but neither made eye contact. I pressed on. "I was wondering if I might ask a question?"

The bigger, hairier of the two scowled and said, "Do you mind? We're having a private conversation here."

Yeah, well, you can fuck off, I thought, but what I said was, "Oh, sorry." I resumed tapping my finger on the bartop to the glacial tones of Slint's *Spiderland* playing start to finish on the house P.A. *Jesus, I hope it isn't always like this.*

Several beers later, I was about to return to the hotel when another white guy arrived with an attractive Asian woman. I saw them coming up the stairs and re-took the barstool like musical chairs. They seemed to be happy, easy-going folk, together but not "together." They took a few moments to settle on a good spot, finally sitting at a table near the back of the bar. I heard the guy order their drinks from the waitress in Mandarin. It was the first time in three days that I heard a foreigner speak decent Chinese. The guy was obviously North American and doing his best to convince the woman of something. Sleeping with him was my first guess. He was short and stocky but not fat. There was more of a thickness about him. The woman was thin, well-kept but not overly manicured, in her early 30s, and smartly dressed in feminine business casual. *An office lady.*

I signaled the bored waitress for another beer. She came over and spoke to me in Mandarin. The gist of it was, "Order it from the bartender next time, dick." Another 20 minutes passed when I heard the office lady say to the short stocky guy that she had to get going.

You might consider it devious, but I was waiting for that moment. I don't know much about life or people in general, but I know that men are almost infallibly on their best behavior when trying to make it with a woman for the first time. So, when the stocky white guy came over and closed out his tab with the bartender, I knew it was my chance. He chatted with the bartender in English, and from their familiarity, I surmised they'd known each other for a long time. I was ready to pounce.

"Excuse me," I said to the stocky dude, maybe a bit too excitedly. "May I ask you a question?"

The guy ignored me for a moment, nodded to the bartender, exhaled and turned to me. "What's your story?" he asked, a grim expression on his face.

"Me? Just having a few beers," I replied, nodding and smiling politely. "Do you mind if I..."

"No, I mean, *where are you from?*" He was mildly annoyed, looking me over.

"San Francisco."

"Oh yeah? Nice place. What are you doing here?"

"Well, you see..."

"Let me guess, it's your first day in Taipei."

"Third."

"You have that look."

"What look?"

"The look like you just arrived in Taipei, and you don't know what the fuck is going on yet." I had to admit, he was right.

"Well, yes," I stammered. "It is...a bit...overwhelming at first."

"Listen, man. I've been here seven years. I *know* this town."

"Really? Wow, that's cool. I've been looking for someone just like you."

"What do you mean?" his eyebrows raising.

"I mean, like, someone I could ask a few questions, you know, about living here, getting a job.... It's a concrete jungle out there," I chuckled.

"No doubt about it," he said, and now I knew he was Canadian. "Listen, man. I'm trying to make it with this lady right now." He turned and motioned to the woman sitting at the table. "Here's my card. If you have any questions, give me a call and I'll do what I can to help you out."

I took the card. "Great! Thanks! I'm sure I'll be calling you sooner than later."

He looked me over again, not quite rolling his eyes. "You do that."

We shook hands. "Stephan." His bear-like paw crushed mine.

"Charlie."

Stephan left with the woman. I looked at his business card. It read: Stephan Belanger—Musician, Teacher, Thinker, Lover of Life.

★✸★

It's a good thing I kept a journal from the very beginning. In hindsight, it was good to set aside several hours each day to write down my thoughts and impressions because I wasn't taking notes on the fly. It was also a good thing I had a few friends waiting for regular updates from me. I kept my parents in the loop, too. *And then there was the missing Mao-mao.* I couldn't keep him out of my head. Every message to Tom Taylor started with: "Any sign of Mao-mao?"

Suddenly, I developed carpel tunnel syndrome in my right wrist. It was completely out of the blue. I wasn't writing *that much*, and I never had a problem with carpal tunnel. Perhaps all the stress had concentrated in one spot? The pain was intense. Of course, I didn't have health insurance or any idea where to get medical attention in Taipei, so I went to the hotel manager and told her my story. She called ahead and sent me to a traditional Chinese medicine clinic around the corner. The doctor examined my wrist and wrote a note to the hotel manager that said I needed to visit the clinic every 12 hours for herbal mudpack, cupping, and acupuncture treatments. And they wrapped my wrist in gauze. Neither the doctor nor the nurse ever asked me a question during the treatments. I could only point to my wrist and say, "*Zheli tong.*" (It hurts here.) None of the treatments worked. The pain went away on its own about a week later.

The clinic incident reinforced the biggest crunch of culture shock: the language barrier. Both the *Lonely Planet Taiwan* and *Insight City Guide: Taipei* said that English is spoken by a relatively decent number of Taiwanese people, especially in Taipei, which didn't seem to be the case during the first few days, except in the bars and hotels.

All things considered, life at the YS Hotel was pretty good. I left the hotel room TV on 24/7, even when I wasn't in the room. Mostly CNN, but now and then, I'd watch HBO or Cinemax. I'd seen *Ghost Rider* starring Nicholas Cage twice already. The room had one of those keycard systems where you gotta insert the card to get the lights to come on. They gave me two keys, so I just left one plugged in all the time. It gave me a bit of comfort to hear spoken English when I walked through the door.

I would have listened to the radio, but there was only one English-language station, ICRT (International Community Radio Taipei, 100.7 FM), and they played the shittiest music ever made. I didn't know the goddamn Carpenters would be the most popular band in the country—Air Supply running a close second. People were really excited about The Osmonds coming to town. They'd already sold out two nights at Taipei Arena, which seats up to 15,000 people. One night, I was at a bar that would become my hangout "spot" behind the Red Theater, and I sat through Kenny G's Greatest Hits and ABBA's Greatest Hits—twice for each. And nobody (locals) except my buddy Johnny Wong had ever heard of Jane's Addiction or The Cure. Green Day was considered punk rock. I saw several kids in Linkin Park T-shirts. I couldn't tell you how many times I heard "Loving You (Is Easy Cuz You're Beautiful)" in bars, train stations, clothing stores, and of course, TGI Friday's. I heard a Muzak version of "Norwegian Wood" and teared up.

Once my hunger reappeared—vaguely—I ate at the McDonald's in Ximen where the staff didn't speak any English. It took a heroic effort to order two cheeseburgers, but at least I got something into my belly other than beer.

A week had passed when Johnny called and said, "Hey, I want to take you up the mountain"—meaning Yangmingshan Mountain, which lies north of central Taipei. We had all but exhausted the must-see sites in scooter-distance, not the least of which was a brand-new Costco way out in the northern suburbs of Neihu. Taiwanese people were *psyched* about that Costco! Anyway, a few nights earlier, I was hanging out at my spot behind the Red Theater, where I got friendly with a group of people— men and women—one of whom happened to be a French dude from Switzerland named Pierre who was vacationing in Taipei with his boyfriend, Justin, a Taiwanese twink from somewhere in southern Taiwan.

At some point, Pierre mentioned Switzerland and Sandoz Laboratories—the famous birthplace of LSD. He asked if I had ever tripped before and I said, "Of course, many times." Pierre dug through his fanny pack and produced a small plastic bag containing a white paper square embossed with a repeating logo motif. I recognized it instantly as acid.

"Interested in some blotter?" Pierre asked, breaking off a smaller square from the sheet. "It's very clean."

"Are you serious?" I was stunned. "You mean right now?"

"Well," Pierre demurred with a wink, "you don't have to take it right now."

"In that case..." I said, shrugging and glancing aside. "Sure, why not?"

Pierre handed me the blotter, which I slipped into the plastic wrapper from my pack of cigarettes, took it home, put it in my backpack, and forgot about it. Until Johnny called and said, "Let's go up the mountain. Meet me at the coffee shop."

Johnny scooped me up on his Yamaha 150cc scooter and we drove north to the Tianmu Circle on Zhongshan North Road. After parking the scooter, Johnny said we'd take a bus up to Yangmingshan Flower Clock and Fountain—part of the larger Yangmingshan National Park. While we were waiting for the bus, I discreetly slipped the tab of acid under my tongue. *Well, this ought to be interesting.*

It took a good 30 minutes for the bus to wind its way up the mountain. We disembarked in front of the fountain on Huashan Road, where a few tourists were posing for pictures. As Johnny led me around the park, pointing out various statues and monuments, and telling his stories, the LSD started to kick in.

After another half-hour of wandering around, I said to Johnny, "Hey man, this is great. But let's head back down the mountain. I'd like to see more of Tianmu, to tell you the truth." Tianmu was a well-heeled suburban enclave of the Shilin District, featuring wide, shady streets lined with boutiques, restaurants, and cafés. As Wilson said, it's where all the rich foreigners live—home to the Taipei American School, which ran about US$30,000 in tuition per year, per kid.

"OK," Johnny agreed, "there's a TGI Friday's right by the Circle. We could do an early happy hour."

"So, let's go back to the bus stop?"

"Forget the bus," Johnny said. "I know a shortcut."

The acid was in full effect. The colors of the foliage were vibrating. The humid air was heavy and pulsating. As we started walking down a trail that started (inexplicably) at the end of a road, we descended into a wilderness. Time was elastic. After several meters of cutbacks, we arrived at some stone stairs, carved out of the mountainside. Along the way, Johnny told me how the stairs had been built by Japanese soldiers and used as a secret passage to get messages and supplies to the top of the mountain, where the military commanders resided. He also said that back in his day, Johnny and his friends used to party up there. We followed the stone trail, some of the passages steep and treacherous, for what seemed like an hour, until we arrived at a clearly marked trail, otherwise known as the Yangmingshan Steps.

43

It was the first warm day of spring, with temps around 27°C/80°F, so I was dressed in shorts, a T-shirt, and flip-flops, and sweating profusely. The flip-flops were wreaking havoc on my feet.

"Dude," I said, "I wish you'd told me we were going hiking. I would have worn shoes."

"Come on, man," Johnny said. "This isn't hiking. Don't be a pussy. You told me you like walking."

"I do. On flat ground, chief."

We arrived at the bottom of the stairs and my upper thighs and lower calves were screaming. The soles of my feet had been rubbed nearly raw. I had half a mind to jump in a taxi and head straight for the hotel, but the acid was making the decisions. For the first time since arriving in Taipei, I was *genuinely* enjoying myself, aside from the physical discomforts. And Johnny was intent on hitting TGI Friday's.

I didn't want to be there when we entered the building. The hard gloss of the shopping mall environment gave me cold vibes. Johnny went through the motions of introducing me to the wait staff while I ordered—uncharacteristically—a Long Island Iced Tea.

Another part of my discomfort stemmed from Johnny's penchant for repeating a couple of weird English catchphrases. His primary catchphrase was "Hello, pretty girl." We'd be walking down the street and every other girl we saw, he called, "Hello, pretty girl." Sometimes, they'd smile, and sometimes, they'd start walking a little faster. After that, he used "Spicy girl," reserved for girls he instinctively knew wouldn't respond to "Hello, pretty girl." The third and most annoying catchphrase was what drove me away from him. Every so often, unprompted by anything, he'd say, "You're V.I.P. Very important pig." I didn't get what he meant, and he always laughed when he said it. I figured it was something he saw in a movie and repeated out of habit.

After sucking down two of those Long Island Iced Tea monstrosities, I didn't feel the alcohol buzz, so I decided to switch to beer. The bartender came over and spoke Mandarin to Johnny, who turned to me and said, "She wants to buy you a beer."

"Well, how about that?" I smiled at the bartender and nodded in acceptance. Turning to Johnny, I said, "Maybe she likes me?"

And then he said, "You're V.I.P. Very important pig," and laughed.

The bartender brought the frosty mug of beer, which I pounded in two massive gulps, and said to Johnny, "Let's get out of here."

We walked back to the parking lot, and I had a sudden premonition of doom. I didn't want to get on the scooter. Johnny was perplexed and irritated. "What? Don't you think I'm a good driver?"

"No, it's not that. I think I'd rather walk back to the hotel." In truth, I hated riding the back of that scooter with every fiber of my being. Every second in traffic was pure torture. Every turn seemed like a Dead Man's Curve. Every passing truck scared the living shit out of me.

"You're going to walk back to Ximen—*from here?*" We were standing approximately 12 km from the hotel. On a good day, in familiar circumstances, I could do that walk in three hours, max. According to the mental map in my mind, it was a simple straight shot south. Like, if I just stayed on Zhongshan North Road, I'd eventually wind up at Taipei Main Station, and from there, I could hop on the MRT Blue Line and ride one stop to Ximen.

"Yeah."

"But you've been complaining about your feet since the stairs. Now you're gonna walk home?"

"I don't know. If I get tired, I'll hop on the bus."

"Do you know which bus goes to Ximen?"

"The 699?"

Johnny scoffed. "There's no 699 bus, you clown."

"Well, regardless. I'm going to start walking in that direction," I pointed, "and see what happens."

"You're crazy," Johnny said, donning his helmet. "If you get lost, don't call me. I have to work tonight."

"Don't worry. I'll be fine."

I left Johnny standing next to his scooter and started walking south down Zhongshan North Road. I don't remember how long it took me to get back to the hotel, only that I somehow found my way back. It was nearly dusk. The LSD was still active in my system, but the peak had passed. For that brief window of time, I felt relaxed and hopeful.

And it was at some time during the walk that I had an epiphany of sorts, or at least got a grip on the direction of the trip. First, I had to abandon the idea of traveling around Southeast Asia. That wasn't going to happen just yet. The culture shock was kicking my ass. Second, regardless of how I felt about the urban environment, I had to stay in Taipei for as long as possible. I remember thinking, "Stop treating this like a vacation." And suddenly, everything seemed easy—for lack of a better phrase. I mean, I knew exactly what I needed to do. Start looking for a job and a permanent place to live and keep making personal connections.

Above all, only a week into the trip, still completely driven by anxiety, adrenaline, and fear of the unknown, I thought about the promise I made. No matter what happened, I couldn't go back to San Francisco. I couldn't go back to waiting tables. If that meant teaching English in a cram school, so be it.

I didn't talk to Johnny for a while after that—maybe two or three weeks. I already had a job the next time we met. One night, I was at Carnegie's for Ladies' Night, and I had a feeling he was going to show up. Aside from TGI Friday's, hitting Ladies Night was Johnny's favorite pastime. And sure enough, Johnny came hobbling through the door on crutches, his left leg in a cast. We greeted each other and I bought him a beer.

"Dude, what happened to your leg?"

"Um," Johnny smiled. "Remember that day we went up the mountain?"

"Yeah, of course."

"Well, I had an accident. Some idiot in a Porsche ran a red light and T-boned me in the intersection."

My mouth dropped in horror. "Dude..."

"I know," Johnny said. "You would have been on the bike." He shook his head and patted me on the back. "The good news is the guy who hit me is rich. He's going to pay—big time."

"Well, well. Who's the V.I.P. now?"

3

Taipei, With the Wind at My Back

The most interesting and controversial advice I received since embarking on this journey came from a middle-aged Dutch woman during my first month in Taipei. She pre-empted said advice with a disclaimer that giving advice was neither her mission nor specialty. However, her advice was to avoid other foreigners as much as possible since many foreigners in Taiwan were ugly, spiteful, negative sociopaths who resented other foreigners for encroaching on their "Asian Experience" (with finger quotes!). And for the most part, she was right. But that didn't mean I took her advice, either—at least at first. It took me several hundred co-foreigner interactions to understand exactly why it was good advice.

The big pink elephant in the room of questions facing certain, mostly Western expats, is why would you want to leave your home country in the first place? Now, if there are any correct answers to this question, it takes a particular type of person to give an *honest* answer. If your answer is money, that pretty much wipes out the rest of any contingent questions anyone might have, but it doesn't work for English teachers in Taiwan because they don't make a lot of money, certainly not the kind of money they could make at home, doing the same job. Another potential correct answer is a desire to see another part of the world and experience a foreign culture. But what you learn, time and time again, and what you see, over and over again, is the expats who claim "wanderlust" are the "My Asian Experience" expats who complain the most and stubbornly refuse to part with certain aspects of their home culture, i.e., they insist on bringing Alabama to Taiwan, or worse, expecting Alabama customs to be followed. I still see this today.

My Asian Experience was part wanderlust and part life or death, but I learned to let go of the idea that this was "My Asian Experience." A billion Asian people were having the same experience. Thousands of expats were having the same experience. The Dutch woman said *many* foreigners in Taiwan were awful, but not *all*. Instinctively, I knew that meeting other foreigners would help me far more than it could hurt, and the key to foreigner interaction wasn't avoiding each other; it was empathy.

When I said that "everything seemed easy," I meant in the hypothetical sense. Nothing came easy those first few weeks. Without Johnny Wong to lean on for simple daily tasks such as making a copy of my passport, I floundered at the beginning. Every available job was teaching in a cram school, which wasn't very encouraging. Finding an apartment seemed to be considerably easier, but even then, the landlords were asking for two-month deposits and one-year leases.

I called Stephan Belanger a few times, but he never answered. I left brief but friendly messages. Meanwhile, I got in touch with Wilson's friend, Martin, who coincidentally lived very near my hotel. Martin was good for moral support and not much else (at the time), and I stuck with Wilson's warning about not counting on anybody except in emergencies. Most importantly, Martin had a weed connection, and he promised to hook me up. "But only after you've been here for a month." So that was something to look forward to, even though I'd been managing just fine without pot.

Looking back on it now, the desk clerks at the YS Hotel were just a little too nice. They were just a little too amused by my presence. Their smiles were just a little too bright. They were too happy to write destinations in Chinese on the back of stray business cards. I probably should have noticed something odd about them and the hotel, but I didn't. In addition to its improved location, the YS seemed like a decent place.

Light-years better than the Good Ground. The room was nice, although I did notice the abundance of heart-shaped pillows and love motifs scattered about the room. A lot of red, gold, and white furnishings, too.

I checked into the first room—an upgraded executive suite. *It's certainly worth 60 bucks a night. Big bed. TV in the bathroom, too. Jacuzzi and shower set-up. What's this, a bidet? Cool. Nice sofa and coffee table ensemble in the foyer. The internet's fast. But what's this funky-looking chair over in the corner? Ankle straps and a doughnut seat? It sure doesn't look like something I'd be sitting in.*

About an hour later, I went down to the lobby and the woman at the front desk asked, "Are you happy with the room?"

"Yes, but...what's that weird-looking chair in the corner?"

A mix of horror, confusion, and amusement barely registered in her eyes. "It's, um, a Chinese exercise chair?"

"Exercise chair, huh? OK."

I went for a walk around Taipei Main Station. After a few hours of exploration, I returned to the hotel, where I was greeted by the same front desk clerk.

"Excuse me, sir. There's a different room available if you want it." Was it a suggestion or was she telling me they were moving me to a smaller room?

"OK..."

I didn't think anything of it until about a week later when Johnny said, "You know that joint you're staying in is a love hotel, don't you?"

I had never heard the phrase "love hotel" until then.

The tenth day marked a crucial turning point: I went to my first job interview and got booted from the YS Hotel. That morning, I went to the front desk to inquire about extending my stay. The manager came out of the office and said, "How long are you planning to stay in Taiwan?"

"I dunno. Why?"

"If you're planning to stay for a couple of months or even longer, there are plenty of studio apartments available that would better suit your needs."

"Yes, I've been looking into that already."

"I see. So, tonight will be your last night."

I was taken aback. "Well...I was *hoping* to stay a few more nights. I don't have anything else lined up."

"I'm afraid that I don't have a room available to you after tonight."

Later that morning, I contacted several apartment agents. By the end of the evening, I signed a short-term lease for a studio apartment deep in the Wenshan District, which was close to the Wanfang Hospital MRT Station on the Brown Line, but nothing else. Pretty much the middle of nowhere. But I didn't care. It was a nice enough place. The rental agent was a kindly older woman who told me I could stay as long as I wanted, or not.

In the afternoon, I went on a job interview cum teaching demo at a school in Haishan, an hour southeast of Taipei City proper, which was way out past Banqiao near the end of the MRT Blue Line. One hour each way on the MRT was too far of a daily commute, but it was my first nibble of employment, and I had nothing better to do. Plus, I could get acquainted with the Taiwanese workplace. The teaching demo was...*interesting*. After a brief introduction, they shoved me in front of a dozen 11-year-old students and told me to start writing words, any words, on the board and ask the class to pronounce and repeat them. For 15 minutes. The first word I could think of was "sun," so I wrote "sun," followed by "sunshine," "sunset," and "sunlight." When we got to "sunspot," a boy raised his hand and asked, "What's that?" I drew a crude marker outline of the sun with a black spot when I realized I didn't know how to explain a sunspot to an adult, never mind a cram school kid.

I told them, "It's a scar on a part of the sun that died," which isn't even close to the real definition of a sunspot.

It was a grueling 15 minutes, but I got through the teaching demo. The observing teacher said, "You've got potential." They offered me a part-time starting position on Monday, Wednesday, and Friday, three hours per day, but they didn't want to sponsor my work permit and ARC, so I turned them down.

Several other job responses arrived during the day. It seemed like the ball was rolling.

The next day, I moved into the apartment and continued the job hunt. Ensconced in my new digs, I celebrated the newfound stability of having a "home." Another week went by; it was more of the same: looking for a job during the day and meeting people in the bars at night. I went on half a dozen interviews and turned down every offer for one reason or another. I kept leaving messages for Stephan but he never called back. My circle of acquaintances was expanding, so screw him. I didn't need that guy.

During the third week, I scored a series of interviews with a large cram school chain in Taipei City called Global International, and they offered me a job. There was one final interview and documentation hoops to jump through. They assigned me to work at the Gongguan location directly across the street from the Guting MRT stop on the Green Line, which was a scholastic hotspot with National Taiwan Normal University (*Shida*) and National Taiwan University (*Taida*) nearby.

I quickly realized my current apartment's location was too far from the "action," so I started looking for a new place on the Green Line. I found a fifth-floor rooftop flat in the Wenshan District near Wanglong MRT Station, three stops from the Gongguan Global International branch. From the photos, the apartment looked old but in good shape—and I loved the idea of a rooftop apartment. So I responded to the Craigslist ad poster, an American woman in her mid 20s, and planned for a viewing. When I showed up to see the joint, I was greeted by the woman, Lisa, and her boyfriend, Jacob. They said they were bailing out of Taiwan for Indonesia, and I recognized the scent of patchouli.

We started talking as they showed me around the place, which was huge compared to the studio. Lisa said she was from Portland, and Jacob said he grew up in the western suburbs of Chicago. That pricked my ears.

"Where in the western suburbs of Chicago?" I asked.

"Clarendon Hills," Jacob said, "which is technically part of Willowbrook now."

"What high school did you go to?" the pitch of my voice rising.

"Hinsdale South. Class of 2000."

I just about choked on my tongue. "Dude, I grew up in Clarendon Hills and graduated from Hinsdale South in '86. What's your last name?"

"O'Leary," Jacob said.

There were several O'Leary families in the area. "Where did you live?"

"Clarendon Hills Road and 79th Street. There's a white house on the corner."

"Come on now, Jacob. I lived at William Drive and 80th Street." I knew the white house on the corner—it was about three blocks from my parents' crib.

"Hey," Jacob said, "my mother's maiden name was Ramsey. She's older than you—Class of '81—but maybe you know her?"

"Get the fuck out of here!" I shouted.

"You know Victoria Ramsey?"

"I dated her younger sister, Jessica, in high school."

"You're kidding. You dated my aunt?"

"Dude... I'm not kidding." I literally sank to sit Indian-style on the bare floor.

Jacob asked, "What's your name again?"

"Charlie Birch."

"Oh, I've heard of you."

To make a long story short, Jacob got on the computer and emailed his aunt, Jessica, now living in Seattle. Jessica replied in a matter of minutes. She wondered what happened to Charlie, she said, and she was sad we lost contact.

"You have to take the apartment now," Lisa chimed in. "It's fate!"

We arranged to meet the landlord and sign the lease the following night.

When I got back to the joint at Wanfang Hospital, I found Stephan's business card in the side pouch of my backpack and decided to give him one last call. He didn't pick up, so I left another message.

An hour later, Stephan called. His name flashed on my cell phone, and I almost didn't answer. "Hey, Stephan, great to hear from you!"

"Yeah, what's going on with you?"

I told him about the job and the apartment.

"No shit," he said warily. "So, you've got all that going on already."

"It was pretty easy, actually."

"How long do you plan on staying in Taiwan?"

"I'm not sure. I don't have any plan to leave, if that means anything."

"It doesn't but...I wouldn't sign that lease or that cram school contract if I were you."

"Why?"

"Look, man. I've lived in this town seven years..." and from there he launched into a two-minute spiel about his experience of moving from Canada to Taiwan. None of it, I might add, was of any use to me. He ended it with, "So, there you go."

"The apartment is month-to-month," I explained, "but tell me, why should I not sign the teaching contact? They're going to sponsor my ARC."

"That contract is illegal. The school knows it's illegal, the government knows it's illegal, but they play this game of cat-and-mouse. The whole system is designed to screw the foreigners who come over here to teach English. If you decide after a month to bail out on the school, they'll yank your ARC, you'll have 15 days to leave the country, and if they're really assholes about it, they can blackball you from working in Taiwan ever again."

"What am I supposed to do? I need a job."

Stephan spent the next five minutes schooling me on the ins and outs of cram schools in Taiwan. He was nothing if not convincing, and later, with experience, I discovered that a lot of what he said was true. But I wasn't going to take his word for it.

"Look, man," he said. "Here's what you do. Wait—how much money do you have?"

"I've got enough to survive for another four months or so, but then, without a job, I'd be fucked. And then there's the issue of doing a visa run."

"Got it. First, bail out on the apartment. Did you sign a lease yet?"

"Tomorrow night."

"Don't do it. Call the landlord and tell him you're sorry, but you've changed your mind. That way, if you decide you want to stay in Taiwan, you can always call him up and ask for that apartment. Trust me, they deal with flakey foreigners all the time. And *shhhhhiiiiit*. Eighteen thousand (Taiwan dollars) a month is way too fucking expensive, man.

There's a cheap hostel just down the street from the Guting MRT stop. You can get a room for seven hundred a night. Get on the internet and try to find a roommate situation. Next, forget that cram school. Don't even go back there, man. Don't return their calls. Forget about it. You don't want to teach at that school. Get on Craigslist and start looking for private teaching gigs. That's where the money is. Find a few students and fly under the radar. Stay out of the system."

I didn't like Stephan's tone. I specifically didn't like that he assumed I was a "flakey foreigner" when I was the one who made it a point to get in touch with him. And he didn't even know me. I could have been called a lot of things, but flakey wasn't one of them. Plus, Stephan wasn't just offering advice, he was telling me *how things were going to be*. It was a cross between a crystal ball and a chip on his shoulder. I was interested in his opinion, but I didn't ask him to provide me with a game plan. And as it turns out, Stephan didn't exactly follow his own advice.

I took the job and the apartment. I'd start the gig next week and move into the apartment at the end of the month.

* ✱ *

Right about then, the panic attacks subsided, and the anxiety disappeared. Man, I could feel the wind at my back. The momentum was undeniable. And my hunger returned.

I wasn't trying to learn Mandarin out of cultural sympathy or a desire for social acceptance. Certainly, the Taiwanese people appreciate a foreigner who's trying to speak Mandarin, but most foreigners didn't spend 12 years in a cram school learning the language, like Taiwanese kids and English. My primary motivation for learning Mandarin (without a language class) was to meet my immediate needs. Everything beyond that—for example, current events—was frivolous. When I wasn't out walking around or having drinks, I was studying useful vocabulary in the phrasebook, thinking ahead to the next time I'd roll up on the night market and buy one of those grilled Taiwanese sausages with wasabi sauce.

Despite my painful lack of Mandarin skills, I became more adventurous when it came to food. Previously, I wouldn't approach any food stalls that lined the streets of every neighborhood in Taipei. Aside from TGI Friday's, I'd eaten at the McDonald's in Ximen for the first ten days. I lived on cheeseburgers, which is the only thing I could manage to order from the menu.

One night, I went to the little ad hoc night market in the alley outside my apartment and bought a bunch of food. I learned to say "I'd like X number of those" in Chinese while pointing, and I was getting better at numbers. However, as soon as the vendor started talking to me, I was lost. So, I'd just hand over the money and let them sort it out. I felt like a savage, you know? Only capable of grunting. Now, I knew they were usually asking me stuff like, "*Xuyao la bu la?*" (Do you want it spicy or not?) or "*Xuyao dazi?*" (Do you want a bag?) but it was no use. I just repeated, "*Wo bu mingbai*" (I don't understand) and shook my head. Nevertheless, I walked out of the market with a bunch of local delicacies—some tasty, some atrocious. You live, you learn.

I also started going to a vegetarian buffet near the hospital, with only a vague idea of what they were serving. A lot of tofu-based sausage and meat patty stuff. When I filled my to-go container, I took it to the lady at the counter and she looked it over and decided what to charge. On a typical day, I'd fill two hardcover book-sized boxes with pineapple, broccoli, leek dumplings, and noodles, and she'd charge me a whopping TWD$60 (US$2) per box. I was spending 20 times that amount on booze in the bars and convenience stores every night.

In general, my diet was improving from what it was in San Francisco, where I survived on restaurant food, basically. I didn't know that I lost 12 pounds until they weighed me during the health exam for ARC application.

Even though I ignored Stephan's warnings about the job and the apartment, he invited me to meet him for a beer at a bar called Roxy 99. On the surface, Stephan was a nice enough guy. In hindsight, I'm deeply grateful for his time and support, but he was kind of a condescending prick. And it wasn't just toward me. As a control freak, Stephan was never completely happy unless he had a solid grasp on the situation. Therefore, he complained. A *lot*. At Roxy 99, he complained about where we sat in the bar. "Let's move over there, no, over there...no, that's not good." He complained about the temperature of the beer and scolded the bartender. "What you should do is keep it in the cooler overnight." He complained about women. "Taiwanese women are afraid of commitment." I hardly said a word, edgewise. I simply nodded and looked at my hands, hoping he would settle down and we'd talk about something useful or actionable.

When we got down to basic life stories, I told him how I wound up in Taiwan, leaving out all the stuff about being a musician and raging drug abuser. Stephan often mentioned his parents, usually in a self-affirming way. "Well, I had great parents, so that's why I'm such a good guy." I'd never met anybody who said they had great parents, let alone used it as a justification for their social superiority.

Stephan used keywords like integrity and commitment, which, of course, I found suspicious. He said would take me "under his wing," but he didn't want to waste his time. He'd seen hundreds—maybe thousands of guys like me come and go. I felt like he was selling me a life insurance policy. And I wasn't buying it.

He had every right to treat me with indifference like any newly arrived expat. He didn't owe me anything. He was, in fact, doing me a favor by offering, however tenuous, his uncensored opinion. But there's nothing worse than accepting a favor from someone who makes it clear that they're going out of their way to do you a favor. And while Stephan had every right to be condescending and wary of my motives, he sincerely believed I was an idiot. The way he looked at me, *I could see it in his eyes.* The way he spoke to me, *I could hear it in his voice.* What he failed to recognize is that I held even less regard for him than he did for me.

4

In the Doldrums

The feelings of hope and positivity lasted for maybe a week, which is how long it took to complete my teacher training at Global International in Gongguan. By the time they had me scheduled to teach a regular class, I was already looking for another gig—even though I signed a one-year contract. First, just being in a classroom dredged up a bunch of unsavory feelings from my prior experience as a substitute high school teacher in the U.S. On top of that, I hated the cram school—the institution and everything about it. And the act of setting foot inside a cram school made me hate myself. All those warm and cozy feelings of making it in Taipei were disappearing, fast.

But then again, I was beyond determined to see this thing through. *I took the job, now I'm going to attempt to do the job.* Fortunately, during my travels through the bar circuit, I met many expat cram school teachers who gave me a lot of advice. Some of it good, some of it not so good. But perhaps most importantly, I learned a valuable piece of information. The first thing that goes out the cram school window is the notion of being a good teacher.

I was assigned seven classes, including this one class of 10-year-old kids on Tuesdays from 5:30–7:30 p.m. I was the third teacher assigned to this class in a month. The other two quit. On the day my predecessor quit, an Australian guy named Leslie warned me about the class. Of all the things Leslie said, only one thing stuck—something about these kids "taking a sense of pride" in scaring off foreign teachers.

"Thanks for the tip, Les," I said with unearned confidence. "They won't scare me. More like the other way around."

When I arrived at my assigned Global International school, the other foreign teachers gave me the coldest shoulder I have ever experienced in my life. It was worse than the time I showed up at my sister's second wedding, so strung out that my relatives didn't recognize me. On my first day of training, I walked into the teacher's room, and it was so frosty I could see my breath. The disdain was palatable. *Goddamn. Why are these people so fucking sour?* I didn't know that teaching at the Global International Gongguan branch did that to people.

So, I tried to break the ice with every teacher and came away with nothing but ice chips. "Can you recommend a good place to eat?" I asked Ronald, the most American-looking guy in the room. Ronald sneered and said, "That depends if you can use chopsticks." The other teachers were just as rude. I asked a morbidly obese woman named Rebecca if she had any teaching tips, and she said, "You should probably wear a hat, so you don't blind the students with the reflection coming off your bald head." Even the Taiwanese co-teachers ignored me with prejudice. During the two months I spent at Global International, I'm pretty sure the only other teachers who spoke to me were the ones who left, like Leslie.

Likewise, the training sessions were torture. They made trainees observe countless classes, take detailed notes, and write up class activity plans. It was all a load of bullshit once you were up in front of the kids.

Ten minutes into the first class with the abovementioned 10-year-olds, I wasn't so sure about my ability to control the classroom atmosphere. Those little punks were so unruly and disrespectful that I stopped turning my back—always keeping them in front of me. It got to the point where I wouldn't even write on the dry-erase board. Looking over my shoulder, I could only keep one eye on half of the room.

To their credit and the depth of my teaching experience, pre-teen Taiwanese cram school kids weren't anywhere near as uncivilized as American kids could be at that age. This bunch just wouldn't sit down and shut up. I couldn't blame them, really. Cram school kids don't want to be there; they have no other choice. They left home for school at six in the morning, spent all day in a series of psych-ward, fluorescent-lit classrooms, and returned home late at night, well past dinnertime, six, sometimes seven nights a week. It was common to see middle school students toting heavy book bags on the MRT after 10:00 p.m.

And so, despite the odds against success, I tried to placate the Tuesday 5:30–7:30 kids. I was obliging. We played games, I told stories, they were allowed to speak Chinese, and I looked the other way when exercises weren't finished. We had fun, or as much fun as one can have in a cram school classroom with your clothes on.

The peace lasted two sessions until one of the parents from the 10-year-old class complained that I wasn't teaching by repetition. A co-teacher pulled me out of class and escorted me to the office, where I was reprimanded by the branch manager, Geraldine.

Rule 1: No improvisation.

Rule 2: No spoken Chinese, which was a rule almost impossible to enforce in this classroom.

Rule 3: A repeated warning to follow the curriculum.

The dirty little secret of cram schools is the students aren't taught to speak English, they're taught to score well on the entrance exams to junior and senior high school and college. The exams have a heavy emphasis on grammar, reading, and vocabulary, and the questions are almost always written by professors at universities, and severely lacking in what you and I might call "practical English." They're testing kids on an approximation of English.

Another thing I learned about this form of babysitting is that every so often, you had to let them see you get angry. You had to give them a taste of the wrath hiding behind your pleasant demeanor. It wasn't like teaching in the U.S., where you had to show up ready to fight Mike Tyson every day. But you couldn't be a doormat, either. If you let the cram school kids walk all over you, they have impunity, and you have no recourse. When you spend all your time being the good cop, the bad cop routine isn't believable.

The other thing was you couldn't kick the little bastards out of class, no matter what they said or did or refused to do. The parents would be in the office screaming bloody murder. The funny thing is it was never discussed during any interview or training session. It was so unthinkable that it didn't need to be mentioned. Nobody told *me*.

One evening, I bounced this fatheaded prick named Peter Chien from the high school class. Aside from Peter, most of the high school kids were cool and smart. They asked questions, which was almost unheard of in my other classes. When Peter was in attendance, all bets were off. I spent most of my time and attention trying to get Peter to adhere to the program and leave everybody else alone. His parents must have been going through a divorce. It was a thrice-weekly class, and Peter always came in late and defiant. This one night, he came in, slammed the door, walked across the room, emptied the books from his backpack across the floor, kicked one toward me, and roared, "*Ahh-hahahahaha!*" like he won a poker game.

I went to the door, held it open and said, "No dice, boss. Go see Geraldine."

The kid challenged me right then and there, putting up his dukes in a fighting stance.

"Peter, Peter..." I said, chuckling and looking down at my feet. "You have no idea how much I would *love* to knock you the-fuck-out. But that's not going to happen. Now pick up your books and get the fuck out of my classroom and don't come back without Geraldine and a parent."

There was stunned silence. Peter made a big show about picking up the books from the floor.

"Move it, chief," I said. "I'm not fucking around. This isn't a joke."

"*Move it, chief,*" he mocked.

A few titters spread around the room. I shot a look at Ashley, Classroom Enemy #2, another attention vortex. "Don't even think of opening your fucking mouth, Ashley, so help me God." Peter eventually sad-sacked his way out the door.

Many cram school classrooms have eye-level windows that open into the hallway so parents can ostensibly observe what's happening. It gives the teacher a feeling of being in a fishbowl, looking out at the pinched faces of half a dozen Asian mothers, while trying to communicate with their shell-shocked and psychologically destroyed children. During the Peter episode, no fewer than three obsessive-compulsive parents had their faces to the glass.

"Good," I said with an indignant snort. "I hope they're enjoying the show."

Later that evening, I was sitting in the hallway outside the main office, grading papers, when I overheard a man screaming at Geraldine. Somewhat disturbed by the intensity of the man's voice, I went to one of the nearby Taiwanese co-teachers and asked if she knew what he was saying.

"He said we're wasting his money."

"Oh? Who is he?"

"Peter Chien's father."

When Peter's father stormed out of the office, Geraldine came to me and snapped, "You can't remove children from your class! You must learn to control them!"

And so, I never bounced another kid from one of my classes. Not even Peter Chien, who was transferred to a different class a week later.

In general, most kids were smart enough to realize how far they could push a teacher before he or she lost their composure, and the 10-year-old Tuesday 5:30–7:30 class reveled in reaching that watermark. Leslie was right on the money about *that*. However, they got quiet when I showed visible anger or raised my voice. During my two-month stint at Global International, I would like to think that I had a few moments of actual teaching. However, they refused to ask questions. If something confused them in their lessons, they would raise their pencils and say, "Teacher?" and point to the problem. The only questions they ever asked were: "What happened to your hair?" and "Why did you come to Taiwan?" Other than that, most of my kids never once asked a question pertaining to English.

Frankly, I didn't give a shit what was happening in the class. My days were numbered in the single to double digits. I knew that. So, I just let them do whatever they wanted and talked over the din, basically ignoring them. When the troublemakers started making trouble, I walked to the window and said to one of the women with their faces pressed to the glass, "Is this your kid? If it is, straighten him out!" They didn't appreciate that. Within days, Geraldine called me into the main office and told me to stop talking to the parents. Bristling from yet another scolding, I went to the next class and invited all the parents in the hallway to come sit in the classroom. Geraldine was outraged and threatened to fire me, to which I shrugged and said, "Go ahead."

No longer caring if anybody learned anything, I was focused on getting my ass out of there. Like the parking meter cop who casually strolls down the street, writing ticket after ticket, impervious to all outbursts of anger and pleas for mercy, I was just doing my job. I'd cue up the lesson on CD, say, "Lesson 16, page 34," and hit **PLAY**. If they didn't follow, then screw them. At some point during every class, it was as if they all got tired of messing around at the exact same time, and suddenly the room would be quiet, and they'd do their exercises.

Outside of the teaching job, it makes me smile to say that things might not have been going much better.

Two nights after moving into the new rooftop apartment, I began seeing a woman named Ivy, who was around my age, divorced, had a 12-year-old son, and lived about 30 minutes north of Taipei. We were originally introduced two weeks earlier by Johnny Wong at the TGI Friday's on Zhongxiao East Road. We met again by chance at Carnegie's on a Ladies' Night. I asked her out to dinner, and she said no. Rebuffed, I said, "OK, no worries." Thinking the conversation was over, I turned away. There was a tap on my shoulder. Ivy asked, "Do you live alone?" Turning back, I said, "Yes, I do." She said, "Well, I like to watch movies."

At first, it was cordial and casual; she'd come into the city, and we'd hang out at my rooftop and watch movies together and do stuff you do with someone you're seeing. A week later, it progressed to her sleeping over, and then one day, she just stopped calling or returning calls or texts and I never heard from her again.

I didn't care about the relationship. The lack of communication bothered me, which seemed to be the rule of law in town. If she was like, "Hey, dude, I'm busy," or "I'm not into you," it'd be cool. Any reason or excuse would suffice. What bugged me was the complete lack of respect. I don't know any other way to put it.

It became a pattern with new people, particularly women. I met a girl named Nina. She invited me to a place called Brown Sugar on a Sunday night. That Sunday afternoon, all contact with Nina stopped cold. She blocked me. Not even a measly text message. It made me not want to trust people. It made me not want to get involved with people. I could only hope there were people in town who didn't make San Franciscans seem like responsible adults.

Oddly enough, once I had the job and the rooftop pad, Stephan called me every other day. This forced me to create spontaneous excuses for declining invitations to ride mountain bikes, watch hockey games, and treat restaurant servers like beggars in the street, which we'd already done in the space of a few weeks.

A few days passed since the last time we hung out. Stephan called with another activity.

"Hey, there's an open mic night over at the Drunken Bear," he said. "Care to join me?"

"Um...sure."

"Sign-up for the open mic starts at eight o'clock sharp, so don't be late if you want to get a slot."

"Are you performing?"

"Yeah, of course. I'm working on a couple of new tunes."

Proverbially rubbing my hands together, I couldn't wait. Parade balloon disasters are the only thing more dreadfully entertaining to witness than an open mic in a neighborhood bar. Karaoke is shadow puppetry by comparison. Regardless of how I felt about Stephan and his condescending attitude, I couldn't skip this open mic event.

I arrived at the Drunken Bear around 8:12 p.m., missing the first performance, a duo of Taiwanese guys covering Billy Joel songs, which Stephan described as "well-intentioned." I ordered a beer, and we jockeyed among what seemed like every foreigner in Taiwan for a place to sit.

"Crowded tonight," I half-shouted. I'd never been to the Drunken Bear before. I had no idea if 50 people meant crowded.

"This is the most popular open mic in Taiwan," Stephan said with a smug, self-congratulatory smile—a non-verbal crossing of arms over the chest. "I'm an insider. Don't you respect me?"

A trio of female expats took the floor and warbled their way through a dissipated rendition of "Hold On" by Wilson Philips, accompanied on acoustic guitar by a goateed Taiwanese guy wearing a beret. I recognized one of the singers from a cram school advertisement plastered around the city.

"I haven't seen or heard anything this bad since a talent show in high school," I quipped.

"I'm next on the list," Stephan said, gleaming. "I'll show those guys."

"Girls," I said.

"What? Who?"

"They're girls. Women. Of the opposite sex."

Stephan looked at a spot about three meters behind my head. "I'm up next."

There were problems from the minute Stephan took his prized Washburn acoustic out of its case. He argued with the sound guy about monitor levels. There was a deafening screech of feedback when Stephan tried to plug his guitar into the P.A. system, which he did three or four times before the sound guy came over and told him to stop.

Joyce, the owner, came out from behind the bar and got involved. Stephan stood with the guitar around his neck and his hands out, palms up at his side, giving the crowd a "What the fuck?" impression while Joyce and the sound guy tried to locate the source of the feedback. Meanwhile, the problem was obvious to me, but I wasn't about to intervene.

This is strictly for egghead musicians and sound techs, but Stephan insisted on running an unbalanced line-level 1/4" guitar cable (aka Hi-Z) from the built-in preamp on his guitar, directly into the mixing board via high-impedance mic channel rather than agreeing to use an XLR converter into the direct box, which Stephan claimed "kills the tone." However, it would have handled the impedance problems that arise when two preamps, the guitar and the mixing board, are acting against each other. The sound guy's solution was to simply drop the fader on the guitar channel and force Stephan to strum it out.

The three of them went back and forth until finally, the sound guy snapped, "*Just play!*" and Stephan introduced himself and the first song.

"My name is Stephan Belanger, and I'm from Toronto. This is a song I wrote about my ex-girlfriend. It's called, 'Pink Slip'."

And away he went.

The first 30 seconds of his "new" song consisted of Stephan strumming a D chord as if he invented the D chord, followed by an abrupt switch to an arpeggiated A minor chord, thus introducing the first verse, which, mostly paraphrased except for the hook and chorus, went like this:

I treated you / like the queen you want to be

64

I put my self-interests on a shelf / and devoted myself to you
You paid me back / my generosity
By shitting on everything / our relationship stands for
That's why I'm giving you a pink slip / a pink slip

It was one of the funniest things I'd ever heard in my life. I'll never forget that line: "I'm giving you a pink slip." I made a peripheral scan of the room to see if anyone else found it amusing, but mostly, I saw the blank, disinterested faces of the crowd. And then, in one of those uncanny moments that make you think the universe is tuned to your conscious inner dialogue, the power went out.

A half-groan half-cheer spread across the bar and I heard Stephan say, "That's just fucking great." The emergency lights came on, the boss lady started waving a heavy-duty flashlight around, blinding several people at the bar, and suddenly three Taipei policemen in full riot gear burst through the front door, announcing in Mandarin what I'd only heard rumors about.

It wasn't so much a raid as some sort of random shakedown of the bar owner. The cops checked the IDs of a few locals and all but ignored the majority of foreigners present. I didn't even reach into my pocket. Several minutes later, the cops decamped, and the power came back on, by which time, Stephan was in a heated argument with the sound guy over whether he could continue. The sound guy kept pointing to his watch and saying, "Your ten minutes are up." Stephan protested in full Shakespearean mode.

"What!? I cannot believe this! Is it my fault the cops came in and disrupted my performance? *I think not.* I should be allowed to continue from the moment I was interrupted."

The sound guy was resolute. "Time is time." I liked that sound guy. He was funny.

"This is no way to run an open mic! No wonder the cops pulled a raid on your bar!" Stephan howled. The boss lady Joyce came over and waggled a finger in Stephan's face, to which he responded by shaking his head and laughing facetiously. Having lost the battle, he put his guitar back in its case and made his way over to where I sat.

"Good effort," I said.

"Let's bail," he replied. "This place has no class."

We wound up at a trendy nightclub called Velvet on the other side of town, which, true to its name, featured a lot of velvet. The drinks were pricy, the sound system was bumping, and the attitude was thick. Despite my repeated attempts to lighten the mood, Stephan was still seething about the open mic debacle. And I'm just guessing that women on the prowl at Velvet outnumbered men by 5-to-1.

"Dude!" I yelped. "Are you seeing beyond your rage? This place is slamming! Good choice!"

I bobbed my head to the Gnarls Barkley "Crazy" remix and sipped my beer. Everywhere I looked, women. There was one I found attractive, so I got up and introduced myself to her. "Hi, my name is Charlie," I said, almost shouting, extending my hand. "What's yours?"

"Iris," she said and smiled, softly clasping my hand.

"Listen, I was wondering if you might like to join me and my friend for a drink?"

"You want to buy me a drink?"

"Yes, I do."

Iris accompanied me back to the table where Stephan sat glowering.

"Stephan, this is Iris. Iris, Stephan." Iris reached her silky-soft paw across the table, which Stephan ignored. I turned for a split-second to signal the cocktail waitress.

"What do you do?" Stephan asked sharply.

"Excuse me?" Iris replied, taken off-guard.

"What are you doing here?"

Iris retracted her paw and laughed, slightly insulted. "I came to dance and have a drink."

"What you're saying is that you came here tonight to be approached by foreigners who will buy you drinks all night."

"Easy, chief," I said nervously. "He's just joking," I said to Iris. "He's had a bad night. In a black mood."

"No," Stephan said, growing angrier, "I want to know what kind of a person just accepts a drink and an invitation to converse from a complete stranger in a nightclub?"

Iris looked at me. "Who does this guy think he is?" And she walked away.

"What the fuck was that?" I was furious.

"She had it coming."

"*No.* She *didn't.*"

"Look, man. I've been in this…"

"Fuck off, dude. I don't even want to hear it." I left a 1,000-note on the tabletop and walked out.

After the Velvet incident, I stopped answering Stephan's calls for a few days. One morning his number popped up. I was bored and felt a little guilty about avoiding him.

"Hello, Stephan."

"How's Global International treating you?" he asked, disregarding the traditional greeting.

"It's alright, not bad." *Lie.* "But the other foreign teachers suck." *Truth.*

"You're a writer and you have a bachelor's in English, right?"

"Yeah, in creative writing, to be exact."

"Listen, I may have a writing job for you. The school I work for is looking for a full-time writer. You have a resume and a copy of your degree? How about writing samples?"

"Yeah, of course."

"OK, I'm going to give your number to this woman named Daisy, and she's going to give you a call to set something up. Don't say anything about it to Global International."

"Oh, I won't."

"What are you doing this weekend?"

"No plans yet."

"The Canadian Association is having an ice-skating pancake breakfast fund-raising event at Taipei Arena on Sunday. Five hundred Taiwan for two hours on the ice and all the pancakes you can eat—with *real Canadian maple syrup.* Wanna come?"

"Wait a minute, did you just say ice-skating pancake breakfast?"

"With real maple syrup."

5

Captain Felix & Knowledge Press Ltd.

The woman named Daisy called a few minutes after I hung up with Stephan.

"Charlie!"

"Yes. Daisy?"

"Yes, hello, how are you!"

"Fine, thanks."

"Stephan tells me you're a writer."

"Yes."

"Do you want to write for us?"

"Umm...I don't know... *Do I?*" I was genuinely surprised.

Daisy sounded convinced. "Can you come to the office today? We can have lunch, and you can meet the boss."

"Uh...today is...not..."

"How about tomorrow morning?"

"OK. What time?"

"Come around 11:45. We have lunch at noon. Do you have the address?"

"No. I don't even know the name of your company." Stephan had mentioned the name of the cram school, Zhang Yi English Academy, but indicated the publishing company was a separate entity. The entire operation was run by a guy named Captain Felix who was something of a celebrity on the island. That's all I knew.

"Do you have a pen and paper?"

"Yeah. Go ahead."

Daisy gave me the address, which I promptly typed into Google Maps. Taipei's street numbering system is bewildering at first, with lanes, alleys, sections, and north-south-east-west indicators, but after a while, it becomes quite logical. The address she gave me looked like this: 7F-1, Apt. 1, No. 63, Lane 65, Sec. 3, Anhe Road.

"Got it now."

"Great!" Daisy exclaimed. "See you tomorrow."

The next day was a relatively pleasant morning, so I rode my bike to the meeting. Arriving at the location indicated on the map, I found a stereotypical red brick, gated residential high-rise—estimated height: 20 stories. I pedaled back to the nearest main intersection and double-checked my map. Nope. That must be the building. I circled back, dismounted, and locked my bike to a light pole. The front gate was open, but the cranky old security guard stopped me with a raised hand. I tried speaking Mandarin, but he didn't understand a word of it. Then I pulled out the Google map. He simply shook his head and said, "*Bu zai zheli.*" (Not here.)

I dialed Daisy's number. "Charlie! Where are you?"

"I'm not sure, Daisy. I think I'm standing outside an apartment building."

"Wait a minute." There was a long pause. "I'm going to have Veronica call you right back."

"Who is Veronica?"

The line went dead.

A minute later my cell rang. It was Veronica. I'll get to her in a minute.

"Hi, Charlie!" Veronica said. "Do you know exactly where you are?"

"Well, I'm at the address Daisy gave me, but it looks like an apartment building."

"Do you see a place called Café 55 on the corner?"

"Yes."

"OK. You're in the right place. Just tell the security guard '*Zhang Yi*' (djahng-yee) and come up to the seventh floor."

"Johnny?"

"No, *Zhang Yi*."

"Chon-yee?"

She laughed slightly. "Just stay where you are. I'll come find you."

Veronica had a nice voice, but I was completely unprepared for the woman who approached me on the sidewalk. "Charlie?"

"Yeah. Veronica?" *Oh my God. She's gorgeous. Like, what the fuck is this?* We shook hands, exchanged smiles. "Follow me," she said.

There was a bit of small talk, but seven floors went by like a heartbeat.

"Oh, you're from California?" Veronica asked.

"Uh-*huh*."

"I've been to Los Angeles."

We alighted on the seventh floor, and she led me to a door, which looked no different than any other residence.

This must be an elaborate joke. There's no way this woman is taking me to a publishing company. Of course, I was completely uninformed about Taipei's mixed commercial and residential zoning policies.

We entered a dark foyer where Veronica instructed me to take off my shoes and put on a pair of *lanbai* slippers (house slippers). The office was a spacious (by Taipei standards) three-bedroom condominium. They busted out most of the walls adjoining the living room, leaving only the kitchen intact. The main space contained a dozen or so cubicles, flanked by three smaller offices with large windows facing in, and two bathrooms—one in the executive office. The occupants of said cubicles, as far as I could tell at that moment, were female, between the ages of 19 and 50-ish. Veronica led me into one of the smaller offices, where she introduced me to Daisy and immediately slinked away. Daisy was an adroit, stern-looking woman with close-set eyes on a broad face framed by a Cultural Revolution bobbed haircut. This was apparently the executive office—Captain Felix's control center.

Daisy told me to sit on a chair against the wall and again asked, "Do you want to write for us?"

"Sure," I said, shrugging. "What do you want me to write?"

"Felix will tell you." The slamming of the main office door gave me a start. "Speak of the devil, and there he is."

The most unpredictable and sometimes troublesome aspect of the psychedelic drug experience is/are the side effects. You may have heard somebody describe an "acid flashback" as an intense recollection of sensations uncannily like the real thing, occurring a certain amount of

CAPTAIN FELIX & KNOWLEDGE PRESS LTD.

time after the drug has cleared your system—weeks, months, even years. A flashback can last anywhere from a moment to a day and range in severity from mildly entertaining to downright horrifying. Flashbacks can be triggered by a wide range of stimuli, from smoking weed to the chorus of a song. On one hand, a flashback can be fun because you never know when it's going to happen. On the other hand, it's not fun for the same reason. In my experience, acid flashbacks have generally been mild—very rarely, terrifying—and appeared during moments of increased stress, anxiety, or uncertainty.

I don't know what it was about the phrase "speak of the devil" that triggered me, but as soon as the words came out of Daisy's mouth—and just a moment after the door slammed, but before Captain Felix appeared in the executive office—my sensory perception underwent that familiar psychedelic sea change. The ambient light of the room flipped to an opaque hue of fluorescent green, while the outlines of human figures had electric blue auras. Time was a giant elastic sheet of tarpaulin; space was a matrix of ribbons supporting the ground beneath my feet. Every word, movement, and living cell in the room appeared to be interconnected by a series of fractals, constantly swirling at random, yet, in perfect harmony—almost like there was some grand design behind the whole gambit of life in general, and it was created by somebody or thing who really liked geometry and video games.

As far as I know, nobody can tell if you're having a flashback just by looking at you. I've seen a couple of guys have flashbacks accompanied by irrational behavior. Most of the time, somebody going through a flashback will say, "Jesus Christ, I'm having a flashback," staring at the palms of their hands. "These...things...are not...real!" Sometimes, you'll be able to talk them down and out of it. And then there will be rare cases where Frankie is pacing up and down the hallway, reciting the Boy Scout Code of Honor, frantically scratching his forearms. Somebody grabs Frankie and say, "Come on, now, kiddo! Let's sit down over here and talk."

If one of my friends had been sitting next to me, I would have said, "Shit's fuckin' weird, man, but I'm rollin' with it."

Stephan had given me the barest of information about Captain Felix and his operation. Stephan described Felix as a "kooky, old, semi-famous

Taiwanese English teacher dude with more money than God," which leaves a lot to be desired. In a place like Taiwan, guys like that could be around every corner. Likewise, Stephan never said anything about the working environment. He taught at the cram school and visited the publishing house once a month or so. "They have a couple of really hot translator chicks" was all he offered.

Nor did I think to ask Stephan any pertinent questions. Just based on the brief phone call with Daisy, and now, the first impressions of the office and the people, I didn't care if the writing position was legitimate. *This is laughable. Why am I even here?* First, who offers a writing job without a description? Second, who offers this gig to someone they've never met? Ultimately, I assumed it wouldn't amount to anything.

Standing five-foot-five in *lanbai* slippers, Felix was average height for a 65-year-old Taiwanese man. A retired captain of the Taiwan Air Force who also received training in the U.S., he walked with a distinctive, steady shuffle—his heels barely left the floor. Aside from his penchant for slamming doors, the shuffling sound was the only way you'd know he was coming. Felix was balding but kept his hair in the grand Chinese tradition, e.g., what little hair he had left, not enough for a combover, he let grow to 3.2 mm and cut according to lunar phases. He wore giant Peter Fonda-style glasses that darken to an unsettling orange-beige in the presence of ultraviolet light. His wardrobe was "golf casual," though I could tell he'd only ever been on a golf course to see if he wanted to buy it. He reminded me, at first, of a Taiwanese Kim Jong-Il—with maybe a little more on the ball.

Now, his name—what everybody called him—was either the Chinese honorific of *laoshi* (teacher) or Felix. I added the "Captain" moniker after I found out about his military service and saw a picture of him in uniform. His Chinese name was Zhang Xiaoming, but he was widely known in Taiwan and China as "Zhang Yi," a courtesy name to be used later in life. After 20 years of age, the courtesy name (zi) is assigned in place of one's given name as a symbol of adulthood and respect. Primarily used for males, one could be given a zi by the parents or one may adopt a self-chosen zi. According to *The Book of Rites*, after a man reaches adulthood, it is disrespectful for others of the same generation to address him by his given name.

Much, much later in this story, I asked him, "Why did you choose Felix for your English name?"

"When I was stationed at Edwards Air Force Base," Felix said, referring to his time in the military, "we had one black and white TV in the barracks that we could watch on Saturday mornings. It wasn't allowed, but our commanding officer gave us a break because we were Taiwanese and so far from home. Of course, there were only two channels, and we always watched cartoons."

I cut in, "Don't tell me you named yourself after Felix the Cat!"

"You know it?" Felix beamed.

"I thought you hated cats."

"I do. But Felix was a funny guy."

I chuckled lightly. "Have you ever seen *Baby Felix?*"

"Baby Felix, yuck," he spat. "No! What's that?"

"A Japanese version for children. It's unbelievable. Brilliant show."

"No," Felix scowled. "I don't know."

Behind his back, his employees referred to Felix as "the tail of the dragon" because (a) in Chinese culture, the dragon is a symbol of power, strength, and good fortune; and (b) you never knew where the hell he was, what he was doing, or when he'd show up next. From the cram schools to the publishing office, every employee was on razor's edge when Felix was around. Subservient and supplicant, they jumped before he could even finish saying their names.

I stood to greet Captain Felix, and we shook hands. "Charlie, that's your name? So good to see you." He looked me over briefly, seemingly disappointed, and moved to his desk.

"Yes, I'm Charlie," I said, trying to establish direct eye contact. "It's a pleasure to meet you."

Felix looked at a piece of paper on his desk. "We need someone to write for us."

"OK..." I slowly sat back down in the chair.

"Can you do that?"

"I think so. But..."

"Good," Felix said, pointing to the main office and cubicles, "there's a girl out there who will tell you what we need." *I hope it's that Veronica chick.*

Meanwhile, Daisy got up, left the office and came back with a red envelope, which she handed to Felix. He reached into his wallet, produced two blue 1,000-notes, put them in the red envelope, and handed it to me. "This is for you," he said. "It's just a little something to get you started. We're happy to have you onboard."

"Thanks!" I said, somewhat amused. Examining the envelope, I saw the company's logo embossed in gold in the lower right corner. *Knowledge Press Ltd. So that's the name of the publishing company.*

Felix relayed an order to Daisy in Mandarin, and she said, "OK, got it."

Daisy circled back around to her desk and said, "Charlie, let's go upstairs to the lunchroom and dormitory and I'll show you around."

"Sounds good," I said, turning to Felix. "I'll see you at lunch? We can talk more?"

Felix had already forgotten about me. He looked up abruptly and said blankly, "Yes, lunch." And then he snapped into focus and added, "Of course, we'll talk later."

Daisy and I took the elevator up to the eighth floor, where she gave me a tour of the property. About five minutes later, the whole crew from the seventh floor came up to the eighth floor and assembled in the dining room for lunch. The flashback was still in effect.

⋆✳⋆

Later that evening, Stephan showed up at my apartment unannounced.

"How did it go at Knowledge Press?"

"Dude," I sighed, "that place is bizarre."

"Isn't it?" Stephan smiled mischievously.

"Why didn't you warn me? Dude..." I trailed off. "Felix? That guy is something else."

"Oh," Stephan leaned back. "You haven't seen anything yet. The question is, did you take the job?"

"Yes, I think I did. They gave me two grand in a red envelope as a welcome gift."

"That means you got the gig. You're in the family now."

"But they never told me what I'm supposed to be writing. And that lunchroom scene? Christ, that was too much, man."

"When are you starting?"

"Tomorrow afternoon, I think?"

"Don't worry, you'll find out then. Daisy will probably arrange everything. Just show up on time. Felix hates tardiness."

"Daisy—wow! Where did that chick come from?"

"She's an odd duck, isn't she? Mainland broad. She's actually one of the more competent people in the whole organization."

As promised, Martin hooked me up with some weed exactly one month to the day of my arrival, which was how long it took for him to feel he could trust me. I purchased 10 grams of high-quality hydroponic for TWD$10,000 (US$320), which was more than three times what I'd pay in San Francisco for the same dope. And Martin made a big deal about the drop, too. From the very beginning, weeks before he got me the weed, Martin repeated the warning: "Don't talk about this to anyone." That meant *anyone*—other foreigners included. "Especially foreigners," Martin stressed. He also warned me not to ask people (strangers) in bars. "They'll take your money and turn you into the cops."

We used coded SMS messages and never mentioned money or weed while speaking over the phone. For the first drop, we met at my spot in the courtyard behind the Red Theatre, a two-minute walk from Martin's home. After one drink, we left and made walking loops about the neighborhood. He stopped to buy a bubble tea for his wife. We continued walking until we reached a quiet alley.

Martin quickly pressed the package into my hand and said, "Don't give me the money yet." I had a wad of crisp bills folded in my right front pocket. We kept walking, turned a corner into a blind alley, and he said, "OK." I handed him the money. He put it in his pocket, and we continued walking.

After a few minutes of aimless wandering, Martin finally said, "All good, gotta get home." We shook hands and parted.

Now, to me, that seemed like an excessive number of circles to complete a drug hand-off. However, I gradually began to understand Martin's extreme caution: Taipei has CCTV cameras on just about every corner.

Having weed was a major game-changer because it put my feet firmly on the ground. Everything I needed "to succeed" was now in my possession. It also meant spending more time at home alone and less time out in the bars, where I was burning through cash. Money is always a concern, no matter how much you have. We used to have a saying back home: You can never have too much toilet paper or too many ice cubes. Same goes for money. I had more money coming in than going out, but it occurred to me that I would need a lot more cash if I wanted to do some traveling, which was temporarily cut from the list of priorities.

It was also during this time that I was able to breathe and take stock of the last month. Thus, I got high and wrote every night—journal entries and letters to my friends—which helped me reckon with my feelings about the trip in general. Although I was no longer disappointed in myself for having panic attacks, I wasn't happy—not in the true sense of the word. Having conquered most of my fears and anxieties, I became more like myself, for lack of a better term. As evidenced by my cram school experience, I went from caring about every crack in the sidewalk to not giving a single fuck if I got fired or kicked out of the country.

Another idiosyncrasy of the expat experience emerged from the chaos of the previous month. I was frequently hanging out with people I wouldn't ordinarily chat with or hang out with back home. For example, if I'd crossed Johnny Wong back in S.F., I'd have shooed him away like so many flies. It seemed like I was gravitating toward people (mostly expats) who were in the same boat, mainly because we had one—and only one—thing in common: our presence in Taiwan. Otherwise, I secretly despised at least half of the people in my regular social circle. For a while, Martin, an inveterate Taiwanese-Canadian stoner from Vancouver, was the closest thing I had to a friend in Taiwan.

Once I got back into my little marijuana thought bubble, I reckoned, you know what? *I don't need any of this shit. I've already proven to myself that I can survive.* There's no point in going out of my way to make anything happen from here on out. I adopted a mantra of sorts: *If it's not fun, I'm not doing it.* Of course, "fun" can be defined in myriad ways. The crux of it was more about letting things unfold without any effort on my part. And in this way, I acknowledged my belief that 90 percent of life was showing up. The rest was how you behaved when you got there. We were now very much in the "got there" stage.

On the morning of May 16, I received an email from Tommy with the subject heading: Dude You Won't Fucking Believe It!

When I first saw the heading amongst the other messages, I had a couple of random micro-thoughts. One, something catastrophic—like the house had burned down. Two, he won the lottery. Three, one of our friends died. By the grace of God, I was wrong on all accounts. **Mao-mao had come home!** Nearly two months after his initial disappearance, Tommy said early that morning, Mao came in through the back door, meowing intensely. He looked to be in good condition, but he had lost a considerable amount of weight.

Over the next few weeks, Tommy took Mao to the vet and nursed him back to health. He would be back to normal in time for summer. We never did find out where the cat had been for two months.

With that news, I felt a major rush of homesickness. I desperately wanted to fly back home to The Cave, hang out with Mao-mao, and return to a semblance of my old life—with or without the restaurant gig. While I'd managed to glean myself from opiates and pharmaceuticals, my life in Taipei wasn't all that much different than San Francisco—it was simply 7,000 miles away.

✳

The writing gig at Knowledge Press was originally unveiled by a young woman named Celeste, who was assigned to be my "editor," but her job was formatting. Barely 25 years old and fresh out of college, I hardly thought she would be a wise choice. It turned out that Veronica was a teacher from the cram school and didn't have consistent duties at the publishing house. *Rats!* Stephan said she was only there to impress me.

"That's how Felix rolls. Anytime there's a new guy, he brings out the sexy bitches. You'll see. Get used to it."

Nevertheless, Celeste explained what they wanted me to do. My first project was to write and assemble a TOEFL prep book, otherwise known as a mock test. TOEFL (Test of English as a Foreign Language) was designed for university-bound overseas nationals wishing to study in the U.S., administered by a company called Educational Testing Services (ETS). It didn't matter, Celeste said, that I had never taken the TOEFL, let alone recognized the acronym, or never written any sort of educational material before. Only two, maybe three things mattered to Captain Felix, Celeste let on. One, you're an American. Two, you have a bachelor's degree in English. And three, you showed up. Celeste handed me a copy of the TOEFL test, giggled and said, "Good luck!"

I was assigned to a desk—not a cubicle—in the main room. It was mostly used to park random visitors waiting to meet Felix in the executive office. There was a PC tower, monitor, and a couple of reference books on the desktop. Daisy said they would find me a permanent workstation as soon as possible.

Later in the day, the Captain rolled into the office, and made a big show about greeting me. "Charlie! So good to see you! Do you know what we need you to do?"

"Um...kind of? You want me to make one of these," holding up the TOEFL exam, which I'd spent the afternoon reading and taking.

"Yes, that's it!" Felix said. "It's a tough job. Do your best."

And that was it. For the first week, I came into the office to write and edit. Felix was wary but welcoming. At the end of the week, I had written five essays and corresponding questions completely from scratch. I did legitimate, painstaking research on every subject. Genuine works of academic journalism.

The next Monday afternoon, Celeste found me in the break room, sipping a cup of coffee.

"Charlie?" she began, timid and shy. "The boss...says...expectations have been raised," she half-mumbled, half-giggled. "He wants a minimum of 12 essays a week. You should...borrow stuff from here and there..." I enjoyed watching Celeste squirm and blush as she tried to get the point across.

"No way. Can't be done. At least by me."

Celeste giggled again. "What am I supposed to tell the boss?"

"I dunno. Tell him what I just said."

Captain Felix was out of the country on one of his frequent junkets to China. He wouldn't be back until tomorrow.

Back-handed pressure—sending an underling to deliver a message—was the type of shit I wasn't going to stand for with Captain Felix. I was teaching 25 hours a week at Global International, doing 10 extra hours a week of unpaid prep work, and then putting in another 20 at the publishing office in the afternoons. I'd never worked more than 40 hours per week at *any* gig. Now, suddenly, I was doing nearly 60 hours and making half the money. I went back to my desk and played online solitaire for the rest of the afternoon.

The next day I didn't show up to teach my classes or go to the publishing office. The first to call was Geraldine, the scheming branch manager of Global International, and she was seriously freaked out. I apologized and said I misunderstood my schedule because she changed it, which was true. Geraldine changed my schedule so many times I wasn't even sure if I was playing hooky. "Can you come in right now?" Geraldine pleaded.

"No, I'm sorry. I'm far from the school this afternoon. I'll see you tomorrow. I'm teaching 5-A at 11:15, right?" Silence. Geraldine had hung up. *Fuck those people. Let them fire me.*

Around 3:30 p.m., Daisy called, not quite as upset. A little more annoyed. "Are you coming into the office today?"

"I wasn't planning on it."

"W-w-ell," she stammered, "Felix wants to know where you are and why you aren't here." Her urgency didn't faze me.

"I need a day off."

"Oh." A short pause. "Will you come tomorrow?"

"Yes. I'll be there in the afternoon. Around three o'clock."

"OK," she said warily. "Bye-bye."

Felix was in the office when I showed up the next day. Before I could sit down at "my desk," Celeste rushed over and said I had been moved to a desk in the control center, kiddie-corner to the Captain's desk. I shrugged and said, "Whatever. Lead the way." Felix didn't acknowledge my presence as I sat down and powered up the PC. I started working on something when Felix asked, "Is everything OK? Is everything all right? Is there anything I can do for you?"

"No, thank you," I said and smiled. "Everything is fine."

"Do you understand what I want you to do?"

"I think so..." I let it hang there. "I'm assuming you want me to basically poach articles from other sources and do as little original writing as possible. Am I right?"

"Uhh, yes..." Felix said. "I want you to work faster. Take little bits from here and there. Change everything."

"I understand."

"Don't copy. Not one line can be the same. Our company will get sued for plagiarism."

"Yes, of course."

It didn't take a genius to recognize what they wanted, so I got good at poaching in a hurry. By the end of the next week, I'd cranked out a shitload of material. All the while I kept my activities at the publishing company from the people at Global International. Another week went by, and Daisy said, "Felix wants to know when you are going to leave the cram school and work for Knowledge Press full-time."

"I'd leave Global International tomorrow if it weren't for the contract."

"What contract?"

"The contract I signed. It's good for a year. If I quit before the one-year period, they can take my ARC and keep the last two week's salary."

Daisy was outraged. "That contract is illegal. They can't keep your money!"

"Would you like to see a copy of the contract?"

"I don't need to see the contract. Felix doesn't use contracts."

Captain Felix arrived ten minutes later. Instantly, Daisy attacked him with what I'd just told her. "*Mei guanxi*," (no problem) he said. "We'll get him another ARC." He leaned toward my desk while Daisy told him about the contract, which stipulated that I forfeit my last two weeks of salary in case of breaching its terms. "*Mei guanxi*," he said. "How much is two weeks' salary?"

Daisy looked at me and said, "I don't know. Ask Charlie."

"Fifteen thousand Taiwan dollars," I said. That's about US$500.

"No problem," Felix said. And the matter was dropped until the next afternoon, when the office lackey, Mr. Chu, came in and presented me with an envelope containing fifteen 1,000-notes.

"I want you to quit that school," Felix said. "Just tell them you want to leave the country. Do not mention Knowledge Press."

"Really? It's as simple as that?"

"Don't worry. I can help you. I will take care of it."

Quitting that miserable teaching gig would prove a little more difficult than advertised. It was a couple of weeks before I started full-time at Knowledge Press, and the transition was bumpy, at best.

✦ ✱ ✦

Captain Felix was the king of an empire that included one of the most famous and popular cram school chains in Taiwan called Zhang Yi English Academy, and the affiliated publishing house aka Knowledge Press, Ltd. that supplied the schools with books and assorted learning materials. The same books could also be found in airports all over Asia with such titles as *Polite Visitor Etiquette*, *Surviving the Airport*, *The Most Common 7,000 Words in the English Language*, and *A Dictionary of English Composition for High School Students*, to name but a few. I was told that Felix was worth hundreds of millions of U.S. dollars, and I had no reason to doubt it—at the time. It would be a month before he and I had a conversation about anything unrelated to the job.

In reality, the Captain's empire was a labyrinth of corporate entities, financial holdings, and investment properties only Felix and maybe one other person on Earth could navigate: his estranged wife, Lorraine Wen. Felix's personal assistant-slash-secret lover, Daisy, was in there pretty deep, too, but she wasn't abreast of Felix's shadier dealings and whatnot.

Felix's speaking voice was neither passive nor aggressive until he was provoked, which could happen at any given moment. I had seen him angry a few times, usually on the phone, with one of the workers at the cram school(s). His voice went from mild-mannered to extremely irritable in just a few words. Otherwise, Felix laughed frequently with a deep bellow that suggested he understood the darkness behind the humor (of a situation). Another conversational characteristic was he almost couldn't let you finish a sentence before interjecting, "Right" or "That's good" or "No problem" in mid-sentence to whatever you were saying. "No problem" (or *mei guanxi*) was his mantra. No matter what I told him, he said, "No problem."

That hooker pulled a knife on me. "No problem. We can fix her."

I owe the government a million Taiwan in back taxes. "No problem. I have friends in high and low places."

For Captain Felix, everything was either "no problem" or a "tough job" for someone else to deal with. Over time, I learned to avoid speaking to him unless he spoke to me first, especially when traveling together. I didn't ask: "How's business?" "Where are we?" or "What's going on?" unless it was urgent.

Above all, Captain Felix was a red-blooded product of his generation and culture, so he both coveted and subjugated women at every turn. The Knowledge Press staff was 4-to-1 in favor of females. And there were 15–25 female cram school admin workers who came into the office daily for whatever reason, but only a handful of men. Of course, no one did shit unless Felix told them to do it.

Now, it's kind of a pain in the ass, but you must understand some of the logistics of the publishing company and the dormitory. The office was located on the seventh floor, and the dormitory, an enormous, eight-bedroom, four-bathroom flat with two huge dining rooms and a recreation area, was located on the eighth floor. The main dining room on the eighth floor seated 30 people comfortably—that's where we had lunch. The units on both floors were owned by Felix and his estranged wife. Felix didn't live there, but he designated one of the master bedrooms as his crash pad. That's where V.I.P.s stayed when visiting. Daisy claimed one of the other suites. Otherwise, only two of the six remaining dormitory bedrooms were permanently occupied. One, by another translator-editor type, Carmen, who hailed from a mountain village in central Taiwan. And two, anywhere from one to three Southeast Asian housemaids, who always shared a room.

Every day without fail at 11:59 a.m., Gretchen, the office manager, unceremoniously turned off the seventh-floor office lights, signaling the start of the 90-minute lunch break. Regardless of whether Felix was around, the whole crew usually trudged up one flight of stairs for the meal prepared by the housemaids. When Felix was on the scene, lunch became a mandatory ordeal. Once he sat down, everybody sat down. There were additional guests about three times a week—you never knew who the fuck was going to be at lunch. Bankers, real estate agents, teachers, investment partners. Some of the seasoned veterans like Gretchen, Ms. Chu, and Sally the Rat would start eating before Felix did, mainly because he was busy holding court, talking shit, and they were greedy, hungry savages at heart. But most of the staff would never lift a chopstick until Felix did. And *nobody* got up from the table until Felix said, "*Zou le.*" (OK, lunch is over.)

Meanwhile, there were two tables stratified by social rank within the company. Felix helmed the big round table with a lazy Susan, surrounded by his favorites and guests, while the nobodies like Coco, Celeste, Sonya the Cat Lady, and Lonesome Carl were parked at the rectangular table off to the side.

On the day I showed up for the "interview" and lunch, the dining room was packed to the rafters with Knowledge Press staff and a handful of women from the cram school, e.g., Veronica, Crazy Tooth, and The Predator. I'll talk about them later, don't worry. Anyway, during that first luncheon, Felix and Daisy hammered me with question after question—highly personal questions like, "How many Taiwanese women have you slept with so far?" and "Do your parents have a lot of money?"

Not to forget that every eyeball in the joint was trained on me, sitting there like a dummy. Veronica and the others sat directly across the circular table, looking at me like, "*The fuck* is up with this guy?" except Veronica seemed to be genuinely friendly. To my immediate left was one of the few men on staff, Lloyd, the Captain's (paternal) nephew and all-around problem solver. Lloyd didn't really have a gig. He sat around waiting for shit to go sideways, and then he'd go about solving it as best he could. Lloyd spoke good English, so between bites of food, he was talking in my ear about the wonders of Taiwan and some other foreign dude who used to work for the company, a guy named Eugene. And I couldn't help but continue to sneak looks at Veronica, man.

After 20 minutes of speaking only in English, Felix switched to Mandarin, delivering a 10-minute monologue, of which I understood maybe 0.3 percent. He occasionally stopped talking to gesture in my direction. Everybody sat in stone silence, staring at me when I wasn't looking at them. Now and then, Gretchen or The Predator would raise their eyebrows or make some kind of grimace. *Whatever this dude is saying, it can't be good.* Finally, Felix called the game, and we dispersed. Before I left, he stopped me in the foyer and said, "I can feel it. You're a genius. You're a one-in-a-million character."

I sighed sharply and said, "Oh, I'm definitely not a genius, Felix. And one-in-a-million would be pushing it. But hey, thanks for the compliment."

Felix put his hand on my shoulder. "You're my kind of guy. Stick with me. The best is yet to come."

Hitting the sidewalk, I was still shaking my head as I cycled down the road. *That was fun. Fucking bizarre, but fun.*

Because I worked in the afternoons, that was my only appearance at lunch for a while. Once I started working full-time, lunch became a daily ordeal for me, too. Seated immediately to the left of Felix, I'd have to wallow there for half an hour, not eating anything because the food was bland rubbish, listening to Felix yammer at everybody.

Felix developed a habit of calling me out to the new people, especially the females. Employee turnover was high, so there was a new woman at lunch almost every day. Felix would introduce me and then say to her, "This guy is untouchable. You can look but you can't touch." He would go on at length about my position in the company. "Charlie is very valuable to this company. His time is precious. Don't waste his time." Inevitably, the new girl would smile and nod and have the same *What the Fuck?* look of confusion that was plastered on my face.

About a month into the full-time gig, we had a visitor, a Canadian-born Taiwanese woman named Carly. She spoke perfect English and poor Chinese. Carly said she came back to Taiwan to "reconnect with her roots." After Felix gave her the Untouchable speech, Carly looked at me, sort of sneered and said, "Oh, don't worry. I wouldn't touch *him*." She meant it, too.

The next day when Gretchen hit the lights, I stayed in my chair. Five minutes passed and no one noticed. At the 10-minute mark, Lloyd came downstairs, stood at the door, pointed at the ceiling and said, "Lunch?"

"No thanks, Lloyd. I'm good. Really busy today, chief."

Lloyd paused and smiled. "But...the boss wants you upstairs."

"Like I said, Lloyd," I leaned my head to one side, "I'm really busy today."

Lloyd disappeared upstairs. Five minutes later, Deborah appeared and said cheerfully, "Felix wants you to join us upstairs for lunch."

I did another one of those Hollywood good-guy side glances. "Like I told, Lloyd, Deborah. I'm really busy today. Thank you."

At the 12:30 mark, Felix himself came back down to the office, which he almost never did after lunch, and said, "Sir, I know you're busy. But we missed you at lunch. You're welcome to join us."

And right there I set the course for years to come. I recognized that by not going to lunch, I could cause Felix to lose face. If I was sick or something, then there'd be a good out for him. "The foreigner is boycotting lunch" would make him look bad. And I don't know how I recognized it, either, because I didn't know shit about the whole "face" thing in Chinese culture. My gut was telling me to make it something self-deprecating.

Felix eyeballed me for a moment, and I said, "Felix, I really don't like Chinese food. You see that I never really eat anything up there anyway, don't you? Even the smell of Chinese food makes me nauseous." This was a bald-faced lie. I was very fond of Chinese food.

A look of acknowledgment yet concern on his face, Felix said, "I had a feeling you didn't like Chinese food. You should have said something. You're too polite."

Obviously, I was sick of being the target of attention at lunch. But Felix got exactly what he wanted. He summoned Deborah, Celeste, and Lloyd into the control center and said, "We have the answer! This guy doesn't like Chinese food. That's why he wasn't at lunch."

And that's how I wound up not going to lunch anymore. And the next morning and every morning for the duration of my time at Knowledge Press, Mr. Chu would give me TWD$200 (US$7.50) in cash. Felix felt bad about the lunch situation, so he said, "If you can't eat with us, I'm going to give you money for lunch. Get something nutritious. It's on me."

★✳★

It was my last day with the 10-year-olds at Global International. As part of our civilized parting negotiations, Geraldine made me promise not to tell the students I was leaving. She said it would create panic and uncertainty because the kids were used to me. The revolving door of teachers upset the parents, too, so it was best to maintain discretion. I would simply disappear, and another sucker would take my place.

The first hour went relatively well. After the break, they came back and no matter what I said, they wouldn't cooperate. Some kids wouldn't stop talking, others were doing their math homework, mocking my speech patterns, generally laughing and giggling. Every other second, one of the boys would get up and smack another boy. I pleaded, scolded, and raised my voice. Nothing fazed these little bastards. The worst thing is those kids were the brightest of all the classes I ever taught. Their language comprehension was better than the high school kids in Half Moon Bay. I stood there snapping at them for five minutes like a fireman putting out fires he thought he put out a minute ago. Finally, I gave up. I snatched a nearby desk and dragged it into the middle of the room. I sat down in the chair, folded my arms, crossed my legs, and proceeded to stare at the boy giving me the most grief: a smart-ass little punk named Andy.

I'm guessing that half the class, mostly the girls, noticed what I was doing. The boys danced like pygmies around a campfire.

Thirty seconds into my gesture, most of the class, save for Andy, had returned to their seats and quietly opened their books to the appropriate lesson, watching me. Finally, Andy, having no one left to dance with, scanned the room and begrudgingly sat down. This is where it got ugly. This is another one of those parts that's going to make me look bad. And I'm not proud of it, but it happened, and you deserve to know.

I didn't say anything for a long time. One by one, I made eye contact with every kid in the room. If a kid refused to make eye contact, I called him or her out, "Hey, you! Yeah, you, Norman. *Look at me.*"

Once I went around the room and it was silent, I got up and moved my desk to the corner where the main troublemakers, Andy and Catherine, were seated. For that brief moment, every one of the kids in my peripheral vision looked scared out of their fucking minds. I wasn't about to waste that power.

Andy stared at me with typical absent-but-present pre-teen confusion. He knew what was going on, but at the same time, really didn't know what was going on. In his mind, all he knew for sure was some American asshole with booze and Marlboro on his breath was about to humiliate him in front of his peers. He squirmed. I leaned forward, elbows resting on his desktop.

"So, tell me, Andy, why are you here in this room right now? I know why *I'm* here right now. *I'm* here to teach you how to read and write and speak English. I'm here to teach but I feel more like a babysitter. I want to teach you something but if you don't want to stop playing grab-ass with Pudgy or even make it *appear* that you're trying to learn something, what can I do? If you score poorly on the junior high school entrance exam, I still get paid, brother. So, it doesn't matter to me if you wind up working at a car wash or a shoe store. Are you here because your parents say you have to be here? Or are you here because you really want and need to learn English? My guess is that your parents make you come here, and you really aren't interested in learning English at all. In any case, you're wasting your time and your parents' money, not mine. So, Andy, tell me, if you could be doing anything other than this, what would it be?"

Andy didn't shit his pants while the question lingered, but he didn't have a smart-ass reply in his book bag. I repeated the final question: *If you could be doing anything other than this, what would it be?*

Andy mumbled something to the effect that he'd rather be playing video games, which I accepted as a legitimate alternative to not learning English and praised him for having the guts to answer the question. "Right on, Andy! That's a solid answer. I don't blame you. I'd rather be playing video games right now and I don't even play video games!" The rest of the students laughed cautiously. They knew it wasn't over yet.

I abruptly spun around on the chair and faced Catherine, the cherubic and adorable ringleader of the girl faction in class. Even though she never, I mean *never* stopped chatting in Chinese, Catherine's English was good. If anybody in the room knew what I was talking about, it was her.

"Catherine, Catherine. Tell me, honey. Why is it that every...single...fucking time I politely ask you to stop talking, you act as if you can't hear me? Did it ever occur to you that there's a reason I'm asking you to stop talking? Did you ever once think about what it must be like to be me, standing up here, trying to do my job, while you mock and ignore my requests for silence and attention? Do you have any idea how frustrating it is to try and teach this class? *Do you?* [Catherine shook her head.] No? I thought not. Because, you see, if you had considered my feelings, you wouldn't be sitting there with that sorry look on your face. But you know what, Catherine? In approximately 45 minutes [I paused to say it in Chinese, *sishi wu fenzhong*], I'm going to walk out the front door of Global International and never return. And if I'm lucky, I will never set foot in a cram school for the rest of my life. So, I guess I should be thanking you, Catherine, and Andy, and Pudgy, and Ivan. Thank you for teaching *me*. I learned something from you, which is more than y'all can say about our time together. I learned that I never want to put myself in this position, ever again. That's huge! It's a major milestone of knowledge acquisition. Thank you, thank you, and thank *you*, Andy, and especially you, Catherine. And so, good luck with whatever you're doing and wherever you're going. I'm gonna to sit here for the rest of the class and think about where I'm gonna be tomorrow. You should probably do that, too."

6

Settling Into Taipei

The rooftop apartment came fully furnished but without a decent sound system, so I bought a stereo and a stack of CDs. Even though I would download some records from the web, having a physical copy was preferable. It was a relic of my vinyl-collecting days. I still don't like streaming or virtual album sales. Anyway, musically, I chose a mix of old favorites and newer, less familiar stuff: Black Sabbath, *Vol. 4* and TV on the Radio, *Return to Cookie Mountain*; greatest hits collections from artists that hadn't previously moved the needle for me, like Guided By Voices, Radiohead, and Talking Heads. I even bought a Tool album, *10,000 Days*, which was *unthinkable* just a few years ago, and the record was surprisingly good. I loved a song called "The Pot". Fucking *loved* that jam! If I was home, there was music. Most nights I'd fall asleep to the back end of one record or another. And despite the local radio station's questionable penchant for Air Supply and Journey, I tuned in frequently. Music was the one thing that kept me tied to my past, my identity, and my dreams. *If I can't be making music, I can listen.* Those records became the Book 1 soundtrack to this remarkable journey, and whenever I hear songs like "14 Cheerleader Cold Front" and "Pyramid Song", I'm transported back to the rooftop.

* ✳ *

It took a month to sort my work permit and resident certificate and get acclimated to the full-time KPHQ environment. Nine-to-five office life revealed a different kind of culture shock—a mild but enduring flashback to a previous existence under the fluorescent lights. I struggled to find a balance between the Taiwanese concepts of personal and professional space. If I hadn't been keeping a journal, I wouldn't remember very much from this blurry period.

Once I was officially part of the "family," Captain Felix added a new wrinkle to the fabric of our universe. He told Daisy to get cozy with me—strictly platonic, of course. "He's alone here," Felix reasoned. "He's far from home. He needs someone to look after him." So, Daisy did some looking after. We started hanging out, going to the night market, and having dinner, sometimes with Stephan. She helped me with a bunch of expat technical bullshit like banking and getting new eyeglasses. Eventually, Daisy and I became friends. When Felix wasn't in the office, we often passed the time in conversation. Within a few months, I knew more about Daisy than Felix probably did—even though he was sleeping with her. And for the most part, Daisy had my back. If I had an issue with someone or something, I didn't go straight to Captain Felix—I'd run it by Daisy first, who never failed to pick up the ball where it had been strategically dropped.

Despised by nearly every other employee, Daisy was the most single-minded person I ever met. Born and raised in Beijing, she looked down on the Taiwanese people as "barbarians." As far as Daisy was concerned, China was the answer to every question.

Plain faced, quick tempered, easily offended, and fiercely loyal to Felix, Daisy's personal history is a tough read. After graduating from Beijing University at 21, she moved to the U.S., alone, to escape an abusive relationship and the iron claw influence of a domineering father. Driven and ambitious to the point of obsession, she scored two master's degrees from the University of Georgia. At 25, she met and got impregnated by a sociopath American serviceman from Texas; they married shotgun, and she gave birth to a son. Daisy stayed in that loveless marriage as long as possible. Divorcing at 35, she found herself adrift in the black hole of the U.S. legal system with nobody but mediocre lawyers on her side. The dickhead husband got everything—custody of the kid, the house, the bank accounts. Broken yet vaguely relieved, she returned to Beijing without her son to stay with her parents. That's when Felix, a longtime friend of Daisy's father, came to the rescue, bringing her to work in Taiwan as his personal assistant. Their physical and emotional relationship developed roughly three years before I arrived on the scene.

I loved Daisy's brutal honesty, but she never let anyone change their mind about anything. Her whole purpose in life seemed to be detecting your inconsistencies and pointing them out. One time, we had dinner at a hot pot joint, and I ordered noodles. Daisy ordered rice. "Don't you like rice?" she asked.

"I much prefer noodles," I replied. "I'll eat rice, but I prefer noodles."

A month later, we went to a local teppanyaki joint where I ordered a fried rice dish. "Hey!" she cried. "You said you don't like rice!"

"I said I *preferred* noodles. Sometimes I eat rice." This incongruity was impossible to reconcile in her mind.

In addition to Daisy, Felix wanted another personal assistant in the office whose sole job was to sit at her desk and "look pretty." That was it—no other task. Daisy and I raised objections with Felix—for different reasons, obviously—but he didn't give a shit, and just kept luring in all these women to "work" for him. Captain Felix routinely asked my opinion about any one of the dozens of women who catwalked the Knowledge Press gauntlet. Regardless of the woman or context in question, I always agreed with the Captain's visual assessment. If he thought she was beautiful, so did I.

I don't remember how it started, but one morning, Captain Felix and I had that first conversation about our lives. He might have said something like, "Did you know that I spent six months in the U.S. when I was in the Taiwan Air Force?" At any rate, we got to talking and he said, "You're an interesting guy. Do you want to make some extra money? I have a job for you."

"What kind of job?"

"I want you to start a conversation class at the cram school."

"As you already know, sir, I'm not a cram school teacher. And I don't care if you say these kids are better than the punks at Global International. You hired me as a writer. I want to help you, I really do, but I don't think it's a good idea."

"Oh, no—it's not teaching. I want you to go down to the cram school and talk to the students. Make some friends."

"That sounds an awful lot like conversation class." I scowled, adding sarcastically. "*Make some friends.*"

"I'll make it worth your while. I'll pay you one thousand an hour. Six hours a week."

I looked at the ground, scratched my neck and said, "Just talking? No structure?"

"Just talk. No structure. You go around, meet the kids, and make them feel good. Make some friends."

"That's an extra six grand Taiwan per week." (US$200)

"You'll get the lunch money, too."

"OK, I'm in."

Captain Felix valued my straightforward attitude. "Ask Charlie a question, and he'll give you an answer," even if the answer is not what you wanted to hear. There was no gray area with me, Felix said. "When you say yes, you mean yes. Everything is black and white. I know where I stand with you." And for the most part, I was honest with him. Aside from Daisy, not a single person in the Captain's circumference had the gumption or the motivation to say anything he didn't want to hear. Of course, for inconsequential and superficial cordialities, I'd go along with the program—or, in this case, *if he made it worth my while.* That extra $200 a week was already adding up in my mental bank account.

That Saturday and Sunday morning from 9:00 a.m. to noon, I went down to the flagship school near Taipei Main Station—Cram School Central—hundreds of competing schools within a few city blocks. Aside from haggling with Felix about what I would and wouldn't do, I was looking forward to seeing more of Veronica and the legion of female teachers and admin staff. Meanwhile, Stephan worked at the school, and he said it was "like shooting fish in a barrel." I wasn't interested in shooting or fishing. My motives were purely voyeuristic.

On Saturday, I walked around the hallways and study areas, accosting students by forcing them to engage with me. *Hey, how ya doin'? What's cookin'?* Few students were interested in practicing their conversational English with a greasy foreigner. And vice versa. The students wanted me to hold their vocabulary dictionaries and quiz them on memorization—spelling and alphabetical order.

I slipped out maybe a few minutes before noon. My cell phone rang at 12:10 p.m. It was Felix.

"Charlie! Where the heck are you?" He was nearly shouting over the background noise of the school.

"I just left the cram school. I'm sorry. I didn't know you were coming."

"No problem. It's lunchtime. How was the conversation class?"

"Great. Just great." *You're going to hear otherwise from the students and admin.* "Tomorrow will be better."

"Right. No problem. Do your best."

Sunday morning got off to a bad start. Lonesome Carl, the on-duty cram school manager, set a chair near the front desk with four chairs fanned out like an audience. He said I should sit there and welcome the kids as they came off the elevator. We argued because Felix said I should just walk around and mingle with the kids. *Fuck that, Carl. I'm not sitting there like a dummy until noon.* Carl was adamant that he was acting on orders from the Captain. Eventually, I capitulated. As students came out of the elevator, I said, "Hey, join me for the conversation class!" Once again, few students wanted to talk with me. They wanted to practice their memorization. It was an agonizing three hours, and I even stayed until 12:30 p.m., just in case Felix showed up. He didn't. *Of course.*

Monday morning at KPHQ, I said to Daisy, "Listen, this conversation class bullshit isn't happening. I didn't make any friends, if you know what I mean."

We made eye contact. She said, "You don't want to do it anymore."

"No."

Daisy repositioned herself in the chair and straightened her back. "Don't worry. I'll take care of it."

Felix came breezing into the office and Daisy waited all of a minute before saying, "*Laoshi*, Charlie doesn't want to do the conversation class anymore."

Felix moved toward me and put his hand on my shoulder, saying earnestly, "The students like you. Try to smile more. Tell jokes and stories."

"Come on, let's be honest about it. They were *terrified* of me."

"He's a writer, Felix," Daisy cut in. "He's not a teacher."

"No problem," Felix said, waving us away. He didn't seem disappointed, but I knew he *really* wanted a foreigner who wasn't Stephan down there at the cram school. For unrelated reasons, Captain Felix didn't care for the Canadian with great parents. But Stephan's classes were somewhat popular and that's all that mattered—butts in the seats, dollars in the bank.

"Listen, Felix, I feel bad for letting you down, so...I have a buddy—an American kid from Sacramento. He's twenty-six, smart, so much better looking than me. Blonde and blue-eyed, super nice, loves to chat with people. His name is Carter Dietz, I met him at Global International. I know he's looking to pick up some side work. I've already pitched him on the idea."

"Can I meet this guy? Can you ask him to lunch? When can he start?"

"I'll call him now."

"But I'm only paying him five hundred an hour. Cash. Same hours."

"That's decent money. He'll do it."

"And I want you in charge of the conversation class. You run it. You make sure the guy shows up."

Carter was the only person from Global International who didn't disappear into the ether. He started at Global about a month into my tenure, receiving the same frosty reception in the teacher's room on his first day. *Except from me.* As Carter appeared in the office, surveying the tabletops, I said, "Hey, kid. Have a seat next to me. Let's talk." We quickly bonded over beers at one of the local bars, having common experience in California. Carter bounced from the Global International gig before I could extricate myself, but we became friends and stayed in touch.

So, to the extent that I "ran" the conversation group, I'd go down to the cram school on Saturday and Sunday at noon to see how Carter was doing, and he was doing great. He had a whole posse of girls fanned out in a circle in front of him, waiting their turn to speak. I'd give him a wink and thumbs up and make a beeline for the teacher's room to see if Veronica or Crazy Tooth were around. In fact, I usually didn't have to go looking for them.

* ✷ *

If I stood five-foot-nine, Veronica was five-foot-eight-and-a-half—just a finger width shorter than me, so face to face, our eyes were dead level. At first, it seemed like we were communicating with visual cues, but I quickly realized that any attraction on Veronica's part was my imagination. Felix said, "She knows *how to look* at men."

Felix had a rule against fraternization at the cram school and the publishing company: no organized socialization between co-workers. You weren't even supposed to go out to lunch with a co-worker (unless sanctioned by Felix). If three or more co-workers got together for any reason outside of the school or the office, they had to put it in writing before they did it. Dating between co-workers was strictly forbidden. If you dated someone in the company and got caught, one of the two would have to resign on the spot or "take a vacation"—unpaid and involuntary leave of up to a month. According to Felix, my relationship with Daisy was exempt because she was my "temporary personal assistant."

Veronica was/wasn't flirting with me. It was impossible to say without asking. She mentioned a long-term boyfriend. We were friendly, but I didn't say *shit* about myself. Just the basics. *Age, origin, why I'm in Taiwan...* And it wasn't about respecting the Captain and his rules. On a superficial level, Veronica was out of my league. Women like her generally didn't date men like me.

Meanwhile, Stephan began "secretly" seeing one of the school admin girls, Black Betty, a hardened city girl type with a tiger shark smile. Black Betty scared me, frankly, so I stayed away from her. Of course, Stephan had to boast of his sexual conquest with Betty, dropping the kind of details I'd rather forget, but I can't.

7

The Real China (Not My Fault and It Was Like That Before I Got Here)

It took a few months before Felix warmed up to me, i.e., *I could be trusted.* By mid-summer, I made tremendous progress on the TOEFL mock test, and (according to Daisy) Felix was pleased with my work ethic and perceived efficiency. "He likes you," Daisy said. "That's important."

The 2008 Beijing Olympics were a massive deal in Asia. Of course, Daisy was beyond excited about it.

One early July morning in the office—Felix hadn't arrived yet—Daisy asked, "Hey Charlie, are you planning to see the Beijing Olympics?"

"It'll be on TV, so I'll probably see some parts of it, I suppose."

"I mean in person!"

"No... Why would I do *that?* I'm not going to *Beijing.* I don't even have a Chinese visa."

Daisy harrumphed. "Well, wouldn't you *like* to see the Beijing Olympics?"

"Of course. I'd love to."

"Well..." she stalled. "*You should.*"

The Captain breezed in at 11:39 a.m., preoccupied, as usual. I had a dental appointment, so I excused myself at 11:45 a.m. The dentist was around the corner. I returned to KPHQ just before 1:00 p.m.—teeth in good shape, they said.

Daisy was gone but Felix was still perched on his throne. Peering over the edge of a magazine, he asked, "Have you ever been to mainland China?"

"No." It seemed like a stupid question. Felix knew I'd never been to mainland China.

"Do you want to go? I will take you there. You need a break."

"Sure, I'll go." I shrugged. "Are you talking about the Olympics in Beijing?"

"Yes. But first, I will take you to a special place. See the real China. No foreigners ever go there."

"Sounds cool. But I need a Chinese visa."

"Oh! You don't have one?"

"No."

"Lloyd!" he called out and Lloyd came scrambling in. Felix told Lloyd that he was responsible for getting my Chinese visa. Lloyd looked at me like, "*What the fuck is this guy talking about?*" and I gave him a shrug and held my palms to the sky. While Felix rattled on, a total of four employees were summoned to the control center—Susie, Gretchen, Deborah, and Yvonne—all looking like they'd never seen me before.

Pointing at me, Felix said, "Get this guy a Chinese visa!" Lloyd and the crew had a little scrum as they simultaneously attempted to flee the office and back to the safety of their cubicles. That little scene prompted my nickname for the Knowledge Press team: the robots. They only knew how to obey a very discreet set of directives, which they did, routinely. But if you gave them an order that went beyond their robot algorithm, they malfunctioned, slamming into each other, bumping into walls, and displaying error messages.

Meanwhile, Daisy popped in, fresh from her badminton lesson, decked out in standard professional athletic wear. She got wind of the Chinese visa issue and expressed her doubts.

"They," she semi-whispered, pointing toward the main room of cubicles, "don't know *anything* about China." Fortunately, old Lloyd was on the case, and he got me a Chinese visa.

Felix announced the plan. Daisy would fly ahead to Beijing a week in advance of the opening ceremony to arrange tickets and transportation. Captain Felix and I would leave a few days later, arriving first in Xiamen, an up-and-coming city in Fujian Province, and take a two-day sleeper train to Beijing. That way, Felix said, I could see "the Real China." Beijing and the Olympics, packed with travelers from around the world, wasn't "the Real China."

Daisy had several clear objectives, so she was off in her little world—always on the phone. Since Felix and Daisy had multiple properties in Beijing, accommodation was covered. We'd stay at Daisy's crib. They haggled all the details. I bought a copy of *Lonely Planet China* and read it from cover-to-cover.

Traveling with Felix for the first time, I was keen to go along with whatever he said. I kept questions to a minimum.

"Don't worry about money," he said. "When you're with me, I'll take care of everything." Felix always booked separate hotel rooms, insistent that they be on different floors—for reasons that didn't take long to figure out.

We left from the office after lunch on a hot August afternoon, boarding a chartered DC-10 out of Songshan Airport (IATA code: TSA) in Taipei, which landed on the single runway at Kinmen Airport (IATA code: KNH), a tiny island about 5 kilometers off the coast of Fujian Province. Kinmen is claimed by Taiwan and serves a symbolic military purpose. From Kinmen, we took a one-hour ferry boat to Xiamen. It was dusk by the time we cleared immigration, and Captain Felix was in a rush to find a hotel for the night.

Waiting for a taxi on the sidewalk, Felix asked, "Do you have any recommendations for a good hotel? What does it say in your book?"

Eager to flex my savvy, I said, "There are more than a few places near..." My voice trailed away as I moved to retrieve the *Lonely Planet China* book from my backpack. *Wait a minute, boss. Aren't you supposed to be the one with the inside dope on China?*

It didn't matter anyway. Felix walked off and approached a fellow passenger on our charter from Taiwan.

Felix waddled back to me and said, "This guy is a local. He knows all the best spots in Xiamen. He's going to take us to a nice hotel."

The three of us piled in a taxi—me, in the front seat. We arrived at a nondescript office building, according to my bearings, quite a distance from the city center. The local guy stayed in the taxi when Felix and I got out. The taxi drove off.

Felix said, "This is a special hotel. It's an apartment complex for traveling businessmen. Only locals know about it."

We took a very slow elevator to the 18th floor, where we were greeted by woman with a clipboard. Felix did all the talking, of course. The woman led us down the hall to a corner where a series of doors faced each other. I took a quick look around and it appeared that Felix was right on target. New carpet in the hallways, numbers on doors, and a distinctly discrete business hotel ankle-level lighting.

"I told her I want to see the room first," Felix said. "Make sure it is safe. Always check." I stood in the hallway as they entered a room. Felix came out very quickly with a scowl on his face. "Let's get out of here."

"Why?" I was somewhat alarmed by his reaction.

"It's a trap. They want to rob us."

The woman called after us, but we were already at the elevator. Felix said, "You can't trust these people. They'll cheat you without blinking an eye. They'll kill you like a mosquito."

During the glacial elevator ride down to the ground floor, I had an opportunity to check the guidebook.

"Says here there are several good places on Hubin North Road, near the harbor."

"Right," Captain Felix said. "We'll do some reconnaissance. Check out the scene."

What scene? The fuck are you talking about?

Felix ignored my suggestions and asked our new taxi driver for *his* input. Thankfully, this guy took us to a legitimate place near the airport. It had the all-purpose café-slash-restaurant-slash-bar, so I was happy. Felix was happy because there was a sauna house on the fourth floor. We checked in and went to our rooms. Maybe ten minutes later, I was in the bathroom when the phone rang. What do you know? There was a telephone next to the toilet.

"Hello?"

It was Felix. "Charlie! What are you doing tomorrow morning?"

"Uhh...I thought we were leaving for Beijing in the morning."

"There's been a change of plans. Don't worry. I've taken care of everything. Our flight doesn't leave until two in the afternoon. You'll have plenty of time to explore."

"Our flight to *where*? I thought we were...?"

"It's the Real China. A happening place. You'll see."

"Well, tomorrow...I guess I'll just take a taxi downtown and..."

"Do you want an English-speaking tour guide? I can get one for you."

"Um, not really."

"No? I can get you one if you want. I'll take care of everything. Leave it to me."

"Well... OK."

"Alright, I'll call you back." Click. Ten minutes later. "Charlie! You must be in the lobby tomorrow morning at seven-thirty. There will be a nice girl waiting to take you around Xiamen."

"Really? I mean, no, that's great. I'll..."

"Is it too early? No problem. You can come later."

"Are you going with us?"

Felix laughed. "Ah, no."

"Well, I guess seven-thirty is fine."

"I paid for the tour service in advance. The rest is up to you. Meet me back here at one o'clock." Click.

The rest of what?

Captain Felix was accommodating his guest, which can sometimes drive you mad. Later that night, I went in search of nightlife but found KTVs and discos. *Yuck.* I closed the hotel bar, retiring before midnight.

The phone was already ringing when I entered my room. Every time I answered, the person on the other end would rattle off a bunch of Chinese. Tired from the travel, I just hung up. The damn phone must have rung 20 times before I took it off the hook.

The next morning at 7:20 a.m., I went bleary-eyed down to the lobby where I was met by a cute woman wearing a laminated ID card hanging from an orange neon shoestring around her neck. I strained to see the words "China International Tourism Service" on the card and relaxed. *That looks official.* It turned out that she didn't speak a word of English other than "hello" and that CITS placard was bogus. After the initial awkward greeting, the woman motioned for me to sit and wait on the shiny leather couch of the lobby.

I took a seat next to three Chinese guys who were dressed almost identically and smoking those cigarettes that smell like dirty asshole, obviously playing hooky from their *ganbu* (tour group). A healthy segment of tourists in China were of the *ganbu* variety—a distinct class of travelers, mostly male, herded around by flag-toting guides in matching T-shirts and baseball caps, very much like a third-grade field trip and most likely all employees of the same company. They're generally harmless and, from what I can gather, they keep the engine of Chinese prostitution running.

This can't be good. I considered calling Felix, but my Taiwan SIM card didn't work in mainland China. And I could have used the in-house phone at the front desk but... *Fuck it. Let's see what happens.* Thanks to the guidebook, I already knew where I wanted to go, how to get there, and how much to pay for it.

Somewhere around 7:45 a.m., we, meaning me, the chain-smoking *ganbu*, a Taiwanese family of four, a sour-faced local businessman, and my "English-speaking guide," climbed into a blue minivan driven by a kid who look didn't look old enough to *know his home address*, let alone drive in China. After an hour of reckless zigzagging through Xiamen, dropping off passengers at various stops, the population of the minivan was down to me, the driver, and the tour guide, who kept eyeballing me in an uncomfortable way.

We arrived at a ferry plaza where I stopped at a tourist kiosk and bought a SanDisk memory card for my camera and a mainland SIM card for my phone. Then I bought tickets for the five-minute boat ride to Gulangyu, which is a minuscule but beautiful island in the Xiamen harbor that was once home to Portuguese nobles. All of this was done, I might add, without any assistance from the tour guide. She was uneasy and distant, obsessed with her cell phone. On the boat, halfway across the harbor, she handed me her phone and nodded, "Here, take this." I put the phone to my ear.

"Uh, hello?"

"Yes, hello," a female voice said. "I am Nicki. You are on tour my friend Bebe, yes?"

I looked the tour guide over. "Yep. That's correct."

"For greatest sympathy I want you ask if there is anything you want say to Bebe?"

"Would you please tell her that I don't need a tour guide and that she is free to go since she was paid in advance?"

"Do you not want Bebe? She is not what you want?"

"No, I don't mean that." I struggled with the words, thinking in English and Mandarin at the same time. "I mean, look, I'm only here for a couple of hours..." and that's where I stopped and handed the phone back to Bebe, who at least had a name now. We spent the next hour walking the narrow, often steep cobblestone streets of Gulangyu Island before I convinced Bebe that I wanted to return to Xiamen and had no interest in seeing any of the so-called "sights." Exactly who was more confused at this point wouldn't shake out for another hour.

We were on the boat back to Xiamen around 10:45 a.m. and caught a taxi back to the hotel. Standing outside of the hotel, I was trying to say "goodbye" and "thank you" but failed, miserably. Bebe squared off on me every time I made for the door.

"Do you want me?" she pressed, and it suddenly clicked. *This is what Captain Felix meant when he said the rest was up to me.*

"No?" I replied, unsure of myself. *That wasn't the right answer.*

She frowned. "*Ni buyao wo le ma?*" (You don't want me?)

"I don't know... *Maybe?*"

I have no idea what she said after that, but I understood what was happening. She grabbed me by the hand and walked me to the elevator. In the elevator, she frisked me for the room's keycard.

When it was over, Bebe handed me her cell phone. A woman on the other end spoke. "Yes, I am Nicki."

"Yes?"

"You will now pay money Bebe?"

"*Duoshao?*" (How much?)

"Three hundred yuan."

"Um, *hen hao.*" (Sure.)

* ✳ *

As we boarded a plane at Xiamen International Airport (IATA code: XIA) headed for Wuyishan, our next destination, Felix asked, "How much did you give her?"

"Three hundred."

"Oh, you were cheated. A girl in Xiamen is two hundred, no more than that!"

"I dunno," I shrugged. "Seemed fair."

"Today, I will take you to a real fucking place." In the Captain's vernacular, a 'fucking place' meant a place where hookers could be found. "Wuyishan is a real fucking place."

* ✱ *

Now is a good time to talk about the fact that the Bebe incident in Xiamen was the first time I ever paid for sex. And that leads me to a proper discussion of prostitution, which I consciously refer to as "sexual economics" when I'm getting particular about touchy subjects. In the case of Bebe, it was a straight-up choice as soon as she took my hand. *Yes, I want to have sex with this woman and I'm willing to pay for it.*

And let's get another thing cleared up. The dark side of prostitution— sex trafficking, human bondage, violation of minors—is pure evil. But it would be hypocritical of me to condemn the sex industry or the act of paying for sex or being paid for sex when I've been a customer. I wish all that evil shit didn't exist, just like I wish fossil fuels weren't being burned to meet my energy demands.

I hope it's obvious that I'm not trying to appear morally or ethically virtuous, but how I made it to 40 years old without paying for sex is somehow relevant. I never had any moral or ethical dilemma with prostitution. It should be legal, and it's not "a sin" if enacted between consenting adults. Prostitution—in addition to being **Not My Fault** and **It Was Like That Before I Got Here**—is an economic rather than moral dilemma. And pornography, though generally hideous, is simply prostitution on camera.

Like sexpats and sex tourism, being involved in pay-for-play sex and being exposed to it are two different things. I was *exposed* to plenty of prostitution. I knew the Times Square hookers were still serious gum-chewing ladies of the evening. I was very familiar with the Tenderloin in San Francisco, where you couldn't be sure who *isn't* a hooker, or a dude. Chinatown, the French Quarter, Vegas, Kingston, Rush Street in Chicago. The abstinence wasn't from a lack of exposure.

The main reason I never paid for sex was a lack of money. If there was anything good about being eternally broke, it kept me from vices like betting on the ponies, paying for lap dances, and picking up hookers. The second and possibly more important obstacle was fear. I was chickenshit. I didn't know how it all worked. I worried about everything from "When do I pay her?" (usually at the end) to "What if I don't want to kiss her?" (no problem) to "Can I get an STD while wearing a condom?" (yes, you can). Without first-hand knowledge of the experience, I was forever on the outside looking in.

And finally, though it means much more to my ego than it does the story, I didn't need a hooker. I was doing fine on my own. I had been tempted to indulge, but I didn't want to spend the money. As I got older, I went to a handful of strip clubs with my friends. I would look but I wouldn't touch. It was none of my business if my friends indulged. I didn't. There wasn't any subconscious Puritanical mind conditioning leftover from childhood. I was not in a position to drop $150 on a handjob. It seemed gratuitous to insult the Goddess of Sex by being greedy with her blessings. And worst-case scenario, I could do it myself.

So, now, of course, I'm assuming the reader's perspective will be to agree or disagree with my position on the subject. That's the whole point in talking about it, really. I just wanted you to know where I stand, so later, you're not asking, "Does this man understand what he's doing?" He does. Moreover, it's not going to make a bit of difference, but I've asked myself, what if somebody wanted to pay me for sex? *What if I was a hooker instead of a john? How would I feel about it?* Well, if somebody wanted to pay me to have sex, first, I'd be flattered. *But what about doing it for a living?* Well, I mean, if I could, you know, maybe I would have done it for a while in my 20s and used the cash to put myself through law school or some white-collar bullshit. As a career, honestly, it doesn't seem any more or less promising than playing in a rock band.

★✳★

Hundreds, if not, thousands of books describe the Chinese countryside in the kind of exquisite detail that I'm neither interested in nor capable of reprising. To me, rural China looked an awful lot like central Oregon with rice paddies instead of livestock pens. The topography was varied and green and surprisingly mountainous. If there was one detail that stands out among all others, it was the mountains. Not for their majesty or their abundance, but rather every other face had a huge chunk missing from where it had been strip-mined, exposing ugly red clay in an advanced state of erosion.

Wuyishan is a difficult place to describe because it's several different places in one area. First, there's Mount Wuyi, one of the most revered peaks in China and part of the Wuyi Mountain range in northern Fujian Province. Then there is Wuyishan Resort Area, an oddly popular tourist destination nearby, known primarily for ripping off tourists, according to my sources. Even Captain Felix said something about getting ripped off in Wuyishan. The entire area is a UNESCO World Heritage Site, which doesn't mean shit anymore because every other village in China has applied for the same status.

And then...15 km northeast of the Wuyishan Resort Area, is Wuyishan City; a county-level municipal region of Nanping, with a population of 200,000 or so; it just seems like a hell of a lot more. There's a small, one-runway airport located directly between the city and the resort area. Either way, unless you make a very concerted effort, you will never set eyes on the actual Mount Wuyi while in Wuyishan.

Most visitors go straight from the airport to the resort area, a not-entirely charmless spread of restaurants, hotels, tea wholesalers, small retail shops, and brothels clustered alongside the Chongyang Stream. A lone highway stretches back to the city; lots of farmland and several factories between the two. The ride from Wuyishan Airport (IATA code: WUS) to the resort area was a harrowing introduction to rural Chinese traffic. Flat and straight, the highway was shared by any number of vehicles—including the four-legged variety—traveling at wildly variable speeds. I was staring out the window at the passing scenery of rice fields and cudding oxen, trying not to question the decision-making process of the bus driver.

We arrived at the resort area and perused a couple of hotels before Felix found one he liked. We checked into the Shengyang International Hotel, but before we went to our separate rooms, Felix insisted that we stop by the "hair salon" to see what was happening. There were two fairly attractive women just lounging on the salon couch—nobody was getting a haircut. The Captain asked, "Do you see anything you like?" and I said, "Nah, maybe later."

"Meet me downstairs at seven o'clock," Felix said. "We'll have dinner. I know you don't like Chinese food, but this place is the best in town."

The landline was ringing when I walked into my room. It was one of the girls from the hair salon asking if I wanted company. I said no. Ten minutes later, another call—different woman. Twenty minutes later, another. It went on for an hour until I took the phone off the hook. From that point forward, no matter where I went in China, the first thing I did was take the phone off the hook or unplug it from the wall, unless I knew Captain Felix was going to call.

We met in the lobby and walked outside to hail a pedicab, which started a mini stampede of idle pedicab drivers loitering around the hotel. A leather-faced woman was the first to reach us. Leather Face took us off the main drag to a restaurant on the river's edge—a lively-looking joint in an otherwise depressing area. Felix was wary of Leather Face, especially as we rode through some dark and desolate alleyways. "It's a good thing you're with me," he said. "Otherwise, I'd be dead right now." *Was it hyperbole?* Yes and no.

We took a table outside the restaurant and a heavy-set, gregarious woman took Felix's order. Dish after dish arrived. Captain Felix was a life-long teetotaler who only drank alcohol during toasts at large gatherings, so I was surprised when he said he wanted to drink beer with me. The food was delicious, and the atmosphere was authentic.

"Do you want to have a smoke?" Felix asked. This also surprised me since he always told me I should quit.

"I'll go have one over there," I said, pointing to an alley about 10 meters from our table. "I don't want to bother you with my second-hand smoke."

"Don't go too far. It's not safe. Stay where I can see you."

A woman came into the alley with a very young boy, and they stopped about two meters from where I stood enjoying a Marlboro. The woman crouched before the boy, pulled down his shorts, and instructed him to squat. He obliged. Then he took a shit. Maybe a minute went by, and the woman hastily wiped the boy's ass with what looked like a single sheet of toilet paper, pulled his shorts up, tossed the balled-up piece of toilet paper to the side, and the two of them walked away. The smell was atrocious. Out of the corner of my eye, I could see Captain Felix arguing with the restaurant owner.

I returned to the table as the proprietor stormed away. "What was that all about?"

"She tried to cheat me," meaning the proprietor.

"Really?"

"Not too bad. Maybe a hundred yuan." I started to talk but he waved me off. "*Mei guanxi.* These are poor people. They're hungry for money."

At the table next to us was an extended family situation. Mom, Dad, daughter, son-in-law, younger brother. Their table was a disaster. Dishes and empty beer bottles everywhere. It seemed like they were celebrating something. One thing was for sure: Joe, the patriarch, was large and in charge. He was really getting into it with the fat-assed proprietor and doing most of the talking (shouting) while waggling the handwritten bill in front of her face. Felix reached across the table, touched my shoulder and said, "Don't go anywhere. Don't move a muscle. Stay where you are."

"What are they saying?"

"I will translate for you."

The proprietor said the price of the fish was 150 yuan but failed to mention that the price was per 500 grams, or *guan*, half-kilo, standard Asian restaurant practice. This oversight pushed the bill to the upper reaches of 1,000 yuan (US$150), which Joe here said was quote, "robbery," and refused to pay. He dined in the finest restaurants from Paris to Honolulu and never so outrageously and egregiously over-charged. He wasn't pissed off about the money. Joe had plenty of that. It was that some saggy-breasted *obasan* (Japanese for 'older woman') in the middle of nowhere dared to foist such a travesty on a cultured, respected man like himself.

The situation deteriorated and I noticed figures leaving the indoor seating section of the restaurant. Joe's wife and kids had disappeared into the surrounding darkness. The air was already hot and thick but now charged with tension. I was spooked. *Where'd everybody go?*

Felix was way ahead of me. "Charlie. Let's get out of here."

We beat it on foot through a dark alley before Leather Face came up behind us on the pedicab.

"See?" Felix said as we got in the pedicab. "They know where you are at all times. You can't escape."

On the ride back to the hotel, I took a chance to ask about the abrupt change of plans. I never asked Captain Felix any unprompted questions if I could help it. With half a beer in his near-virgin belly, I reckoned he'd be jolly enough to roll with it.

"Just curious, but why did you decide to bail out on going to Beijing?"

"The city will be crowded with tourists. Everybody will want to be there. No fun."

"What did Daisy say about us not coming to Beijing?"

"Right. Don't worry about her. I'll take care of her. No problem."

"Is she pissed off?"

"Huh?" Felix squinted. "Is she angry?" His eyes glazed in mischief. "Yes, she is very angry. She's fit to be tied."

"*Yikes.*"

As we boarded the elevator in the hotel, Felix said, "I'm going to leave you to explore on your own for a day or two. You can take care of yourself. I hope you don't mind."

"Not at all, boss," I said. "Thanks for everything. The trip has been awesome so far!"

"You deserve it. You deserve more. Stick with me, the best is yet to come."

I slept through breakfast and wobbled down to the front desk around 10:00 a.m. There was a large kiosk with pictures of local tourist destinations and assorted information. As I pointed to a picture on a travel brochure of the Bamboo Raft River Canyon Trip, one of the two front desk clerks picked up the phone. The other motioned toward the lobby couches.

A black, late-model Lexus pulled up in the turnaround of the hotel. The driver grossly overcharged me 30 yuan (US$4) for a 3-minute ride to the gate of the scenic area. From there, it was fees, every step of the journey. I paid another 40 yuan to get into the park, 10 yuan for a shuttle bus to the river, and another 100 yuan for the river raft. All those travel books were right! Wuyishan was a rip-off. But we were just getting started.

The Bamboo Raft River Canyon Trip on Nine Bend Stream was a 90-minute float down a lazy river that winds through an impressive karst canyon. Highly recommended if you're into karst. The raft held 6–8 people plus one guy to steer it. There were collapsible umbrellas so you could control the amount of sun exposure. Next time, I'm bringing a cooler full of beer. Unless you get stuck with a bunch of chatty tourists, as happened to me, it has the potential to be a very pleasant and serene experience.

At the end of the trip, you take a shuttle bus—for another 15 yuan—to other areas or exit the park. I was already sick of the nickel-and-diming. Leaving the park, I was met by one of the motorcycle taxi drivers who hovered around the hotel. I said, "I want to go eat," but he must have heard, "Take me to another river boat experience" because that's where I wound up, another 100 yuan lighter for the lift.

I paid another 150 yuan to paddle us—myself and the guide—5 km down the southern fork of the Chongyang Stream, in a shitbag inflatable two-man raft. For the first hour, it was just us on the river, exchanging cigarettes, nodding and smiling. I took some pictures. And then we came to a quiet bend in the river. The guide steered us toward the shore. *Great,* I thought, *we're done. This bullshit is over.* The raft floated gently to the riverbank when a guy with a camera popped out of the brush and took my picture. Scared the ever-loving bejesus out of me—I almost jumped from the raft. Like retreating from an ambush, the guide started paddling hard, and soon we were back in the river current.

The high August sun was relentless. The guide sat in back and did zero share of the paddling. I really felt his dead weight during the last half hour. Finally, it ended. We beached the raft, and the guide ran ahead of me toward a makeshift reception area. I hadn't even made it halfway up the beach when the same photographer came out of nowhere—Ambush #2—and snapped another picture. Really pissed off at that point, I took a swing at him and *just barely* missed his chin. Thank God I missed because that hard right cross would have dropped this fucking dude. He was maybe five-foot-three, 120 pounds. He screamed like a girl, "*Waahhhh!*" before scampering up the beach and out of sight.

Up the beach was a single-story multi-family compound and another "tourist kiosk," where a group of five shirtless men sat under a roof shelter on tiny plastic chairs near a glass case, drinking beer from large green bottles and 4-ounce glasses. Chickens and barefoot infant children mingled about. The main man greeted me, offering a cigarette. The photo guy lurked near the shed. They were highly amused by my presence, asking the typical questions, and I tried my best to answer in my terrible Mandarin.

Soon a crusty minivan pulled up into the courtyard of the complex—my ride back to town. The driver approached and said, "Come on, let's go." The main man immediately stood up and protested. It seemed there was unfinished business. The driver pointed at me and said, "You must buy something." I looked at the glass case. There were a couple of T-shirts, bottles of water, cigarettes, and condoms. *Condoms!?* So, I bought a T-shirt and a bottle of water. Another 50 yuan. The photo guy cautiously crept over. I said, "Sorry about that" (*bu hao yisi*) and bought one of the 8"x10" glossy shots of me from the river for 100 yuan. And then the minivan driver hit me up for his 50 yuan, which I guess I assumed was already covered. *Jesus, these people really squeeze you.*

And then—the driver dropped me in front of a restaurant instead of the hotel. A woman came out and corralled me inside. Ravenous anyway, I pointed at some shit on the menu. They brought me chicken, vegetables, noodles, beer, and a bill for 250 yuan (US$35). This time, I protested, and the woman returned with a bill for 180. All told, I spent roughly US$150 on a series of lackluster experiences. Did I get ripped off? *Yes.* Did I care? *Not really.* I thought it was 150 bucks well spent.

Back at the hotel, the ambush photographer was waiting for me, now with 5"x 8" glossies of the same goddamn photos he took and already sold me on the river. *How the fuck did this guy even know where I was staying?*

* ✱ *

Friday, August 8, 2008, was an auspicious day in China. Eight is the luckiest number in Chinese culture and it was the opening day of the Beijing Olympics. The opening ceremony was scheduled to start at 8:08 p.m. Beijing Standard Time.

I spent most of the day lounging around the massive hotel pool and fending off a variety of fixers, vendors, and hookers who furtively approached. At lunch, I started drinking beer and piled on a huge buzz. Somewhere around 3:00 p.m., I went back inside the hotel, all fucked up, and took the elevator to the 11th floor instead of 10. A pair of teenage girls who looked maybe 18 years old, tops, were also in the elevator car. My "age radar" wasn't great in the beginning. Most Chinese women were older than they looked to me. The girls got off on the 11th floor, too. I wobbled around the hallway. "Shit, am I on the wrong floor?" The girls knocked on a door—the Captain's room.

The door opened and I heard Felix say, "Ah, you're here! Come in, come in. Oh, such pretty girls!" The girls entered, the door slamming behind them.

Back in my room, I showered and took a nap. I had a dream about my friend Scottie, who blew off most of his left hand in a fireworks accident when we were kids. It was dusk when I awoke to the percussive sizzle of fireworks going off outside my hotel window.

It was 7:57 p.m. when I stood in front of the hotel, scratching my head. Street traffic was nonexistent, but in every storefront, restaurant, and garage, people were sitting on small plastic chairs, glued to a TV. The men were drinking beer and smoking, the women were eating. Children of all ages sat around, staring at the screens. And the fireworks. They seemed to come from every direction but where? I heard the crackling but didn't see any sparks or smoke.

I crossed the street and took a table outside the biggest and best-lit restaurant on the block. Inside were 20 or 30 people, fixated on a pair of flat-screen TVs. Occasionally, someone would steal a curious glance my way. A woman approached and asked what I wanted. I pointed at several random menu items and asked for beer.

By 8:07 p.m., the few stragglers in the streets found their way to a TV set. The pedicab drivers were nowhere to be seen. A non-stop white noise of fireworks washed across the neighborhood. The frequency of explosions slowly increased. I drank beer and watched the TV through the window. At 8:08, time stood still. I tried to imagine what the people of Wuyishan were feeling in that moment: pride, love, and maybe hope? Other than being in the Bird's Nest during the opening ceremony, I could think of no better place to witness the event.

Surprisingly, a few minutes into the opening ceremony, the server brought a tableful of food. And I lost all interest in the Olympics, concentrating on the grub. Two hours and countless bottles of Wuyishan Beer later, I stumbled back to the hotel.

The next morning, I got up early for breakfast, stopped by the front desk, walked out of the hotel and approached the motorcycle taxi guy who marooned me on that silly river raft bullshit. The front desk lady wrote down the name of my destination in Chinese. I handed it to the driver. We agreed on a flat rate of 200 yuan for a half-day.

I came across some tourist paraphernalia about a waterfall located 20 kilometers away, out in the middle of the Fujian Wuyishan National Nature Reserve, with a man-made trail built into and around the falls, making for a steep but manageable one-hour climb. The rushing water was said to cool the air so you wouldn't suffer from heat exhaustion during the hike. It seemed like a good day trip.

The ride out there was fantastic once I got comfortable on the back of this guy's Kymco 250cc, *sans* helmet, doing 50 km per hour on winding mountain trails and dirt roads. He was a good driver, and I think he sensed my anxiety, so he took it easy. Once we arrived at the waterfall, the driver agreed to meet me in the parking lot in two hours. I paid the 40-yuan admission fee and began the climb, a little surprised by the number of Chinese tourists. These people didn't look like they'd done a lot of climbing in their lives. It was slow-going as I elbowed through the herds of families and stragglers.

I finally reached the top of the waterfall. There was a beautiful wood lodge with a souvenir vendor and benches to sit. A woman was slicing mangoes and watermelon on a table. A couple of grizzled old men sat and watched. The woman told me to sit down and eat but I politely declined. Next to the building was a monkey in a cage.

Otherwise, it was dense forest up there. Wasn't much to see or do. Eat the fruit, feel sorry for the monkey, head back. Starting down the trail, I came upon three women. They said hello to me, and I said hello back. It was a mom, an aunt, and a daughter from Xi'an. The daughter spoke decent English. They weren't interested in eating the fruit or looking at the sad caged monkey, either. The four of us walked back down the trail together, chatting the whole way. We took a couple of pictures together to commemorate the meeting.

The motorcycle driver was waiting for me at the exit. At the far end of the parking lot, a dispute was reaching critical mass. What started as a disagreement over a taxi fare had escalated into a full-blown melee. One guy, who appeared to be a tourist, was getting his ass beaten to a pulp by a group of locals. His hysterical girlfriend or wife was being restrained by a couple of middle-aged women. Another woman was kicking the bloodied tourist guy in the stomach as he lay on the ground. I took out my camera and put it up to my face to take a picture, when the driver put a hand on my arm to push it down and said, "Don't do that."

I returned to the hotel and took a nap. It was after 8:00 p.m. when I wandered back down to the restaurant on the corner. The Olympics were on the TV but hardly anybody was watching. Life had already returned to normal.

I drank a few beers, ate more exceedingly spicy food, and called it a night. We were leaving in the morning.

On the bus ride to Wuyishan City, the Captain surprised me. "Did you sleep with that girl you met at the waterfall?"

"What girl at what waterfall?"

Felix groaned. "Two things you need to know about the Chinese. They see everything and they love to gossip."

"Well, they were wrong. Yes, I met some women at the waterfall, but I didn't sleep with any of them."

"Huh," Felix said. "Strange."

Upon arrival in Wuyishan City, we stopped at a restaurant that was "famous" for lamb. After lunch, Felix said, "Let's go find a sauna house." We grabbed a pedicab and Felix went to work on the driver.

"This guy," Captain Felix said, "is going to take us to the best sauna house in town." Nowadays, I can spot a sauna house a mile away, mainly from the Chinese characters for "sauna house," but this particular sauna house looked no different than any of a hundred other Chinese establishments. It could have been a restaurant, hotel, bus station, shoe store, bank—I didn't know. From the outside, there was no indication of what went on inside. A couple of dim-looking girls sat at the front desk. I stared up at a big board on the wall behind them.

"That's the menu," the Captain said. "They've got everything. You want a massage? You can have massage. You want to take a sauna? You can take a sauna. You want full-service? You can have full-service."

We took off our shoes and the porter gave us a pair of *lanbai* slippers. We were escorted to the second floor "lounge," where the *mamasan* took a wide-eyed look at me and immediately started yapping at Felix. She was alarmed and surprised by my presence. I heard *waiguoren* (foreigner) several times. Felix said *mei guanxi* (no problem) a few times, but the *mamasan* continued to eye me suspiciously. Captain Felix later apologized for not telling me sooner that some sex operations in China are locals only—no foreigners allowed.

"What do you want?" Felix asked. "Do you want a massage?"

"A simple massage. That's all."

"If you change your mind," Felix pointed at the *mamasan*, "just let her know."

"I will."

"You're sure you just want a massage?"

"I'm sure."

"For how long? Forty minutes? An hour?"

"Forty minutes will do."

Felix took care of the details while I was led by a cute woman dressed in a "sauna house uniform" to a small massage room that reeked of stale cigarettes and condoms. There was a small black and white TV in the corner and the massage table looked as if it had recently been wiped down with a greasy cloth. I was instructed to disrobe down to my boxer shorts. Part of me was hoping this woman wasn't going to be my masseuse, and at the same time, the other part was hoping she was going to be my masseuse. It was probably better for both of us if she wasn't.

The cute woman left the room, closing the door. I lay down on the table and waited. About five minutes later, a mannish middle-aged woman came in. There was very little "massage" involved—she pinched and poked and pressed and pulled and elbowed and stabbed and did everything you could possibly do to another human being in the course of a "massage" without crossing into the realm of misdemeanor assault. I cried out during the contortion of my right shoulder. At one point, she was mumbling to herself. *You filthy scumbag, I'm going to make you pay.* She even slammed the door when she left. I dressed and stumbled out of the room, beaten, sore, and humbled.

Returning to the lounge, I sprawled onto a couch, lit a smoke, and gazed at koi fish swimming peacefully in the 500-gallon aquarium. The *mamasan* came in and out of the lounge several times. I heard Felix's laughter and female giggling from one of the massage rooms. The cute woman returned, took me by the hand, and walked me to his room.

"Charlie! Did you enjoy your massage?"

"Sure did, boss. Just what I needed. Thanks."

"Right, right... Sit down, I want to talk to you."

Yet another other girl brought in a plastic chair, and I sat down. She quickly left the room.

Felix lay face-up on a massage table with two girls (young women) in sauna house uniforms sitting at his side, each rubbing a leg. They weren't rubbing his legs as much as they were idling rubbing their hands over his knees while he talked. Felix was wearing only a white towel and his Peter Fonda aviator glasses. I did everything I could to avoid looking at him, but the erection under the towel was unmistakable. The girls smiled and laughed at everything Captain Felix said.

"Was the girl beautiful?" he asked.

"Who?"

"Your massage girl."

"Oh, her? I wouldn't say that."

"Did you get laid with her?"

"No. I did not."

"*You didn't?*"

I nodded towards the girls. "These girls are...legal age, aren't they?"

"Of course!"

"Great. Well, I'm going back to the lounge. Are you just about done here?"

∗✱∗

On the ferry boat ride from Xiamen to Kinmen, between bouts of nausea, Captain Felix mustered the effort to say, "Now you've seen the Real China. You have been where no man has been before."

It seemed like I'd been where a lot of men had been before, but I guess he had a point.

8

Home Again, Briefly

Back in Taipei, the forward momentum continued for several weeks, but I had a lingering notion that some kind of disaster was on the horizon. *This is working out a little too well. Something's gonna give here, sooner or later.* Nevertheless, I was neither concerned nor equipped to do anything about it. Whatever happened was simply going to happen.

Captain Felix started inviting me to dinner once or twice a week in the evenings when Daisy was playing badminton with her friends. We usually had American or Western fare at The Diner, Carnegie's, The Second Door Cafe, Chili's, TGI Friday's, etc. It was pretty cool to have a meal with Felix, shoot the shit, and part ways when it was over. He mostly talked about women and traveling. I did most of the listening.

A week before my first project—the TOEFL test book—was due to be published, Felix took me to a hot pot restaurant, where he uncharacteristically started talking about work. He told me that more than a thousand students had enrolled in the new TOEFL class at the cram school. There was a lot of money involved, both in the production of the book and earnings from the school, and he stressed the importance of not fucking things up.

None of this was news to me. I had a rich understanding of what was at stake. Daisy talked about it all the time. She warned me, "If the class opens and the students start complaining the test is too hard or too easy—your head will be first to roll." *That seems a little excessive, Daisy.*

Meanwhile, the book itself—the physical copy—was already out of my hands since I'd met my deadlines with Celeste, who oversaw formatting.

Before we left the hot pot joint, Felix said, "When it's all over, I'm going to take you on a trip. Let's go somewhere and have fun. You need some relaxation."

"The trip to Wuiyshan was awesome!"

"That was nothing. Someday, I'll take you to the secret island. It's a *real fucking place*—paradise for men, hell for women."

"Uh...yeah. Alright..."

The day before the TOEFL book was sent to the printers, I asked Celeste to print me a final copy, just so I could give it the old once-over. The copy she gave me was flawless. I didn't catch a single typo or formatting glitch. The final proofreading was done by an American woman in Korea named Polly, who had been telecommuting as the company proofreader for five years. The book looked great. I was *almost* excited.

As I came into the office the next morning, Daisy was waiting for me, highly agitated. "Charlie! Have you seen the TOEFL book?"

"No. It's not back from the printer yet."

"*Yes, it is!*" My heart sank. Daisy shoved a copy of the book into my hands. "There's a big problem! Everything is wrong! What happened?"

The initial 2,000 print copies of the test book were loaded with typos and inconsistencies—missing pages, funky typesetting, and Chinese characters where they shouldn't be. It was a mess. The good news was the CDs hadn't been pressed yet, which would have really fucked things up. The bad news was the class started tomorrow.

When word of the misprint spread through the company, Polly quickly produced files via email that showed all the necessary corrections were made. Somehow, Celeste sent the wrong file to the printer. This was confirmed later in the day when Celeste confessed to mixing up the files.

Captain Felix was quick to absolve me of any blame. However, I couldn't help feeling guilty in some way.

"You know, it seems like I deserve some responsibility for this, too." *What a dumb fuckin' thing to say.*

Felix started to speak but Daisy jumped in. "*No!* That girl has been warned many times. I told you she was going to be fired six months before you came here. She has been here a year and hasn't produced a

118

single book. Now, she does something and it's a mess! *It's a disaster!* This will cost the company a lot of money. This makes the company look bad."

"You are the writer," Felix said, "and she (Celeste) is the formatter. Polly is the proofreader."

"What's gonna happen...?"

"No problem," Felix said. "This is a minor setback. It can be fixed."

"You fired Celeste?"

"Don't worry. Her father is a good friend. I will find something else for her to do. She can work in the cram school."

About an hour after Felix and Daisy left the office, Celeste came in, crying and holding her personal effects in a box.

"I came to say goodbye," she said, sniffling. "I know I am careless, and this is all my fault. I'm very sorry I ruined everything for you."

"Aw, don't say sorry," I said. "You don't have to leave. Felix didn't fire you."

"No. I can't stay here any longer. It was a bad mistake. I am careless and unwanted here. I am a poison to the company."

"Don't say that! You are not a poison. Everyone makes mistakes."

"I want to say that I enjoyed working with you, and I'm so sorry."

I felt myself tearing up. From the shadows, Lloyd appeared behind Celeste at the threshold of the office door and gave me a 'wrap-it-up' gesture.

"Felix is coming. She needs to go."

A few days later, I was working on a comprehension test when Felix said, out of nowhere, "I know you like that girl. Don't worry. She will be OK."

"*What* girl?"

Aside from that one comment, Captain Felix didn't look at me or refer to me in conversation with others. Daisy also gave me the silent treatment. Another few days passed and it seemed like the entire company was giving me the freeze-out. Even the cram school admins were giving me a stink-eye. And in my mind, it might not have been my fault, but I was associated with that book disaster, and now, tainted in the company. *It's time for me to bail. The show's over.* So, I called China Airlines and rescheduled the back end of my original return trip to San Francisco for a week from today.

Stephan called after hearing about the TOEFL book disaster and offered his condolences. I told him I was probably leaving Taiwan for good.

"Don't do that," Stephan said. "Go home for a while. Take a break. Felix will get over it. They're promoting the shit out of that TOEFL class. If it blows up, you might be in good shape."

"The only hitch is what to do about the apartment? The landlord is a nice guy. I don't *want* to screw him over, and I really don't want to lose my security deposit. In terms of self-preservation, not giving him notice seems like a smart thing to do. My rent is paid through September, so... I'll leave it as-is, just in case I come back. And if I don't, well, sorry about that. I'm sure they'll figure it out."

"Forget that apartment, man," Stephan said, disgusted. "You're already paying way too much for that place."

When I told Daisy that I was returning to San Francisco for two weeks to take care of some unfinished business, she said, "You're not coming back, are you?"

"No, wait, yes—I'm coming back." I tried to be reassuring. "For sure. I'll be back." She gave me a side-eye and mumbled something to herself.

Captain Felix had an oddly positive reaction when Daisy predictably jumped the gun and broke the news of my departure.

"That's great!" he said. "You should see your family. Take some time off." He asked about the airfare, and I told him it was already covered since it was the return ticket from my original flight.

Felix replied, "I want to know how much it cost. I want to pay for it." And so, an hour later, Mr. Chu came and handed me a thousand U.S. dollars in cash. On the day of my departure, Felix came around and gave me *another* grand in cash. "See you when you get back," he said. Otherwise, that was the only farewell.

The truth is, at that moment, I wasn't coming back.

* ✳ *

The flight arrived at SFO around 8:30 p.m. and Chet Monroe was waiting to pick me up with a fat joint ready to smoke and a six-pack of

Budweiser longnecks in the passenger foot well. Arriving at The Cave, I greeted Tommy with a warm embrace. Less than a minute later, Mao-mao came screaming in through the back door, having heard my voice. The boy jumped into my arms as I bent down to scoop him up. Cradling him as he purred, I began weeping, "Where were you, kiddo? What happened?" The tears were flowing.

I spent a week just kicking around the Sunset District, crashing at the Seal Rock Inn at Ocean Beach, which was expensive, but I reckoned Felix was paying for it. Every morning when Tom left for work, I'd roll down to The Cave and hang out with Mao-mao, clearing the backyard of six months' worth of overgrowth, the neglect of my absence.

It was great to see Wilson, Chet, and Tommy. As far as my travels were concerned, I talked about Taiwan and China in vague generalities, avoiding discussion about Captain Felix and Knowledge Press. They didn't care. They weren't listening anyway. So, I told them that I worked as a writer for this eccentric Taiwanese dude. They said, "That's cool." More importantly, I didn't know what to do: stay in S.F. or return to Taipei.

Finally, Tommy brought up the situation with Mao and The Cave. "What is your plan, chief?"

"Well," I said, "the six-month agreement period is almost up. Have you got any plan to evacuate?"

"That's just it," Tom said, pulling a drag from his smoke. "I don't have any plans to leave."

"Do you *want* to leave?"

"What I want is for you to get that computer desk out of here."

"That's fine," I said. "But what if I don't go back to Taipei? Are you telling me that I have to find somewhere else to live?"

"No, but kind of..." Tommy said, shifting gears. "Are you going back to Taiwan?"

"I don't know."

"Well, that kind of dictates everything else, doesn't it?"

We went round and round about it. "Look, brother, this is *my* goddamned apartment. I understand you did me a favor, but I helped you out, too, man. You never would have left that shoebox in Nob Hill if it weren't for me."

"Sure," Tommy agreed. "But things have changed."

He was right. Things had changed. First, those guys had moved on with their lives, and whether I was a part of it, didn't matter at all. So, there was no point in thinking I had any leverage by coming back and picking up where I left off.

"The question is," Tommy said, "are you staying in San Francisco, or going back to Taipei? Make up your mind, chief. Make up your mind."

I spent the next day looking at the Bay Area job listings. There wasn't much in my wheelhouse. *Fuck it. I'll just move out to Oakland and start substitute teaching again.* Then I called my former boss at Mykonia, Jack Mercer, who sounded happy to hear from me.

"Say something in Chinese," Mercer said.

"*Wo xiang yao yibei zhong de hei kafei jia yidian tang.*" (I'd like a medium cup of hot coffee with just a little bit of sugar.)

Mercer was tickled. "Listen, Charlie, the door is always open for you here. Whenever you want to come back, be it tomorrow or ten years from now, you'll always be a part of the Mykonia family." It was slightly reassuring to know that I wouldn't starve.

My folks were in Phoenix, Arizona, where they lived in a plush retirement community and spent their days in a sun-kissed suburban bliss. Over the years I visited them every so often, for a week at a time, but most of our communication happened via video chat on Skype. Later in the evening, I gave them a call. Without sharing any details, I told my parents that I wasn't sure the Taiwan gambit was going to work out, and I was likely to stay in San Francisco for a while. The only problem was finding a place to live, since Tommy was staying in The Cave, for the time being.

"Have you ever thought about moving to Phoenix?" my mother suggested, knowing that I wouldn't last more than a week in the desert.

"I don't know *what* I'm going to do, Mom."

"Well, dear, at least you had the experience of traveling to Asia," switching to a comforting tone, "which is something you've always, always wanted to do."

My father said, "It sure seems to me, after going so far, it would be a shame to stop now."

In the middle of the conversation, that familiar Skype notification popped up—it was Daisy calling.

"Who's that?" my mother asked.

"A friend from Taiwan."

"Oh really?" She was excited. "Are you going to add them to the call? Oh gosh, I'd really love to meet them!"

"No. It's someone from work. It wouldn't be a social call. I'll get back to them later."

My mother was deflated. "Aw, that's too bad."

The single-minded Daisy didn't take no for an answer. Two minutes later, she rang again. My mother said, "Oh, it might be important, you should take that," so we cut our conversation short, and I picked up the call from Daisy.

"Charlie!" Daisy chirped as she appeared on the screen, broadcasting from the Knowledge Press control center. It would have been 10:00 a.m. in Taipei, right about the time Captain Felix rolled up for the day. "Where are you?"

"Hi Daisy. I'm in San Francisco. Where did you think I was?"

"Well, I don't know. Captain Felix wanted to know where you were."

I smiled and stared into the camera. "I'm...here."

Daisy looked off-camera, and I could hear the Captain speaking Mandarin in the background. "When are you coming back to Taipei?"

"I don't know. I haven't booked a ticket yet."

There was more commotion in the background—Felix talking—and Daisy said, "Don't worry about the airfare. We'll take care of that."

"So, you *want* me to come back? After everything that happened with the TOEFL book?"

"Of course! *That wasn't your fault!*" she shrieked. "You know, Felix has been asking about you every day since you left." There was more background noise and Daisy smiled mischievously. "No, really," she said. "He wants you to come back as soon as possible."

"Tell you what. I've got a couple of things to deal with here, so I'll book a flight tomorrow and let you know ASAP. OK?"

Daisy again looked off-camera and said to Felix, "He's gonna book a ticket tomorrow." Felix probably said, "No problem." And Daisy said to me, "That sounds great! Send me an email with your flight information. I'll have somebody pick you up from the airport."

9

Getting to Know the Crew at Knowledge Press HQ

Even though I was only gone for two weeks, I was pleasantly surprised to see that my rooftop apartment was *exactly* how I left it. And I was satisfied with myself for not making a rash decision about the landlord. I spent the first night on the patio getting high, drinking beer, and gazing at the sky. It felt more than good to be back. It felt *right*. Regardless of how things went down earlier, I was back where I belonged.

Captain Felix was openly pleased about my return to the KPHQ fold. As it turned out, once they got the TOEFL book straightened away, the class was a big success, and the teachers rained praise on the material I poached and wrangled into shape. Felix said, "I want you to do the same thing" for the rest of the standardized ESL tests–acronyms and initialisms that I'm not going to burden you with. In other words, I had job security. There were towering stacks of reference materials on my desk. Meanwhile, everybody else at Knowledge Press treated me like an old friend.

"I didn't think you were coming back," Daisy said tearfully. "I really didn't."

That night, Felix took off for Hong Kong, but he told Daisy to treat me to dinner at Ruth's Chris Steakhouse. After dinner, we went to Tonghua Night Market near the office to visit Daisy's friend, Sasha, who had just opened a dressmaking shop. About a month earlier, Daisy tried to fix me up with Sasha, but it wasn't happening. Daisy asked, "It's not going to bother you to see Sasha, is it?"

"No, why would it?"

"Because she rejected you."

"Oh. Like she's the first?" I laughed. "I don't give a shit, Daisy."

"Well... Even if you're hurt by her rejection, please, just be nice. She's very nervous and excited about her new shop."

Night markets are crowded with people and merchandise. There aren't many open spaces in a night market for long. Somebody closes shop, another somebody moves in. It's all very cyclical. Sasha's dressmaking shop was taking over the space of an old man who'd been selling off-brand watches and jade jewelry. The last remnants of his shop—a display case containing watches and other knick-knacks—were posted in front of the stall, which Sasha allowed as a courtesy to the old dude, who wasn't happy about getting squeezed out. At any rate, Daisy said, "As soon as this old guy sells the rest of his stuff, he's out of here."

I didn't have any use for the dresses or conversation with Sasha, for that matter, so I just lurked outside the shop and waved and said, "Looks great, Sasha! Best of luck!" while Daisy perused the dresses and jawboned about whatever those chicks jawbone about. As I poked my nose into the old man's display case, I noticed a small selection of pipes—the type used to smoke marijuana. So, I reached in and examined a couple of them. The old man scooted over and said, "I'll give you a great deal on those." And I said, "*Xie xie. Bu yao, xie xie.*" (Thanks, but no thanks.) One of the pipes was still in my paws.

Daisy spied the interaction and buzzed over, real quick-like. "Charlie, what do you have there?"

Now, I didn't want to lie to her, and I also didn't want to tip my hand about smoking weed five times a day in the stairwell between the seventh and eighth floors of Knowledge Press HQ every day, so I said, "Oh, I was just looking at these pipes. I used to have these in San Francisco."

"Did you smoke pot in California?"

"Of course. But I wouldn't even think of it in Taipei."

"Well, could you use those pipes?"

"No, I don't think so, Daisy. I—I wouldn't, you know..." And I just let it sit there for a second.

"Hmmph," Daisy huffed. "Don't bullshit me about smoking pot, Charlie. I'm sure you still do when you're out with your friends at the nightclubs."

"Please," I said dismissively, "I don't go to nightclubs, honey. That's for kids. I'm a middle-aged man for, chrissakes."

The old dude interrupted to say, "*Yao buyao ma?*" (You want the pipes or not?)

"No, sir," I said. "Thanks. Maybe some other time."

Again, Daisy hit me with her patented side-eye. "Just get them if you want them, Charlie." And I knew she was thinking, *the sooner this old fucker gets rid of his stuff, the sooner he's out of Sasha's hair.*

"Nah," returning the pipe to the display case. "Waste of money. I'd never use it."

So, that was the end of that. The next morning, I was the first to arrive in the office, or so I thought. Daisy was nowhere in sight. I needed to write something on a Post-It-Note, so I opened the desk drawer to grab a pen, only to find all three of the marijuana pipes from the old man's display case. When Daisy came in a few minutes later, she greeted me as usual, "Charlie! Good morning!" like nothing out of the ordinary, and I said, "Hey," while maintaining eye contact. "Thanks."

Daisy winked and blushed a little bit.

* ✳ *

Felix frequently told me not to waste my time with Taiwanese women. He had his reasons. On the other hand, mainland Chinese women, he said, are simpler. They don't ask for much. They are good at making and raising children. Excepting his workplace demographic, Felix gave me a sweeping generalization that Taiwanese women are back-stabbing gold-diggers—worse than whores. At least whores usually stick to their end of the bargain. They *usually* don't change their minds 20 minutes into your contract and demand more money. But then again, Felix didn't care who I was sleeping with as long as it wasn't someone on the payroll. And I didn't care how or why he came to these conclusions about women.

Felix kept me on a strict need-to-know-basis, and I returned the favor. Though he was always eager to hear about my social life, I generally left out the graphic details and tried to be as vague as possible about who, what, where, when, how and/or why? Every office conversation took place in Mandarin except when it directly involved me. There were plenty of days Felix didn't speak directly to me at all, even though our desks were kiddie-corner to each other. His actual presence in the office was hardly predictable, but I learned to listen for clues as to where he was and if he would come to the office. If he was in Taipei, he usually showed up at 10:00 a.m., had lunch at noon, disappeared, and sometimes returned at 5:00 p.m. Then he and Daisy would banter for half an hour, and he'd say, "*Zou le.*" (Let's go.) Of course, there were variations of the routine, but I got used to their patterns.

There were three things nobody at Knowledge Press would ever know about me. The first and most work-related "truth" was how long it took me to write something, e.g., a collection of essays or a complete prep book, versus the amount of time I allowed to elapse before submitting the finished product. Correspondingly, nobody knew that I was smoking pot every day, and ostensibly, how much pot I needed to smoke to do my job. The third and final thing they never knew was how much Mandarin I understood. Over the years, my comprehension and speaking skills improved, but I never let them see or hear it. Even when they talked about me, I pretended not to know what was happening.

If I *really* wanted to know what was going on, I had to pay keen attention to what was being said, how it was said, and who was saying it. I learned to listen for keywords that indicated they were talking about me, for instance, *waiguoren* (foreigner) or *laowai* (old foreigner) or *meiguoren* (American). If I heard my name thrown in there, *then* I paid attention, but otherwise, after a while, it was too exhausting to keep up. I just kept my head down and continued playing solitaire or clicking Random Article on Wikipedia until I stumbled upon something worth reading or poaching. I was comfortable in my ignorance though it was far from blissful.

When Felix wanted me to do something, be it write a new book, judge a speech contest, or make a ceremonial appearance at the *buxiban* (cram school), he followed the same routine. I could almost predict when it was coming. He'd say, "Charlie, I have a new mission for you. It's not easy. Try your best." And I'd say, "What do you want me to do?" And I did what I could, even if the result was failure. Felix was a greedy opportunist and yet a generous soul. If you had value to him, he treated you very well. If you didn't have a perceived value, he ignored you. Over and over, I kept replaying what he said about having a Western face, being "The Real McCoy." Felix had many stereotypes about foreigners. Americans were at the top of the English food chain. However, the whole lot of us, in his opinion, were marauding spend-thrifts who couldn't be trusted. Yet Americans, Felix said so many times, know how to enjoy themselves. He respected that. "You live for today," he said. "Tomorrow may never come."

To Felix, having a Western face meant that I spoke directly and never bluffed. When asked a question, I said yes or no or whatever was required. When declining an invitation, I kept it very simple and honest (as far as he knew). When I wanted something, I asked for it specifically. Most of all, I had no sense of what Asians call "face," which, to this day, is one of the damnedest things for me to explain, let alone understand. If I accept your invitation to a party, I will show up, no matter what. You will see my face.

The people at Knowledge Press seemed to know what they were doing, but many times, I wasn't so sure if they had *any idea* what they were doing. The company published dozens of books a year, most in English with Chinese translation. They published a lot of glossaries and dictionaries and mock test books. That's all I knew. I was spared the drudgery of everyday gossip and conditions of bowel movements, of which there were plenty.

In many ways, everybody who worked at Knowledge Press was a robot of sorts—including me. We were programmed to move under precise conditions yet unconcerned with outcomes.

Felix had two classes of robots working for him, Alphas and Betas, followed by the ever-growing group of former employees, the Pariahs, who weren't de-programmed since leaving, and some were still hanging around the periphery of the empire.

Alphas and Betas were unequivocally submissive to Felix and his whims, having earned his respect and trust through loyalty. Felix might've argued with an Alpha, but he almost never yelled at one on purpose. This was the primary survival mechanism of the Alpha Class. Do what he wants, show him some value, and he'll be nice to you.

The Betas were the true workhorses of the office. They said nothing and stayed out of the way. The last thing a Beta wanted was to attract the attention of the boss. It was a good month for a low-level Beta if you didn't make eye contact with Felix.

The Pariahs did something to piss Felix off. That's the only way you became a Pariah, except by choice, and the Taiwanese, passive-aggressive, occupational version of *hari kari* was bloodless.

Working closely with these people, I began to identify and categorize both personalities and our interactions. There were dozens of other names and faces, but these were the main players during the early days.

The Alpha Class

Daisy

The undisputed queen of the robots, universally despised by everybody except for me and Felix. Despite our co-working relationship, Daisy and I had moments of sibling rivalry, vying for the favor of Captain Felix, even though I eventually developed and enjoyed a strange indifference to any preference.

It took four months or so before Daisy and I had our first real "episode" where she got upset over something I said. The first time was right after the tainted Chinese milk scandal broke in the late summer of 2008. Suspiciously, the whole story didn't come out until after the Beijing Olympics were over. Chinese officials knew the milk was tainted back in May but covered it up—again, it had to do with that whole thing about Chinese "face."

We were sitting in the office one day, and I was reading an article about a group of parents whose children had been poisoned by milk and died. They went to Beijing to petition the government to (a) take responsibility and (b) give them some sort of compensation. What happened to those parents? They disappeared. Look, you don't need a bozo like me giving you a primer on human rights in China.

I turned to Daisy and said in a very humble way, "Can I ask you a question about China?"

"Oh, I don't know," she said warily and genuinely suspicious. "You might be a spy." Any other human being says that to me, and I would have known they were kidding. But not Daisy. She was dead serious.

"I'm not a spy. Look at me. Do I look like a spy? Do you really think the U.S. government has any interest in anything I might be able to tell them? Who, exactly, would I be spying on? You? Felix? His *buxiban* (cram school) empire? Come on, Daisy. You can't mean that."

"Well," she said reluctantly, "all right. If you say so." She didn't look convinced. "What is your question?"

"OK, now, don't take this the wrong way, but I really want to know, what the hell is wrong with the Chinese government?"

"What are you talking about?!" she cried. *Uh-oh.*

"No, I mean, wait, I'm just, I'm talking about the tainted milk scandal. Why did they wait until after the Olympics to admit there was a problem?"

"I don't want to talk about this. You have no right to say anything about my government. You don't know anything about it. How can you say anything when your government is the most hated in the world? You start more wars and kill more people than my government ever will."

"Correct me if I'm wrong, but you're a naturalized U.S. citizen, am I right? Yes. That means you're familiar with transparency and due process. I'm very aware of the heinous crimes the U.S. government has committed. The only difference between China and the U.S. is that Americans generally try very hard not to kill our citizens. At least we do a good job of making it look that way. That's why we start wars. It's OK if we make sausage out of other people, but not our own. For whatever reason, your government treats its people like the enemy, and in the U.S., it's the other way around."

"Don't talk to me anymore. You have no right to say anything. You're a foreigner!"

"Is that a quote from the *Little Red Book?*"

Well, that did it. Daisy stormed out of the office, slamming the door. The next day, Felix asked me to apologize to her.

"She's very quick to anger," he said, chuckling. "You have to be careful what you say to her." Slowly but surely, I began to understand why Felix kept Daisy around and on a very short leash. She was as fiercely and blindly loyal as any German Shepherd I ever met.

Daisy grew envious about any and every little thing Felix gave me—attention or otherwise. Felix routinely gave me a red envelope (*hong bao*) whenever I finished a project or he was pleased with something I did. If he gave me a *hong bao* with TWD$3,000 in Daisy's presence, that meant he'd already given her the same amount. Otherwise, she'd freak the fuck out.

One day, Daisy's chair broke, so she went out to get a new one. She returned with a well-designed but armless modern office chair she bought a block away on Furniture Street. Daisy sat proudly pecking away at her computer for an hour before announcing that she "hated this chair."

I glanced over, shrugged, and said, "Take it back."

"No!" she snapped.

Completely uninterested in the chair dilemma, I ignored her. Five minutes later, I noticed her laser-focused in my direction. Daisy was purely reactionary–like a gun–and possessed few wiles or what I would call street smarts. She was sizing up *my* chair.

"That used to be my chair," she said, stiffening her back and looking blasé in the other direction. "I gave it to Eugene."

"If you want to switch chairs," I said, "I have no problem with that."

Daisy was pleased. We switched chairs, and I found the new chair to be quite comfortable, if not unnerving, for the lack of armrests. I figured I'd get used to it.

"Aw, this is nice," I said, smiling. Daisy looked content for the moment.

An hour after we made the switch, Felix rolled into the office, and Daisy set upon him like an excited puppy.

"*Laoshi, ni hao. Ni he shenme?*" (Hello, sir. What would you like to drink?)

"Where's your new chair?"

"I bought the new chair, but I didn't like it, so I switched chairs with Charlie since the new one was uncomfortable and doesn't have arms, and now Charlie likes the new chair, which isn't right. It's supposed to be *my* new chair, not Charlie's. Now I'm using Charlie's old chair, and I don't like Charlie's old chair. It smells like farts."

Felix released that unmistakable, deep, resonant laugh and pointed at me, smiling broadly.

I stood up, pointing at Daisy, and said, "Get up. I want my old chair back. I never asked for a new chair!" Hesitant at first, it took her about five seconds to make the switch. She said something about "it's not fair" while smiling like an idiot.

Felix was tickled about the whole exchange.

"You are sharp," he said to me. "I like your style. You ask for nothing and get everything! Stick with me. The best is yet to come. Stick with me, and you will grow rich! One day, you will wake up a rich man, and you won't even know how it happened." He laughed and laughed. I laughed with him.

This little moment pushed Daisy over the edge. "He gets everything!" she cried, pointing at me. Felix kept laughing, mocking her. Daisy pulled her signature move: storm out of the office and slam the door. I quietly got up and switched our chairs back. Felix nodded in approval.

The next day, Felix made a big production about rolling in a new chair for Daisy that he picked out for her. She sat there like a smug little girl for the rest of the day.

Daisy's main problem with me was that I was not picky about anything. You could tell me I'm a genius or a piece of shit, and it wouldn't matter one way or the other. Felix always said, "You are free to come and go as you please. This is your home. We will be here when you come back." That line of commentary used to drive Daisy up the wall.

Gretchen
The *de facto* office manager and a top-ranking Alpha. She'd been with Felix for nearly 20 years and was one of two people he trusted with the combination to the safe, where he kept a ton of cash. Even Daisy didn't know the combination. Gretchen was a smart but demure, slightly chubby woman in her late 30s and much more attractive than she gave herself credit for. She never married, and Felix said she never had a boyfriend, either. I suspected that something bad happened in her childhood. Gretchen did not like to be touched at all. No handshakes, no hugs, nothing. Felix said, "She puts a mountain in front of everyone."

Gretchen worked long hours. Exactly what she did in the office was a mystery that I gave up trying to solve. But she was filthy rich. Felix once told me that he sometimes had to borrow money from Gretchen at the end of the month. I never saw her wear the same expensive outfit twice. She was always cordial to me but hardly what you might call "friendly."

Susie

The unusually cheerful office accountant who was also responsible for answering the phones with an endearingly sweet and cute voice. She was the second person trusted with the combination to the safe. We didn't have a lot of interaction in the beginning, but one day, I had a doctor's appointment in the morning that took longer than expected. I came into the office around mid-afternoon, and a minute later, Susie emerged from the private bathroom, smiling like a moron, followed by an ungodly stench. Susie was also in sole possession of the Yellow Sheets, which were companywide directives and/or disciplinary measures issued by Felix, usually in a fit of rage or panic, but often used to inform people that they needed to work overtime. A Yellow Sheet could also be used to fire somebody.

Whenever Felix wanted to issue a Yellow Sheet, he'd call Susie into the office, and she'd dictate the message. When it was finished, Lloyd was in charge of circling the office and making sure everybody signed the sheet in acknowledgment.

Lloyd

Aside from Daisy, Lloyd was the only robot who was not visibly intimidated when I approached him to ask a question. Another long-serving employee and the only Alpha Class male at KPHQ, Lloyd's "official" duty was "oversight of the marketing department," and he shared one of the other two private offices with Susie and Coco. In practice, Lloyd didn't do anything except damage control. His English was excellent, which is why Felix made him the liaison of all my visa, residency, and insurance issues with the government. Lloyd got the job done, unlike his predecessor, Wayne, who bungled my first Alien Resident Certificate (ARC) application so badly that I almost had to apply for a new passport. It was Lloyd who rolled up his sleeves, made a few calls, and discovered both the passport and ARC had been languishing in someone's outbox at immigration. After that debacle, Wayne got shipped off to the cram school, where his accomplishments included wiping out the entire student database.

Sherry

Technically a robot but the Golden Goose of the entire operation, Sherry was a former flight attendant, and one of the most popular cram school English teachers in Taipei. She was also a woman who, a decade earlier, was offered up as mildly scandalous fodder in the Taiwanese tabloids for having several affairs with high-profile government officials and giving birth to a child without disclosing the name of the father. Sherry was what I call "situationally attractive." The Asian female obsession with porcelain white skin meant Sherry used industrial strength skin whitener—bleaching lotion—and she was never seen without an umbrella during daylight hours. Her perfect C-cup breasts, which she had no compunction about displaying, were not all-natural, and no doubt her face had come under the discreet blade of a plastic surgeon. Underneath the Gucci and Prada was, from my viewpoint, a very vain, insecure, and vindictive woman. She dressed provocatively and her classes were always packed. Like, sold out with a waiting list. She was incredibly popular, and Felix spoiled her rotten to the point that I often wondered, "Is he banging her?" because you don't just give a million-dollar apartment to a cram school teacher, no matter how many students she drew.

While Sherry's karaoke hostess charm seemed to work on the boys at Zhang Yi English Academy (and Felix, who once rhapsodized about her 'dynamism'), I found her grotesque and creepy. Of course, when asked by Felix if I thought Sherry was attractive, I would always answer, "Why, yes. I think she's very spicy." But Felix was under the illusion that I meant it in a Ginger Spice sort of way, not in the diarrhea-inducing, colon-cleansing way I wished to insinuate.

As the Golden Goose, Sherry was ruthless in disposing of other robots she considered a threat. Next to Daisy, she had the second most personal clout with Felix. Even Gretchen couldn't (or wouldn't) spar with Sherry. Countless robots had been fired because she went to Felix with some dirt on them (see Veronica) or a petty complaint. A month after I started working at KP, several robots were missing. I went to Daisy and asked, "What happened to so-and-so?" Daisy replied, "Oh, they were fired. Sherry said they were lazy." It went on and on like that. Daisy couldn't stand Sherry, by the way.

Things only got personal when Sherry came after me. One of her cronies, a weasel-faced woman in her early 20s, had erroneously heard (through the cram school grapevine) that I was dating Veronica, which was patently false (even though I could only dream of being so lucky). What happened is that Veronica and I ran into each other at a mall and had coffee at a Starbucks. It was completely innocuous and coincidental. But Sherry brought her little weasel buddy into the office after lunch and had her spill the beans.

Had the Weasel not kept glancing nervously at me while she talked to Felix, I probably wouldn't have given it a second thought. I started picking up little bits of sentences and heard her mention Veronica's Chinese name and Xinyi-Warner (the name of the mall), and then she looked at Sherry and said, "That's all I know." Sherry then tore off a bit about the Weasel's friend who works at Xinyi-Warner and went to high school with Veronica and recognized me from pictures at the cram school. The informant said she'd seen us (Veronica and I) several times. Yada-yada.

Felix sat quietly, not smiling, kind of smirking, and Daisy just nodded and said, "Mmm." Felix didn't react for few moments. Suddenly, he ripped off a stream-of-consciousness rant that came as a shock considering Sherry's Golden Goose status. And it became obvious the discussion was about *me*. It was all in Mandarin, but I understood him to say, "We want to make this guy feel welcome. He is a long way from home. He doesn't have any family here. He doesn't know anybody here. This guy is very important to this company. He does a good job." And then Felix broke into English and pointed at me, saying, "You should be nice to this guy. He's lonely. He needs friends." Sherry and the Weasel were stunned and withdrawn. I couldn't even make eye contact with either of them. Daisy was staring straight ahead at Felix. I simply shrugged.

Felix ordered Sherry and her minion out of the office, turned to me, and said, "Is that true? Are you dating Veronica?"

"You're kidding, right? Veronica is *light years out of my league!*"

Felix scowled. "What does that mean?"

"It means she's way too good for me. She wouldn't touch me with a ten-foot pole. Felix, for real. We ran into each other on a Saturday afternoon and had coffee at Starbucks. That's it. I swear to God."

Daisy interjected, "I've met Veronica's boyfriend. He's very handsome!"

Felix winced, drumming his fingers on the desktop. "OK, OK. *Mei guangxi*. I understand. Nothing to see here, correct?"

"*Absolutely* nothing to see here," I replied, looking at Daisy. "Can you even imagine? Me? And *Veronica?*"

"No offense, Charlie," Daisy said, "but you have no chance with a woman like that."

And that was the end of it until I heard about a Yellow Sheet with Veronica's name on it.

Fair enough, Sherry and the Weasel. But I wondered why they came after *me*. I had never said a bad word about Sherry (as far as she knew). I did all the proofreading she gave to me (even though it was against the rules). In fact, I went out of my way to praise Sherry's ability to "fill a room" when Felix asked what I thought of her teaching prowess. Sherry just didn't like me. So, I sat on it for a few days, trying not to think about it. Felix was extra nice to me. All was a satisfactory limbo. And then that Friday morning, I came into the office to find a stack of papers on my desk and a note from the Weasel, asking me to proofread these tests for Sherry.

Because of the TOEFL book disaster, Felix had issued an official Yellow Sheet declaration that "Charlie is the writer and editor. Polly is the proofreader. Do not give proofreading to Charlie." I even got a copy, the only time in Yellow Sheet History. You see, there was a difference between editing and proofreading. Editing involved making changes to the text—rewriting in many cases. Proofreading was simply checking for grammar and typos. Giving me proofreading work was now a punishable offense. If Felix, by a one-in-a-million chance, looked over my shoulder and asked, "Charlie, what are you working on?" and found out I was proofreading, the offending robot would get an involuntary two-week unpaid vacation. Anyway, I saw this stuff from Sherry on my desk. *Let's play ball, sweetheart.*

And so, I waited. I poked around on the internet and waited for Felix to show up. It got to be after lunch and there was still no sign of him or Daisy for that matter. I checked Daisy's desk calendar, which always indicated her travel dates. She crossed out each passing day with a blue marker, something I always thought was for prisoners or dudes in

Alcoholics Anonymous, and sure enough, she and Felix were out of town until Monday.

Around 3:30 p.m., the Weasel stuck her face around the corner of the threshold and said, "Um...hello."

"Yeah, yeah. Come on in," I said.

"I'm sorry to bother you, Charles, but..."

"Not a problem. How can I help you?"

"Did you finish the work for Sherry?" Poor Weasel was visibly twitching.

"Um, no, I didn't have a chance to get to it."

"Will you finish it soon?"

"What do you mean by 'soon'?"

"Today?"

"I doubt it." I chuckled and pushed away from my desk. "You see, I have this other work that I'm doing for Deborah, and I think it has priority. Plus, I'm not even supposed to be proofreading. Send it to Polly. I've done it for Sherry in the past, but those days are over."

The Weasel's eyes got big. "Sherry said she must have it before class tomorrow morning. Can you stay late and finish it?"

"Tell you what. If Felix calls me and says, 'Charlie, I want you to proofread those tests for Sherry,' then yes, I will stay and do it. Felix has my number. He can call me at any time. But until that happens, I've been told to work on Deborah's root word dictionaries." I gave her the palms up and shrugged. Then I handed her the stack of Sherry's papers, and the Weasel got out of there, fast.

The Weasel must have put out an APB because 20 minutes later, Sherry burst into the office, got on the blower, and tried to get in touch with Felix but couldn't since he'd turned off his cell phone, which I knew because I'd already tried to call and warn him about the impending catastrophe—three times. I even tried calling Daisy but she didn't pick up. Sherry enlisted Gretchen, Deborah, and Gigi to get a hold of Felix, *now!* She was livid. Finally, she came into my office, waving her un-proof-read-tests, and said, "Felix said he wants you to do these for me."

"Do what for you?" I said stone-faced.

"Edit the tests." Notice she didn't say 'proofread.'

"I can't do that. The last thing Felix said to *me* was, 'The Root Word Dictionary is your priority.'"

"I just talked to him," Sherry said, waggling her pink and jewel-encrusted HTC smartphone in my face.

"Really? That's cool. Could you get him on the phone for me? I've been trying to get in touch with him all day."

"He's very busy. He's on a business trip to the mainland."

"That's great, Sherry. But like I told your little friend, unless Felix calls me and tells me otherwise, it's not a priority. And furthermore, this is not writing or editing; this is proofreading. You know it and I know it. So, feel free to take it from here. Send it to Polly." Her nostrils flared and her eyes bulged, but there was nothing she could do. I called her bluff, and she had to fold. Sherry stormed out of the office while I chortled under my breath.

Unbeknownst to me, Polly the proofreader was unavailable for a few weeks. Even robots had real vacations. No one mentioned this fact to me since if they had, I'd have done the fucking proofreading, Sherry-related or otherwise. Felix never called, and I went on about my bad self.

On Monday morning, Felix was back in the office with a glint in his eyes. "Sir, how are you?"

"I'm great," I said.

"You look great. Full of life."

"That's me. The poster child for vitality."

"Sir, I think you need a break."

"OK." *Uh-oh, am I getting fired?*

"Where would you like to go?"

"Go?"

"Anywhere you want to visit, I will buy a round-trip ticket for you." I could see he wasn't joking and he sure as hell wasn't firing me. "Where would you like to go?"

"Let me think about it."

"I will buy the ticket for you."

"Thank you."

"You deserve it. You deserve more. Stick with me. The best is..."

Yeah, yeah, I know, Felix...the best is yet to come. That was the difference between me and the robots. They got fired; I got an all-expenses-paid trip to wherever I wanted.

Deborah

Gretchen's classmate from college and a 17-year veteran of the company. Deborah was smart, personable, and one of my main collaborators on the textbook scene. She returned to KPHQ after giving birth to a son about a week after I started. She ranked just behind Daisy and Lloyd in her comfort level with foreigners. Her English was impeccable but sometimes tended toward a British accent, which Felix routinely bitched about. I did a lot of writing for books that Deborah put together or classes she taught. Felix trusted her to get the job done, and for some reason, we seemed to work together well. Deborah's directions could be somewhat cryptic at times. "Make this better" didn't give me much to work with.

Meredith

The head of the graphic design department and the least robot-like of all; her English nickname was Cinderella, the Disney character she vaguely resembled. I had a slight crush on her until I learned she was married.

The Predator and Crazy Tooth

The Predator and Crazy Tooth were an administrative double-team that ran the Zhang Yi English Academy and always arrived at the office together, usually on Monday, Wednesday, and Friday mornings. They were both in their late 20s/early 30s and attractive, superficially charismatic women.

The Predator (no English name; everybody called her Xiaoxiu) made national headlines when she was busted for having sex with a 16-year-old male high school student at ZYEA and the kid's parents sued Felix. For some reason, she didn't get fired. Instead, they moved her down to the cram school in Taichung, where—I couldn't make this up—she did it again. This time, the kid was 17 and the parents didn't sue. Felix told me it was "a love story."

Crazy Tooth (English name: Peggy), on the other hand, was an outgoing, fun-loving type who reportedly dated Stephan way back in the day, when he first moved to Taiwan, and from the story Stephan told me, CT was just as much fun *in* bed. She also treated him like such a piece of shit that his residual bitterness toward women, in general, will be forever palatable.

Much later, I learned that Crazy Tooth's main job was devising increasingly complicated ways of denying refunds to students who wanted to drop out. The whole deal at the cram school was about recruitment, followed by retention. *Get the money, keep the money.* Crazy Tooth started working at the school as a lowly admin drone straight out of high school, and by the time I rolled up on the scene, she and Captain Felix were tight—like a pair of thieves.

In conversation with Crazy Tooth, I used her English name, Peggy, but all I could think was, "This girl sure has that one crazy tooth sticking out, doesn't she?"

The Beta Class

Mr. Chu

The handyman-slash-errand lackey and Felix's nephew by marriage, which explained why he hadn't been fired. Daisy often complained viciously about Mr. Chu. "He's so stupid. He screws everything up." He was also one of the few people I ever saw stand up to Felix. On several occasions, Mr. Chu was summoned into the office for a dressing-down, only to argue and dismiss Felix with a "Yeah, whatever" and walk out. Good shit, for sure.

Mr. Chu was mostly nice to me for a while, even when Felix ordered him to perform ridiculous tasks on my behalf. First, it was peanut butter. One day, it had to be near the end of the month, Felix (rightly) assumed I was short on cash. I had about 12 yuan in my bank account, not enough to buy a bottle of water. He asked, "What did you have for dinner last night?" and I said, "Oh, peanut butter sandwiches."

"You must be short on cash."

"Well," I said sheepishly, "things are a little tight. It's the end of the month, of course. But I love peanut butter! It's comfort food."

"You really like peanut butter?"

"Oh, sure. I could live on it."

Mr. Chu was immediately summoned.

"Make sure," Felix said, "that there is always peanut butter in the kitchen upstairs."

Mr. Chu blinked, drawing a blank.

"What kind do you like?" Felix asked.

"Skippy," I replied. "Extra Crunchy."

"That's all? Just peanut butter?"

"Oh, and white bread."

And it was so. That afternoon Mr. Chu rode his scooter out to the Neihu Costco and bought an industrial-sized jar of Skippy Extra Crunchy and arm's length sleeve of white bread. I'd sneak up to the kitchen after lunch and make a couple of sandwiches whenever I was running low on cash. On a few occasions, I made the sandwiches, bagged them up and brought them home for dinner!

Another morning, Felix showed up early and spied me eating a banana. "You like bananas?"

"Oh, sure," I replied. "They're nature's perfect fruit."

Once again, Mr. Chu was called in. A week later there were so many bananas in the office they were attracting flies. I said to Felix, "I think you cured my addiction to bananas." The next day, the bananas were gone.

Julia

Julia was one of the first robots in the office every morning and often one of the last to leave—a solid Beta who worked on English-to-Chinese translations. I was told she had a wicked sense of humor. Julia stopped going to lunch upstairs when Felix declared all meals should be vegetarian. I suspect that like me, Julia was sick and tired of the routine. But the fact is, lunch was almost always vegetarian since Felix believed that ingesting protein after 10:00 a.m. was "unproductive." Julia was also nondescript to the point of nonexistent. She spent a minimum of 60 hours a week sitting at her desk.

Several years into my tenure at KPHQ, Julia blew a gasket, and it was unlike anything I'd ever seen. When most people quit (or got fired), there was very little fanfare. They generally disappeared. Julia, on the other hand, went out with a bang. Something happened to earn a Yellow Sheet. She forgot to do something. It was trivial. I heard her grousing at her desk for a while. When Felix showed up, Julia started screaming at him, and of course, I didn't know what she was saying, but it was bad enough that Felix fled the office and called Lloyd and Mr. Chu to escort Julia from the building.

The whole office was rattled for a few days after. Even Daisy was on edge. Captain Felix didn't show his face for a week.

Ms. Chu (aka Chuma)

Ms. Chu was the oldest of the robots, in her late 50s, not related to Mr. Chu. Aside from her infectiously girlish giggle and her unabashed Me-First attitude at lunch, Ms. Chu's other outstanding characteristic was that she stayed as far away from Felix as possible. I never saw them interact. She would not dare use the private bathroom in our office that virtually everybody used when Felix, Daisy, or yours truly weren't around. Ms. Chu deferred to Gretchen in all matters that required Felix's attention. Though she never said a word to me, not even a head nod, Ms. Chu *did* offer me candy on several occasions.

Yvonne

Yvonne was a Chinese editor who spoke six languages, had multiple degrees, and traveled to Europe and the States, but she kind of reminded me of a turtle. She was the first to duck and hide when Felix was on the warpath. However, she always smiled at me when we crossed paths at the elevators.

The Weasel

Despite our communication issues, and even though she was a Team Sherry-recruit, I *liked* Weezie because she didn't wear makeup and came from an aboriginal family in Hualien. She once even offered to set me up with her friend, but nothing ever came of it.

Sally the Rat

I barely cracked the enigma of Sally the Rat. She was on the homely side, probably in her late 30s, didn't really look Asian, and used to work at the cram school. One day she just showed up at KPHQ. From what I could tell, she had no function or purpose except watching everybody else in the office and ratting them out when they made a mistake or showed up late. She had at least three Yellow Sheets with her name on them. Daisy once remarked that she hated Sally the Rat and hoped she never found a boyfriend. *Hmm. Why the bad blood?*

Sonya the Cat Lady
Sonya the Cat Lady was an editor and teacher known for keeping cats. They said she had over three dozen strays and tomcats in her Xindian rooftop studio apartment. Either way, she thanked me for my "efficiency" in helping her. Stephan once told me that Sonya was the first of his KP conquests.

Emily
The second member of the graphic design department. Emily and I were forced to collaborate on a series of children's books. More accurately, *she* was forced to work with me, and I say forced because she was extremely uncomfortable in my presence, to the point that Meredith came into my office and said, "If you have any questions for Emily, you can ask me. Her English is not so good."

Coco
Susie's accounting assistant whose only job seemed to be checking the fax machine twice a day. Yes, they still used fax in those days. Probably still do. Felix was not ahead of any technological curve. If anything, he remained stubbornly behind it.

Gigi
An American-born Taiwanese woman from Texas, a teacher, part-time editor, and one of the two robots who Felix issued a Yellow Sheet for "unapproved friendliness" towards me. Though Gigi and I never officially dated, we met several times at an odd little Mexican restaurant tucked away in an alley off Xinsheng Road. Gigi got the Yellow Sheet and promptly pulled the plug on our assignations. Felix didn't know for sure what went on between us, but that didn't stop him from asking me about her every week until she left the company. My response was always, "Gigi's a very nice person."

Rufus

I don't think Rufus had an English name, so I called him Rufus in honor of Rufus Wainwright, the swishingly gay pop star and opera aficionado. The robot Rufus was like a shadow in the office. He was there but you never noticed him. He did translations and stayed out of the way. Rufus and I had a conversation once. He asked where I was from and I said, "San Francisco." His eyes lit up. "Oh, it's my dream to live there."

Wayne

Wayne was Mr. Chu's nephew, thus making him something like a third cousin twice removed by marriage to Felix, and therefore, despite his unbelievable incompetence, couldn't be terminated. If Wayne was not homosexual, then he was simply the most effeminate Asian hetero male I had the fortune of encountering. But the fact remains that I saw him on several occasions hanging out at G-Bear in the courtyard behind the Red Theatre in Ximendeng, and let me tell you, he was not there for the women or the beer.

Lonesome Carl

A cram school manager somewhere between Beta and Pariah with just a hint of Down's Syndrome. Lonesome Carl was in his late 20s and wouldn't be around too long, leaving to attend flight school in Virginia. His father was in the Air Force with Felix, which accounted for Carl's position at the cram school and his absolute deference to the man in charge. Carl talked shit about everybody except Felix. He wouldn't hesitate to badmouth Daisy, calling her a "washed-up mainland hag." I'd seen Felix pat Carl on the back and scream at him in front of 200 cram school kids within a few minutes. We met during the Make Friends Experiment and frequently crossed paths at the speech contests. Carl's English skills were not as good as I expected from someone who went to high school in New York and attended Columbia University. His tenure as a manager at the cram school lasted a little over a year. Although he wasn't the only Beta/Pariah still hanging around, Carl was the only one who still reported back to Felix as if he never left the gig.

Lonesome Carl often invited me to dinner, and I quickly surmised that his invitations to Japanese BBQ were not necessarily out of friendship or goodwill. Felix told him to cozy up to me and find out if I was a spy. It's laughable now, sure, but at the time they were serious. Since I was already inclined to be suspicious of Lonesome Carl's motivations, I played dumb, always careful not to say anything negative about Felix or the robots or the cram schools.

Carl got the "Lonesome" moniker after he told me that he often spent the night in the teacher's lounge at the cram school because nobody was ever home at his house, and he hated being alone for too long. When I asked if he ever had a girlfriend, he scoffed and said, "Look at me." In that way, I admired his self-awareness.

The Pariah Class

Eugene

My American predecessor, but only in the sense that he was Felix's token Authentic Yankee and occupied my desk for ten years before he was cast out into exile. Eugene was not a writer, a fact Daisy routinely stressed when giving me cryptic and unsolicited assessments of my perceived value to KP and the empire. From what I gathered, Eugene played more of a sidekick role to Felix, and in doing the math, his exit coincided with Daisy's rescue-slash-arrival on the scene.

Eugene returned to visit during the 2008 Beijing spectacle, and I went out to lunch with him once. He gave me some much-needed perspective and dirt on the inner workings of the empire, but nothing major. He hung around the office and stayed upstairs in the dorm for a few days before making his way to the mainland. I got the sense that if I met this guy at a party, I'd be wondering, "What's with this ass-kissing moron!" as well as a sense that *here's* the reason Felix thinks Americans are such addle-brained yahoos. It still burns me to this day that I agreed to let Eugene borrow my brand-new *Lonely Planet China* guidebook just a few days before my first trip to China. He was in the office and saw the book on my desk.

"Hey, buddy. Do you mind if I borrow that Lonely Planet book tonight? I'll return it in the morning?"

He disappeared the next day, so I had to plunk down another 30 bucks for a second copy.

145

Several years later, Eugene returned a few more times, and I can honestly say he's one of the few people I've ever hated with every fiber of my being.

Veronica

The first robot in my file system, openly despised by Sherry the Golden Goose, ostensibly for the fact that Veronica was infinitely more beautiful—inside and out. It didn't take long before I wondered, "What *the fuck* is she doing in a place like this?" With a brilliant smile and a very sociable personality, she was a neon light in a dark room. The more I got to know Felix, the more I understood why he went to great (often covert) lengths to keep Veronica around.

Several months after Sherry and the Weasel tried to get me fired, Veronica asked me to have dinner as a third wheel with her boyfriend, Preston, the son of a famous actor. We dined at the soft opening of a *nouveau* Taiwanese joint owned by Preston's friend. The food was pretty good, we all got fucked up, and Preston seemed like a nice guy. With Veronica, the conversation focused on the office environment, specifically Felix and his tyrannical ways.

I don't know how word got out, but it did. When Felix found out that Veronica had dinner with me, she got a Yellow Sheet and was reprimanded during lunchtime in front of the entire office.

Things took a nasty turn for Veronica when Sherry cranked up the heat, complaining to Felix every single day. She accused Veronica of being "a cancer in the company" who was solely responsible for the declining enrollment rate. And she dug up dirt on Veronica's alcoholic father, which I felt was stooping low, even for Sherry. Finally, she dragged some shell-shocked student from the cram school down to KPHQ and had the little bastard tell Felix that he (and some of his classmates) thought Veronica was a terrible teacher and never prepared for their lessons. The kid said he was considering a transfer to another cram school and one of Felix's most fierce competitors. *That did it.* Felix would rather chop off a finger before losing a student to a competitor.

Veronica was gone a week later. She came into the office to say goodbye. She started crying, my eyes got dewy. I waved her out of the office. It wasn't the last time we'd see each other, but it was heartbreaking, nonetheless.

Celeste

Of course, the editor who messed up my first project and resigned. Celeste's father was a college professor with deep ties to Captain Felix. Celeste and I became quite chummy during her time at KPHQ and stayed in touch after she left. Because there was no rule about dating people who no longer worked at the company, I didn't see a problem with it. We wound up dating for a while, but I'm getting ahead of myself here. There will be more about Celeste when the time is right.

Becky

A teacher-in-training at the cram school and Sherry's right-hand crony. Becky and I frequently worked together on translations. At least twice a week she came into the office and asked me to edit a stack of test materials. Becky liked to flirt, and she knew about my relationship with Celeste. For a long time, I thought I could trust her.

On a couple of occasions, Becky asked me to personally proofread and edit her friend's C.V. or resume, which I obliged and did on my own time. I figured it was the vig on her supposed silence about the Celeste deal. She had, after all, kept the info from Sherry; otherwise, it would have come out a lot sooner. One afternoon she asked me to edit some stuff that didn't look like the typical KP test material. The font was different; the grammar was strange. "Is this ours?" I asked. Becky nodded and said, "Mmm-hmm. It's from the latest high school entrance exam." I knew Sherry taught that class, so I went to work taking it apart and putting it back together in a reasonable form. Maybe it was Becky's unlucky day, but Felix came into the office and pulled a one-in-a-million move.

"What are you working on?" Felix asked as he circled behind my desk.

"Just this test for Becky."

"What test?"

"I dunno. This." I handed him the test papers. The hand-off wasn't even complete and I knew something was wrong. Felix went ballistic. First, he shouted for Sherry, who came teetering in. Becky was summoned. They sat on the bench next to his desk and cowered. It turns out that Becky had long been giving me work to do for some English website her boyfriend was developing. She was taking both outside and KP material and having me rebuild it so no one would catch on. She admitted this to Felix, who every so often shot me a look like, "You're next, buddy."

The women were dismissed, and Felix turned to me and said, "Did you know this girl was a spy?"

"A spy? A spy for whom?"

"Our competitors!"

"What competitors? *I didn't know shit.*"

"You didn't recognize that she was giving you material that didn't belong to our company?"

"Well, I did, but Becky said it was okay. She gives me stuff to do, and I do it. I swear to God that I didn't know she was a spy. She said it was for the high school entrance exam."

"What high school entrance exam? It won't be released until next week!"

Man, I'm telling you I was pretty freaked out by the way he was talking to me. "Felix, look, I didn't know."

Daisy came to my defense. "Charlie doesn't know anything," she said dismissively. "He's stupid. All he thinks about is having sex. These girls can tell him to do anything, and he'll do it." *Thanks, Daisy.*

Felix calmed down. "That's what I thought."

10

Fuzhou

Less than a month after my return from the U.S., Felix was excited. He booked us a trip on the second of the "Three Links to China" via the Matsu Islands. Matsu is an archipelago of 19 tiny islands, dominated by a Taiwanese military base on Nangang Island, located 17 km off the Chinese mainland, a vestige of the Chiang-kai Shek era but still very much a part of Taiwan's defense system.

Our destination was Fuzhou, a sprawling maze of 6.5 million people in Fujian Province. According to our trusty Captain Felix, very few foreigners took this route or went to Fuzhou except on business. Felix made it somewhat clear that once we arrived in Fuzhou, I would be free to do whatever I wanted for the next four days, while he handled some stuff involving a copyright infringement, which I knew was bullshit. There was no such thing as 'copyright infringement' between Chinese and Taiwanese businesses. It didn't exist. When I asked why we were *really* going to Fuzhou, he said, "To look for business opportunities." Good enough for me.

The weather in Taipei that day was fine, so there was no delay flying out of Songshan, but on the descent to Nangang Island, Felix said, "I've got bad news. We might be stuck here."

When the weather is shit, the ferry boat between Matsu and the port of Mawei in Fuzhou doesn't sail. Though the skies were clear, the wind was howling. From the plane, I could see whitecaps in every direction. The crappy Fokker 100 got pushed around during the landing, which felt like a car crash that wouldn't end.

Exiting the airport, we got on a bus and crossed the island to the ferry terminal. The ferry *might* run at 1:30 p.m., Felix said, and if so, it meant we had only an hour and a half to kill.

The ferry terminal was surrounded by a bunch of nondescript government buildings. Conscription-age Taiwanese soldiers in uniform milled about the plaza. There was a 7-Eleven around the corner from the ferry terminal, so I drank two tallboys of Taiwan Beer and looked out over the water. There was really nothing to see. But I was happy to be there. If nothing else, there was gratitude. I was the luckiest guy on Earth. Less than a year ago, my life was a disaster, *and there I was*, about to board another boat to China.

At 1:20 p.m., in my peripheral vision, I saw Captain Felix charging toward me. "Charlie! Let's go. The boat leaves in ten minutes."

The first thing I noticed on the mid-sized fishing boat masquerading as a ferry vessel was a sheath of plastic bags hanging from a hook at eye-level on the back of every seat. For people who travel so often, who have overcome such incredible obstacles in their historical quests to get from here to there, and despite the fact they eat anything that moves, the Chinese appeared to have extremely weak stomachs. They don't do well on boats or buses. A relatively calm, two-hour boat ride from an island to the mainland turns any ferry boat into a vomit factory that rivals the production quotas of any vomit manufacturing plant in Shenzhen.

"Let's get a seat in the rear," Felix said. "It's the best place to sit. It's where you want to be."

Even a seat in the last row couldn't keep Felix from emptying the contents of his stomach—a typical Taiwanese lunchbox called a *biandang*, which he ate during the layover and comes standard on all chartered trips—into a series of pink plastic bags, within minutes after shove-off. I fought off my empathetic nausea by chain-smoking on the rear deck, which was technically not allowed and really kind of dangerous on a shitty boat like that, but when I saw a couple of dudes go out there, I said, fuck it. *Better than sitting in a vomit factory.* An hour into it, the boat's captain joined us. It was fun in an awkward sort of way. Them staring at me, me staring at them. The ride itself was a little rocky at the beginning, but once we got out of open water and upstream on the Min River, I thought it was quite smooth.

At least two dozen dudes were standing outside the exit of the Mawei port, lined up for a makeshift reception—all taxi drivers and private chauffeurs. A well-dressed middle-aged man came forward and greeted Felix. The man looked very professional. "This guy will take us to Fuzhou," Felix said. The man smiled and shook my hand. He led us to a late-model black Lexus sedan. It was the only time I ever let a Chinese taxi driver take my backpack and put it in the trunk.

"This guy used to be the personal driver for my friend in the Air Force," Felix said.

"My name is Jack," the driver said. "I speak a little English." And off we went.

I stayed quiet and looked out the window, taking in the industrial bloat of greater Fuzhou. *Man, it's so hard to tell if they're building up or tearing shit down because it all looks like a maze of concrete tentacles in a state of cardiac arrest.* A series of cables and connections incongruously tangled with all the logic of the average home entertainment system. Half a highway overpass just ends right there. Half-built skyscrapers. Mountainsides recklessly scooped away. The roads are shared by every conceivable car, truck, bus, motorcycle, rickshaw, mule team, and/or pedestrian under the Chinese sun. *Who the fuck oversees planning around here? Fire that guy, now.*

Then Felix started talking about China, telling me this and that. Mostly, he talked about fucking. The dude was 65 years old, and he still thought about sex every moment of every day.

It was late afternoon by the time we checked into the Baihe Hot Springs Hotel, which was famous for its hot spring spa and sauna house girls, per the Captain. He gave me a brief tour of the joint and suggested we meet at the sauna house on the fourth floor in an hour. I took a shower, dressed, and went down to meet him. The elevator doors opened and the college-aged staff in sauna house uniforms took immediate notice. No one said anything. A young woman took my shoes, gave me a pair of *lanbai* slippers, and led me toward the back of the house.

Felix hadn't even gone to his room upstairs. I found him lying on a massage table wearing a white robe and flanked by two young women who were rubbing his legs with hot oil. He looked quite pleased.

"Sir," he said. "Have you eaten yet?"

151

"Well, no. But I am quite hungry." That was a dumb response because Felix wasn't asking if I'd eaten yet. It was the standard Chinese greeting. [*Chi fan le ma?* = Have you eaten?]

"Do you want a massage now?"

"Um, no, not really."

"No problem. You can come back whenever you want. This place is open twenty-four seven."

"Sure. I'm gonna find something to eat."

"Try the restaurant on the second floor."

I went to the restaurant on the second floor because they had English subtitles on the menu, which were hardly accurate but that didn't matter. The first five minutes of every Chinese restaurant experience was still difficult. My Mandarin was choppy, at best. They didn't understand me, I didn't understand them. If I couldn't point to it, I couldn't eat it. The first girl who approached the table may have been as nervous as I was irritated. She asked a series of questions I couldn't answer and scurried away. I saw one of the girls behind the reception desk get on the phone. She spoke into the receiver while staring at me.

Not long thereafter, a skinny woman came to my table and said hello in English. The assistant manager of the restaurant introduced herself as Nana, and asked if she might sit down and talk to me, aka "free English practice." Nana was 24, from Guangdong, and had just finished her studies at the local university. In a few weeks, she would leave Fuzhou for her home near Hong Kong. Her sister had married the Fujianese guy who owned the restaurant, which explained what she was doing in Fuzhou.

I ordered a full bottle of red wine with dinner and poured a glass for Nana. I hardly ate any of the five or six dishes that arrived. For a while, it seemed that Nana was simply taking the opportunity to practice her English. She didn't appear to be a lush or a player, at all. I ordered a second bottle of wine.

Around 10:00 p.m., Captain Felix came in, all smiles. "Ah! Look at you!" he said, oddly proud. "You really know how to enjoy yourself!" Captain Felix spoke to Nana in Mandarin for the most part, so I didn't know what he was saying. But he did say to her, in English, "Charlie is a good guy. He's a genuine person. The only problem with him is he smokes and drinks."

I stayed until midnight talking with Nana, well past the restaurant's closing time. I paid the bill and went to the elevator. Nana offered to escort me to my room, to make sure I got there "safely." Although it seemed for a split-second that Nana was waiting for me to invite her in, we said *bai bai* and parted.

Lying in bed, watching TV about 30 minutes later, I heard a soft knocking at the door, so I got up to check. Looking through the peephole, nobody was there. I opened the door, stepped out into the hallway, and very briefly saw a shadow duck around the corner near the elevator. "Hello?" I called out. No reply. And then I thought it might be some type of robbery set-up. Felix had repeatedly warned me not to open my door unless I knew who was there. Either way, it was creepy—I quickly cut back into my room, double-locking and chaining the door.

In the morning, I went to the restaurant on the second floor for breakfast. Nana was at the concierge desk with a bland smile. One of the other girls took me to my table. Nana came and sat down a few minutes later. "What do you want to see in Fuzhou?" she asked.

The first order of business was to locate and scout a couple of bars. Fuzhou doesn't really have a bar street like other Chinese cities, but according to the guidebooks and the internet, I might find several bars near the West Lake area. Of course, *Lonely Planet* often employs the Chinese caveat: places open and close and reopen under a different name so frequently that even the locals don't know what you're talking about when you say, "The Red Door Pub."

Nana shook her head. "I don't know about any bars," she said, pausing, "for foreigners. There are places near West Lake, but I don't think it's safe for you to travel there alone."

I quickly changed the subject.

Fuzhou is extremely spread out and the air quality is very poor, so walking around is not recommended. However, I had nothing better to do than walk. The Baihe Hot Spring Hotel was fortunately situated in the central part of the city. I figured I could head off in any direction and find something worth seeing.

After breakfast, I set out walking around 10:00 a.m. The weather was cool and pleasant. I made a short list of bars and their addresses. And of course, I had the business card of the hotel, just in case I got lost and had to take a taxi.

I walked for hours and didn't find a single bar, never mind one that was open for business during daylight hours. There were no TGI Friday's in Fuzhou. By late afternoon, my feet began to hurt, so I got in a taxi and went back to the hotel for a nap. I woke up around 7:00 p.m. and returned to the restaurant on the second floor. The girl at the concierge desk said, "Nana isn't here." I nodded and took my usual table. After dinner, I took off walking again, looking for a place called The Red Door Pub, which was supposed to be one of the only true British pubs in all of Fujian Province. I spent an hour walking up and down the road, asking locals, double-checking the address, all to no avail. The place simply didn't exist...anymore. In its place at No. 119 Jintai Road was a shoe store.

While in the area, I stumbled across a place called Jazz and Blues Club—by outward appearance, just another Chinese nightclub. *Nah, maybe tomorrow night.* But I made a mental note of the address.

I finally came across a massive nightclub called BMW Music Club—on the fourth floor of what looked like a factory. At first, I was reluctant to enter, but one of the dudes at the door encouraged me to check it out. "Come in, come in," he said. "Look around." At that point, I just wanted a drink. But I wondered if Bavarian Motor Werks was aware or would even care if they knew a club in Fuzhou had appropriated their logo.

The door guy walked me past the metal detectors and led me up four flights of stairs and into the club. It was a typical Chinese nightclub. Neon and strobe lights, techno music at brain-jarring volume. At least a dozen super-hot girls—I mean, stunners—were sitting around a few tables. The guy walked me over and asked if I wanted one.

"No, no, thanks, I just want a beer." He parked me at a table near the door, away from the bar, where another set of not-quite stunners were lined up. All I wanted was a beer. They brought me 10 bottles of beer for 100 yuan. The club only sold bottles for groups. Every single one of the stunners was staring at me as I sat, embarrassed, behind a wall of beer bottles. I looked up periodically to see two dozen pairs of eyes locked on my every move. A couple of bartenders were staring as well. This wasn't garden variety, what-is-that? staring. This was hardcore, laser-like focus. I could barely breathe at one point.

A few minutes later, a group came in and one of the guys spotted me, stopped, spun around, spied the circumference of the bar, shook his head, and came over to my table and embarrassment of beers.

"My Lord!" he said with a Southern American accent, introducing himself as Doug from Key West. Although I was confused as hell by the scene and a Chinese guy with a Southern twang, I was happy to hear someone speak English.

Twenty minutes later, the place was half-full, and Doug got around to asking me to join his party.

"Do you know what's going on here?" Doug half-shouted above the din.

"I think so."

"Those bitches are fuck toys. You know what a fuck toy is, Charlie?"

"You can play with them and put them down when you're bored, like toys. And just like toys, they don't care one way or the other."

Doug smiled and put a hand on my arm, "*Oooh, I like you!*" he cooed.

"I'm straight, Doug."

"I know. I can still like you, can't I?"

"Of course!"

The music kicked up several notches of volume. All at once, the fuck toys got up *en masse*, formed a little conga line and walked past our table of five Chinese guys and me. Four of the guys picked women—Doug just looked them up and down and shook his head—and the remaining women dispersed. Meanwhile, there was a circle bar in the middle of the club and another smoking-hot stunner got up and did a note-perfect karaoke version of "Complicated" by Kelly Clarkson, followed up by Madonna's "Vogue". *So, there was more than one floorshow tonight?* Even though I had eight beers left to kill, I wasn't planning on sticking around much longer.

Doug's friends were amused by me but preoccupied. The unselected fuck toys were staring at me like Alex in *A Clockwork Orange*—heads bowed, half-moon eyeballs, menacing beyond words. Doug and I were the only two guys in the whole bar without female companions. Doug was parade gay but doing his best not to let his buddies know. Maybe they knew, I dunno. "Tomorrow night this place is happening," he said, while doing a little raise-the-roof move and biting his lower lip.

Occasionally, Doug's friends got up in pairs and headed into one of the V.I.P. rooms in back, as it turns out, to do lines of coke, and they came back all jacked up.

"They're getting high?" I shouted to Doug.

"Yeah! Do want some?

"No, thanks."

Then all four of the guys disappeared with three of the women, leaving me with Doug and the hottest of the women—who slid over and spoke English.

"What is your name?" she hollered.

"Charlie!"

"I'm Gaia!"

"Beautiful name!" I shouted. Gaia was from Inner Mongolia and in Fuzhou to work as a "hostess companion." She pulled my ear to her mouth and said she really didn't like the guy who picked her, and even though it was going to cause her a spot of trouble, would I like to take her out of there?

This raised a series of rash contingencies. *Was this a business proposition? Was there a fee to take her out of the bar? Would there be residual trouble if she left?*

There was a break in the music, so we didn't have to shout anymore. I stood up, turned to Doug and said softly, "Tell your buddy doing lines in the back room that I'm sorry I took his fuck toy, but he left her sitting here all alone."

"You can't take her out of here!" Doug was pissed. "My buddy will lose face. You'll get killed!"

"But she said..."

"Don't listen to her. She's a whore. *Trust me.*"

"OK, man." I sat back down, and we toasted to beer that Gaia poured in our glasses. I turned to Gaia and said, "Look, I'm sorry but I gotta go. Maybe next time."

"Give me your number," she persisted. I gave her a business card with my Chinese cell phone number on it and she rubbed my hand. "Where are you staying?"

"The Baihe Hot Spring Hotel." I shook hands with Doug and left before his friends came back to the table.

An hour later, I was sitting in bed, watching TV, when my cell phone rang. Of course, I didn't recognize the number, but I picked up anyway. It was Gaia.

At 7:59 a.m., my cell phone rang. It was Felix. "Sir, are you alone? Your phone is off the hook again."

"Am I alone? You tell me."

Captain Felix fucking *roared*. Hadn't heard him laugh like that in a long time. "How much did you pay her?"

"A thousand yuan plus taxi fare." (US$150)

"*A thousand!*" That was way more than Felix would pay for a hooker. "You got cheated!"

"I don't think so, boss. It was worth it."

"Right. That's great. You really know how to live. Do you have any plans today?"

"Just to explore the city."

"Meet me in the lobby at noon. I'm going to take you somewhere."

"But I thought you said I'd be on my own?"

"Bring your things. We might stay overnight."

Felix was waiting in the lobby when I showed up at 11:50. "Charlie, so good to see you! The driver is waiting. Let's go."

I didn't see a black Lexus or Jack. "Where's Jack?"

"He will not make this trip. He's booked solid. We can trust this guy." I didn't like the sound of that. Felix didn't seem convinced, either.

A black Toyota sedan pulled up and a nondescript guy popped out. Once seated in the back of the sedan, Felix unveiled his plan. We were going to Shaxian, two hours northwest of Fuzhou. The driver was recommended by his "massage girl" in Taipei, so we could trust him. Otherwise, Felix said, "They kill you like mosquitoes."

"What's this driver's name?"

"His name? I don't know. His Chinese name is…"

"I'm gonna call him Dave, if that's OK."

"Dave! That's a great name. Of course, call him Dave."

Shaxian is a sleepy provincial town of 100,000 or so (documented) residents. According to an article Captain Felix read in one of the hotel magazines, Shaxian was also known as "The King or the Capital of Snacks or Snack Food."

The drive to Shaxian was amazing. The brand-new highway runs through some of Fujian's more mountainous areas. The mountains themselves aren't majestic—they're just plentiful. Every 10 km or so, there was another ramshackle industrial town situated in a valley. I marveled at the idea of ancient peoples trying to make their way across the terrain. Some people wanted to reach the ocean. Some people never made it and settled here. I've been through incredible mountain drives, but Fujian's was different. The highway didn't go up or around or over mountains; the mountains were removed, or the highway went through them.

Toyota Dave passed the exit for Shaxian, even though I said to Felix at least three times, "Hey, that sign says, 'Next exit: Shaxian.'"

"This guy knows where he's going," the Captain assured me.

Sometimes you just hate being right. Almost an hour later, we rolled into Shaxian, and only because I prevailed upon Toyota Dave and Felix. "Fucking listen to me, Dave—we're heading *west* right now! Turn around. Shaxian is back *that way*."

We drove around the town on the north side of the river and finally, Felix said, "Stop here." We were in front of a massage parlor. "What do you want to do?" Felix asked, and before I could answer, he continued, "I'm going to get a massage here. Do you want one? Do you want a girl?"

"No, I think I'll just walk around and take pictures."

"Meet me back here at five o'clock. And take him with you," pointing to Toyota Dave. "It's safer. You shouldn't be alone here."

"Haha, um, no Dave," I said. "He's a liability, if you ask me." Toyota Dave didn't know anything about 'snack foods' or where to find them. He said he knew how to get to Shaxian, but obviously, he didn't. "Tell him to take a nap."

"Be very careful," Felix said, concerned. "Are you sure you don't want this guy to...?"

"I'm sure."

I spent the next hour walking around and taking pictures. Shaxian is a pleasant enough provincial city, neatly divided by a western branch of the Minjiang River, its only drawback being a pervasive Level IV smell of something acrid and burning. I returned to the massage parlor, where Felix greeted me by saying, "This girl wants to marry you," referring to the plain woman who had just given him the happiest of endings.

"That's great." I nodded. "I know you're hungry. Let's eat. Let's get some of those famous *snacks*." I felt stupid saying the word "snacks."

The massage parlor woman gave Felix a list of famous places to eat in town. We piled in the car and rattled Toyota Dave out of his catnap. At this point, I knew more about Shaxian and how to get around the city than Toyota Dave, who was either very stupid or just wanted to make things difficult by dropping us in the middle of a four-lane intersection.

"What's the point of having this driver when he doesn't understand the basics of urban transportation? Why don't we just tell him to take a break and use local taxi drivers? He can take us back to Fuzhou later, now that he knows the route."

"We're safer with him," Felix said. "He comes by recommendation."

We went to a total of seven different establishments, sampling the "snacks," which consisted of myriad dumplings and All Things Goose— Shaxian's other and probably true claim to fame. Even the dumplings were stuffed with goose. The sun was setting, and I began to feel anxious about being in Shaxian. With each place we visited, a crowd appeared out of the shadows, as if the news of a foreigner had spread across the city and everybody was coming out to have a look. By the time we got to the sixth "snack" destination, they'd figured out that our driver was retarded and beat us to the next restaurant. After the seventh place, I was bored with snacks—and pissed off. At least two dozen people were standing outside the window in front, watching us eat shitty pork dumplings and deep-fried goose livers like they were at a zoo, watching the pandas gnaw on bamboo.

Walking out of the last restaurant, Felix asked, "What do you want to do? We can stay overnight or we can go back to Fuzhou. Do you want to explore Shaxian? Or do you like Fuzhou better?"

"Let's get the fuck out of here."

"Yes. I like that idea. This place isn't safe after dark."

It was *countryside dark* when we left Shaxian and got back on the expressway. I could see stars in the night sky. Felix pointed out hundreds of little smokehouses scattered across the farmland. "That's where they smoke the geese."

"And that's where the stench comes from."

"Most of it, yes."

We passed a large orange sign about 10 km down the road. Toyota Dave started talking, Felix got very agitated, and we got off the highway at the next exit.

"The road is closed," Felix said. "We have to get off here."

"What do you mean 'closed'?"

"Closed for construction."

"On a Saturday night?"

Felix didn't respond. Toyota Dave pulled over to the shoulder and made a phone call. He exchanged words with Felix.

"This guy says he knows another way to get back to Fuzhou," Felix said, "but it might not be safe. I'll leave it up to you. We can trust this guy, or we can have him take us back to Shaxian and take a bus in the morning."

"Leave it up to me? *This* guy? He didn't even..." I was flustered. "Define 'safe.'"

"It's the old two-lane highway that runs through the mountains. This guy says he used to drive it when he was younger."

"The question is not whether I trust him—it's do *you* trust him?"

"I don't trust any Chinese. This road goes to the middle of nowhere. He could take us to the mountains, kill us, and they'll never find us. The only thing we have going for us is *you*." Captain Felix laughed.

"Why me?"

"If something happened to you, they would come looking for this guy. They would find him and shoot him on the spot. The government can't allow American tourists to disappear. Too much trouble. Your parents would...the President... It would be on CNN. People might get the wrong idea about China. I'm Taiwanese and I have a Chinese passport. If it were just me, this guy would kill me, and nothing would be done about it. They would sweep it under the rug."

I already knew what Captain Felix was going to say. It was just the first time I ever heard anybody say it out loud.

"Are you serious? Does that shit really happen?"

Felix nodded. "This guy would kill us like mosquitoes."

"I can't believe that people in Taiwan wouldn't come looking for you."

"Oh, they would come and look," Felix said seriously, "but they would never find anything. I would vanish."

"If it were just you? *This* guy?"

"Who knows?"

I didn't get a sinister impression of Toyota Dave. He seemed like an average dumbshit Joe, trying to make a buck. It would hardly be worth his trouble to knock us off for a few thousand yuan.

"Against my better judgment, I think we should take a chance on him," I said. "How bad can this highway be?"

"You'll see," Felix said, "but I like your style. Nothing ventured, nothing gained. If you stay at home, nothing can happen."

"Let me take a look at that map, will you? I was an Eagle Scout."

Captain Felix had a beautiful fold-out map of Fujian Province, but it was in Chinese and the overhead reading light bothered Toyota Dave, so he repeatedly asked Felix if he could turn it off. The map became impossible.

First, we headed east to the industrial wasteland of Nanping City, and from there, hooked up with the provincial road that ran southeast through the mountains and in the general direction of Fuzhou. It was possible, Felix said, that the entire expressway to Fuzhou might be shut down for the night.

Soon, we were up in the mountains on the winding, two-lane road. There were no lights except for those of on-coming traffic, which seemed to consist solely of careening, overloaded trucks driving way too fast in the middle of the road. Toyota Dave was forced at almost every turn to cede his share of the asphalt to oncoming traffic. Cars and trucks passed us from behind, horns blaring in an endless game of General Tsao's Chicken. This went on for an hour, non-stop.

The silence in the car was thick. Dave was focused on the road. Felix had his eyes closed. *He can't be sleeping.* Finally, we came to a security checkpoint booth. Dave got out of the car to ask for help.

"This is not a good situation," Felix said. "Something is wrong. We should have been back on the highway by now." Dave returned to the car and said, "We turn right before the bridge, and it's 20 minutes straight ahead." Half an hour later, we wound up on an unnamed road headed who knows where.

"If we just go back to G316, it runs parallel to the highway," I said exasperated, "and eventually near Minqing, there's an exit for the Jingfu Expressway."

Neither Toyota Dave nor Felix acknowledged me. It had been two hours since we left Shaxian, and from what I could tell on the map, we were still a minimum of 70–80 km away from Fuzhou. We slowed to pass through a tiny, crumbling village. There were signs of civilization. Satellite dishes and neon signs. I asked if we could pull into one of these villages and ask for directions. Felix said it wasn't safe. Toyota Dave pulled over at a clearing on the roadside. He had to piss. So did I. All three of us got out to piss.

A black Mercedes-Benz came around the curve and slowed upon sight of us. It did a U-turn and shined its lights in our direction. The passenger rolled down the window and said something to Toyota Dave. They bantered back and forth for a minute.

"I think they're lost, too," Felix said. "They're Taiwanese. That's good."

Toyota Dave approached the Benz and started talking to the passenger. I took a step in that direction when Felix grabbed my arm, "Stay away from there." I caught a glimpse of the passenger, a young man wearing a baseball cap. The windows were tinted but I could make out the silhouette of three people in the car.

A windowless van pulled up and a couple of soldiers got out. They kept pointing toward the southeast. Felix hustled me back to the Toyota, where I lit another cigarette and watched. Toyota Dave returned, and we took off following the Benz.

"We're going to follow these guys back to the highway," Felix said. "It's safer with two cars."

We drove for 20 minutes down an unpaved, one-lane road that hugged a mountainside. It was more like an access road. Rock piles every so often made passage precarious. Though I could only see what the headlights illuminated, we were headed into even more remote territory with every passing turn, and I was getting more anxious with every passing minute.

"This seems fishy to me," I finally said. "This road doesn't go anywhere."

Another moment in my life when I was not pleased to be right. The road ended in a clearing marked by a pile of rocks and tree stumps. Three guys got out of the Benz and stood around the car, scratching their heads, lighting cigarettes. Toyota Dave put the car in reverse and started a two-point, reverse U-turn.

"It's a trap," Felix said. "I can feel it."

"What do we do now?"

"Nothing," Felix said. "Turn around and go back."

A set of headlights came barreling down the trail, revealing the same van we saw 20 minutes before. It passed the Toyota and came to an abrupt stop at the bumper of the Benz, pinning the car against the pile of debris. Two soldiers got out with guns drawn and rounded up the three men against the passenger side of the Benz. Two more soldiers with guns drawn jumped out of the van and ran toward us.

Felix screamed, "*Gan, gun chu zheli!*" (Get out of here now!) Toyota Dave jerked the steering wheel and hit the gas. I looked back and saw the two soldiers stop, turn around, and head back toward their van.

I gotta give him credit—Toyota Dave showed some skills. Maybe he was just scared and the adrenaline took over, but he got us the fuck out of there in a hurry.

I kept looking out the rear window. "What if they follow us?"

"If they do," Felix said, "we're dead."

Another hour of nerve-wracking mountain passage and we were starting to descend. Passing a large hydroelectric dam, I said, "I think we're coming up on a place called Shuikou Reservoir."

"Shuikou Reservoir?" Felix said. "That's great. You know everything."

Toyota Dave dropped us at the Baihe Hot Springs Hotel just after 11:00 p.m. In the elevator, Felix asked, "What are your plans tonight? Are you going back to that bar?"

"Are you serious? We just survived a near-death experience!"

"The girl you met last night... Will she be at the bar?"

"I don't know. It's possible."

"How did you find the bar in the first place?"

"I just walked around. There it was. So, I went in."

"I want to see it. Is it a fucking place?"

"You might say that."

"Take me there."

"I don't think...you're...going to..."

"Let's go."

On the walk over, I was guessing how long Felix would last inside the BMW Music Club. *Two minutes? Five minutes?* He hated cigarette smoke, and the club was bound to be thick with it. He didn't drink. He hated loud music. We could hear the massive thumping of Chinese techno from a few blocks away. There was a line around the front of the club. As we approached the entrance, one of the door guys recognized me and said, "Hello, welcome back!" He took me by the arm and escorted me past the line. He nodded in respect to Felix, who was impressed.

"Everyone knows you! You're famous here."

As we were climbing the stairs to the club, Felix wore a wrenching look of discomfort. The place was packed, but they cleared a table for us. A line-up of a dozen or so fuck toys assembled between us and the bar.

"I think we're supposed to choose one," Felix shouted. I felt so bad for him. His discomfort made me uncomfortable.

"I don't want a girl," I shouted back. "I want a drink!"

I told the male server that I knew the deal: 10 beers for 100 yuan. "*Yi bei shui, meiyou bing kuai, wo de pengyou. Meiyou niuren, xie xie.*" (Bring a glass of water, no ice, for my friend. No girls. Thank you.) They brought out the beer and the water. Felix and I toasted. The music was unbearably loud. I knew Felix could stand about another minute of it. After the Shaxian ordeal, I was impressed that he wanted to go out *at all*. But then again, after such a harrowing experience, I didn't want to sit in my room and watch TV, either. Adrenaline takes a while to clear your system.

The club was seriously blowing up. Smoke, flashing lights, throbbing beats. We were a matter of tremendous curiosity for the locals. Several familiar faces came by, made eye contact, and pressed a hand into my thigh or brushed a full breast into my shoulder. Over the din, I vaguely heard my name being called out in English. It was Gaia and Doug, leaning against the railing of the upper level. Gaia motioned for me to come over. I waved at Doug and bent up toward Gaia.

"I didn't know you were coming," she said.

"I didn't know, either."

"Is that your boss?"

"Yes."

"I'm sorry. I'm...already...working tonight." She gestured with a slight head tilt.

I looked over her shoulder and saw a very stern-faced dude staring at me.

"No problem," I said. "We can't stay."

Doug said, "Come on up, here, sailor! Have a drink with me."

I ran upstairs, had a short glassful of beer with Doug, and readied to leave. Gaia came over, reached down, took my hand, pressed a bar napkin into my palm, and leaned forward to whisper in my ear. She pressed her lips and nose to the side of my face but didn't say a word. Then she backed away and returned to the couch, seated at the side of her customer. I unfolded the bar napkin and saw a bunch of Chinese characters and an eleven-digit number. I dropped it on the floor. Felix was staring at something on the other side of the bar when I returned to the table.

"Hey! What are you looking at?"

Felix shook his head and made a stink-face. He was done with the experience. And I knew his true motive: check the veracity of what I'd told him. Like me, he wasn't willing to take someone else's word for it. He wanted to see it for himself.

"Is that the girl from last night?" Felix shouted and pointed.

"Yes!"

"Is she beautiful?" Felix had bad eyesight.

"Let's get out of here!" I took a full bottle of beer from the bucket, downed it in three gulps, set the bottle back on the table, belched, wiped my mouth with my sleeve, and said, "Let's go." Felix *scampered* down the stairs and out of the club.

On the way home, he said, "I'm beat. I'm tired. Are you done for the night?"

"No, I'm not. I could really use another three or four beers to take the edge off."

In the lobby of the hotel, he handed me a wad of cash. "Here, have a good time tonight. Paint the town red. Live for today, for tomorrow may never come." It was a generous gesture and solid advice.

A taxi dropped me off in front of the McDonald's across the street from Jazz and Blues Club. Of all the bars I've been to in China, the first time I walked into Jazz and Blues Club was the most welcome I've ever felt. Like many Chinese bars, it was a basement establishment. Four very attractive women worked the rectangular bar, each to a side. Two younger dudes worked as barbacks. One of the bartenders could speak a little bit of English. Her name was Miranda. She was the hottest of the group. They were all hot, as far as I was concerned.

A pair of suited Chinese guys in their mid 20s walked in and sat to my right. Soon, they introduced themselves as Hector and Shark—businessmen from Shanghai. One by one, the staff members came by to check me out. The manager of the bar, a short, butch woman I called Lesbian Panda, came over and introduced herself. Her English was good, and we had fun feeling each other's breast/chest areas to see who was bigger. Everywhere I looked or turned, someone was waiting to talk to me. Every time I took a sip of beer, I was toasting my neighbor, someone would come over and clink my glass. Cigarettes were pushed in my face. Girls came by and rubbed up against me. Twin sisters named Angel and Fiona asked me to dance. "No, I'm sorry, I don't like dancing," I said. They went out on the dance floor and put on a show, man. Then came the spotlight karaoke competition. I lost track of time.

The crowd thinned out and it was getting late. The friendly bartender named Miranda approached me with the bill for 300 yuan (US$40), which was high when you consider the price of a beer was roughly US$1.50. Apparently, I had bought some drinks for Hector and Shark.

"I like you," Miranda said. "You are cool."

"I like you, too," I said. "I think you are very cool."

"Don't leave me."

"Huh? Leave you?"

"Stay here."

Miranda went back to work breaking down the bar and for a long while it was just me and some intense, dour-looking guy I'd dubbed "Bruce" earlier in the evening, staring at each other. The music stopped. Most of the staff had gone home already. Lesbian Panda hovered over the cash register, removed the drawer, and disappeared into the back. Miranda came out from behind the bar and stood before me, tucking her hair behind her left ear, smiling. It was then I realized how pretty she really was. But I could feel Bruce glaring at us. I swiveled around on the bar stool to face her, and she put her hand on my thigh.

"*Hen gaoxing renshi ni.*" (It was nice to meet you.)

"Yes. It was nice to meet you, too." We joined hands.

"How long will you stay in Fuzhou?" she asked.

"I don't know. It depends on the weather. I'm supposed to leave tomorrow."

"I hope you can stay here."

"Me, too."

"Is that guy your boyfriend?" I asked, nodding at Bruce.

Miranda leaned forward and said, "I don't have a boyfriend." Then she walked back behind the bar and started playing dice with Bruce again. Lesbian Panda returned and the lights came up. "It's time to go!" I drank the last of my beer, waved and smiled at Miranda, and left.

Sunday morning was rainy and gray. Man, I was exhausted—almost happy to be going home. I packed and went down to the lobby and waited for Felix to call. When he hadn't called by 10:00 a.m., I went to the front desk and asked one of the clerks to call his room. No answer. Somehow, I knew we weren't leaving Fuzhou. Still holding my room key, I went back to my room, waiting for the phone to ring.

"Charlie! Where the heck have you been? How was your night? Did you have a good time?"

"It was great."

"Sir, we are leaving at noon. The driver will take us to Mawei. From there we will take the boat back to Matsu. Meet me in the lobby."

I returned to the lobby at noon. Ten minutes later, Felix walked in.

"Charlie, so good to see you! Have you eaten yet?"

"Yeah. What's going on?"

"I have bad news. There is no boat to Matsu. The ocean is too strong."

"What do we do now?"

"We can stay in Fuzhou, or we can go anywhere by bus. We can go where the wind takes us. What would you like to see?"

"Well, there's a few places in Fuzhou I haven't seen yet. There's one joint on the south side of the city called Ancient Street, that's like an all-day night market."

"You know that place? You know everything. I will take you there."

"What about the hotel? Are we going to check out?"

"No problem. I extended our stay."

We got in a taxi and zipped down to Ancient Street, which was a typical Chinese pedestrian mall with a little bit of history. We walked the length of the street and stopped to look over the river.

"You need adventure," Felix said.

"I do?" I chuckled to myself.

"Yes. You're still young. You have energy."

"This trip has been pretty adventurous, so far."

"We may be stuck here until Tuesday."

"Really? Why?"

"The flight to Matsu is cancelled for tomorrow."

"How is that possible?"

"Bad weather."

"I mean, how do they know the weather will be bad enough *tomorrow* to cancel the flight?"

"They just do. They know. *I know.*"

"Well, I guess I'm cool with that."

"There's a place not far from here. It's a real fucking place. I want to take you there."

"What's it called?"

"Pingtan Island." An island 150 km away, ironically, not that far from Matsu.

"Is that the secret island you're always talking about? You know, paradise for men..."

"No, that's near Zhuhai. Pingtan isn't far from here."

"But if it's an island, how are we going to get there? The boat isn't running."

"It's an island, but it's connected to the mainland by a short ferry. They put the whole bus on the boat."

"The south station has busses going to Pingtan," I said. "It's not far from here."

"Really? How did you know that?"

"I read about Pingtan. There are some cool rock formations on the north side of the island."

Felix waved me off. "About the bus station? How did you know to catch the bus to Pingtan at the south station?"

"I did my homework."

The south bus station was a chaotic mess. Captain Felix bought two tickets for Pingtan while I went to the bathroom. I came out and Felix said, "We must hurry. The bus leaves now." We scrambled onto a packed bus, Felix leading the way. There were no two conjoining seats available, so Felix sat down at the first open aisle seat.

"Go sit next to that pretty girl," he said. "Make some friends."

Slowly walking to the back of the bus, I cringed as the pretty girl recoiled in horror with every step I took in her direction. I wrestled my backpack off and sat down, placing the pack between my legs. I looked over at the girl, who smiled nervously. *At least she smiled.* A long minute passed, and Felix got up from his seat and made his way to the back of the bus.

"Hello," he said to the girl on my left. "Do you speak English?"

She shook her head "no" and they had a brief conversation in Mandarin.

"This girl wants to be your friend," Felix said.

"She does? She looks uncomfortable to me, boss."

"OK, no problem." He turned and headed toward the front of the bus.

Felix was about to exit the bus when I stood up and barked, "*Hey!* Where the fuck are you going?" Every passenger turned around to look at me.

"I'm too old for this!" Felix said. "You're young! You need adventure!"

"What?! Wait!" I cried. "You can't just leave me on this bus!"

Captain Felix smiled and waved. "You'll be OK! You need adventure. Be back in Fuzhou by Tuesday morning." He walked off the bus. And that was it. The driver closed the doors and proceeded to back out of the station. I was livid.

The bus lurched through traffic for 20 minutes and we were still in the city. We'd traveled maybe a mile in light rain. The girl on my left stared out the window. I began to get a whiff of vomit. We were parked at a stoplight and about to get on an elevated freeway. I grabbed my backpack and bolted for the front of the bus.

"Let me out here," I said to the driver.

"Huh? What?"

"*Da kaimen. Wo buxiang qu Pingtan.*" (Open the door. I don't want to go any further.) The driver reluctantly opened the door, and I bounced off the bus.

At first, I was angry and horrified that Felix would leave me like that. And then I had a change of heart. *Well, he thinks I'm an intrepid traveler.* That kind of bullshit could go either way. On one hand, it might be rude, inconsiderate, and not very friend-like. On the other hand, it could be seen as a light-hearted gesture of good fun—a prank. It could have been a test, or it could have been a trick to knock me off my game. And the more I got to know Felix, there was also the possibility that he had absolutely zero premeditated intent. He might have walked on the bus, realized he was going to be puking for the next six hours, and said, "Fuck this, I'm out. You're on your own, pal. Later!"

Regardless, it broke the circuit of my front-facing thoughts: I couldn't trust *anybody* now, not even old Felix—not that I trusted him unconditionally to begin with. Although the trip had been full of memorable experiences—some good, some bad—my fresh-faced, positive energy was creeping to sullen cynicism. I lost trust in Felix, *forever.* Fuck me? *Fuck you!*

I walked back towards the bus station, or at least what I thought was the bus station. The rain started to come down harder. Soon it was a downpour. I was soaked from head to toe when I hailed a taxi to the hotel.

I dialed Felix's room on the house phone, ready to chew him out, but there was no answer. I went down to the restaurant on the second floor. Nana was there, pleased to see me, I guess.

"Tomorrow's my birthday," Nana said. "I'm having a party. Would you like to come?"

"Sure."

I finished dinner, said goodbye, got in a taxi, and arrived at Jazz and Blues Club around 10:00 p.m. Hector and Shark, the two guys from Shanghai, were posted up at the same corner. Miranda looked great—even better than last night—but she seemed cold. The truth is, I was having a hard time reading her. The light in her eyes flickered. It was weird. Like the way she said she didn't have a boyfriend but then went back to Bruce. There was something there between them. I could feel it. I looked around and didn't see Bruce, but I did see Slim Pickens, Cool Ranch, Sunshine, Lesbian Panda, and Lenny Swish. And Rock Star and Cowgirl. I had nicknames for all of them except Miranda. It was insanely fun.

The twins Angel and Fiona appeared. Angel said she was 23, but Shark said she was only 19. Her English was decent. Attractive doesn't begin to describe her. Fiona was distant and wary of me, but Angel was hardly subtle in her approach. After a brief discussion about her rate (400 yuan for the night), Angel and I were getting ready to move to my hotel room. I signaled to Miranda and said, "The bill, please." She shook her head. I put both my palms up and said, "What?" Miranda turned away.

I got Slim Pickens' attention and said, "*Maidan!*" (Check, please!) Slim shook his head and said, "*Meiyou.*" (I don't have it.) Angel went to say goodbye to her sister who was shaking it on the dance floor, so I waited until my erection went to half-mast and got up and walked around to the side of the bar where Miranda and Sunshine were playing dice with some guy. Miranda made eye contact and said, "Don't go."

"Why?"

"Don't go," she repeated.

"OK, I will stay."

Angel didn't appreciate my change of heart. "Let's dance," she said, frowning, dragging me by the arm toward the dance floor.

"No," I said. "I don't dance." Angel stomped off. Then her sister Fiona approached and spat some nasty Mandarin at me. Miranda came over and chased Fiona away.

By 2:00 a.m., I was done. I couldn't smoke another cigarette or drink another beer.

"Miranda, I have to go now."

"Can you wait?"

"No, I'm sorry." I handed her 300 yuan. "Is that enough?"

"Too much," she said. "Two hundred."

"Keep the rest."

Hector and Shark were fucked up. I bid them farewell and we embraced in a group hug.

Lesbian Panda came over and said, "Don't tell me you pussies are calling it a night?"

None of us left. The farewell was all for nothing. It was 4:30 a.m. by the time Jazz and Blues Club closed. I got in a taxi and headed to my hotel.

Miranda called at 2:28 p.m. the next afternoon, which seemed odd. *Did I give her my number?* I was halfway up Wu Mountain, a 200-meter hill in the center of town that overlooks the giant Mao statue in Wuyi Square. Heading for the White Pagoda—yet another in a series of mundane Chinese temples perched atop a mountain, or in this case, a 200-meter hill called a mountain.

"You come to Jazz and Blues club tonight?" Miranda asked.

"Yes, but...maybe I go back to Taiwan tonight."

"You say you leave Tuesday."

"Um, well, my boss says he wants to go home tonight." Long pause.

"Oh." A longer pause.

"If not, I come see you."

"OK. Bye-bye." And she hung up. Then I lost the steam to continue up the hill and started back down.

Nana invited me to her birthday party, so I wanted to see what *that* was all about. When I returned to the hotel, one of the desk clerks said, "Hello! Hello! *Meigouren!*" She handed me a handwritten message from Captain Felix. I hadn't spoken to him since he left me on the bus. I assumed he knew I didn't go to Pingtan Island. The message said to meet him in the lobby at 7:00 p.m., but I impatiently went up and called his room.

"Charlie! How was Pingtan?"

"I didn't go, Felix. I got off the bus about twenty minutes after you did."

"You have what it takes. You are the master of your dominion. I admire you."

"It's 'master of my *domain*'—not dominion." I rarely corrected the Captain's English, but I was still pissed at him.

"It means the same thing, doesn't it?" I could hear him smiling. "So, what's happening tonight?"

"I got invited to a birthday party."

"By the girl from the restaurant? She likes you. She told me."

"That's nice. Is there anything I need to know about this birthday party deal? Like etiquette?"

"Meet me at the restaurant on the second floor."

Nana's birthday party was held at a KTV joint not far from the hotel. KTV are massive-scale karaoke joints decked out like movie theatres, staffed by an army of kids who do nothing but escort people to and from their rented rooms. Captain Felix told me to make sure I brought a cake of some sort, which I picked up at a supermarket.

Unfortunately, I was the first to arrive, greeted by Nana. She introduced me to her mother, who took the cake from my hands and dropped it on the "gift table" with an inferential *thud*. A few guests arrived. I sat on the couch in the far corner of the room. Nana's friends did a double take when they saw me. "Whoa! What the hell is that?!" Nana came over once to offer a glass of cheap blended whisky, my least favorite of all the alcoholic beverages. Soon, the room was full, and people were singing, and it was awful. Nobody would make eye contact or acknowledge me. It was not a "Hi, my name is Charlie" type of crowd. Sensing some antagonism from the male population of the party, I slipped out of the room unnoticed. I was greeted in the hallway by a young kid who assumed I was looking for the bathroom. "No bathroom," I said. "Exit."

I got out on the street and hailed a taxi. Suddenly, I remembered leaving my camera on the table next to the couch in the KTV room. *Motherfucker, I am not going back there. But goddammit! I had four days' worth of photos in that camera.*

My reception at Jazz and Blues Club was ebullient. Miranda jumped across the bar and gave me a bear hug before planting a kiss on my lips. Bar patrons and staff cheered alike. Hector and Shark were not on the scene but Lenny Swish was over there, making eyes at me.

"You will marry her and take her to America?" Lenny Swish asked.

"Maybe. Who knows?"

It was a night to remember. A new group of foreigners came in and I quickly bonded with a Swedish doppelganger. It was almost 3:00 a.m. when Miranda and I went back to my hotel room. In the morning, we had breakfast together at a café down the street. We shared a long, almost painful embrace.

"I'll be back," I said.

"When?"

"Soon."

"Please don't forget me."

"I won't."

11

Fuzhou Redux (That's a Lot of Climbing to See a Fucking Statue)

Two months passed without major incidents at work or in my personal life. I belonged to a small social circle of expats who couldn't have been nicer people, but I had to watch my step. They were all 10-15 years younger. We had almost nothing in common. I was just happy they tolerated me, and I kept getting invited to events.

The Western year-end holiday season (Christmas and New Year's) approached, and Captain Felix and Daisy started bugging me about my travel plans. They were going to Beijing for Christmas. "You shouldn't be alone during the holiday," the Captain said. "Anywhere you want to go, I will buy the ticket for you."

Miranda and Fuzhou were still very much on my mind. "I'll do that Three Links to China route again."

Felix was delighted. "You are going to the Real China! By yourself! You are not afraid of anything! Traveling alone is dangerous. But don't worry, if anything happens, I can help you. I know people up here [hand above his head] and I know people down here [flat hand near his feet]."

"We will make sure your body gets sent back to the States," Daisy chimed in.

"China can be...a bit of an ordeal," I said, "but come on, Felix, it's not like going to another planet."

Captain Felix flashed a broad smile and blinked rapidly. "If you stay at home, nothing can happen." I waited for him to say "nothing ventured, nothing gained" or one of his other greatest hits of shop-worn clichés and idioms.

On Christmas Day, Miranda replied to my email. She said she "would very happy see me." The next day, I called, and we agreed to meet at Jazz and Blues Club at 9:30 p.m. Later that same night, I received another email with the subject heading of (heart heart heart!) YOU ARE COMING!

"I wait for you me when you are Fuzhou together," read her email.

Getting from Matsu to Mawei to Fuzhou was easy. It was around 4:30 p.m. when I arrived at my hotel, the "Grand Hyatt," but there was nothing grand or Hyatt about it. Last time I checked, it's called the Minjiang Hotel. Anyway, it had all the typical amenities and deformities of a mid-range Chinese business hotel, occupying the 10th through 25th floors of a high-rise near the corner of Hudong Road and Wusi Road. Felix explicitly told me *not* to stay at the Baihe Hot Springs Hotel again. The Grand Hyatt's ubiquitous sauna house down on the 12th floor, judging from the number of dudes rolling up off the street and up to the 12th floor, must have been pretty damn special.

Over the years, I developed this thing about hotel towels. If the towels sucked, I couldn't stay more than one night. The Grand Hyatt's towels were fantastic—new, clean, and fluffy. There was a set of matching white terrycloth robes. The sheets were soft and yet crisp. I was ecstatic. This was going to be one of the greatest trips of all time.

Part of my euphoria stemmed from the fact that I brought a couple of grams of pot and a pipe with me. In hindsight, it was stupid, reckless, and irresponsible, but at the time, I knew I could get away with it. I didn't even attempt to hide the pot—I kept it in the front pocket of my jeans. The clean, unused pipe—courtesy of Daisy—was in my backpack. In Taiwan, they don't care what you take out of the country; it's what you *bring back in*. Comparatively, going through Chinese customs is like walking through the express lane at Safeway without buying anything. You won't arouse suspicion unless you set off an alarm or have a five-pound ham stuffed into your T-shirt.

I stopped to pick up some beer at the Chinese version of K-Mart. I went back to the room, got high, drank the beer, and watched TV—and the clock—until 9:00 p.m. I hit the street at 9:10, and I was sitting at the bar in Jazz and Blues Club at 9:40. There was no sign of Miranda. In fact, I didn't recognize *anyone*. The staff was completely different. Gone were the Rock Stars and Cowgirls and Sunshines and Slim Pickens. The whole bar was staffed by a new crew of girls and boys. No sign of Lesbian Panda, either.

I'm a fairly patient individual. I'll give someone half an hour before calling to see why they haven't shown up. I called Miranda at 10:45 p.m. and got the standard message that the person I was trying to contact was unreachable at this time, i.e., they'd shut the phone off. Please try again later. So, I put in the last call at midnight and gave up. *Wow, I must have really liked her. I've never waited two and a half hours for anybody, ever.* In the interim, I sat there and drank six beers while the bar staff ignored me.

I was about to leave when Angel appeared, and so we shared a beer. As usual, her hands were everywhere but on the bartop. Angel's sister, Fiona, showed up, and we discussed a possible "arrangement." After a few beers, I begged for a rain check, saying I was "too tired to satisfy both." Their demeanor instantly changed from sex kittens to feral cats. They took their business to the dance floor, which, by now, was packed with local revelers. I left the bar in a foul mood.

Miranda called at 7:15 the next morning, and while I'm not sure exactly what she said, I gathered that she no longer worked at the bar, and I would never see her again. I was right on both accounts. Her voice was shaky and sad. "Please wait for me," was the last thing she said. The phone went dead.

My flight back to Taipei was scheduled for New Year's Eve. Faced with three more days to kill, I amused myself by getting high and going to the sauna house on the 12th floor, which was indeed something special. The late December weather was shit—I'd seen everything I wanted to see in town already. I had no plans except to hook up with Miranda.

During the day, when I felt like stretching my legs, I'd make a walkabout. One morning, I went back to Wuyi Square to complete the ascent of Wu Mountain. And finally, sweating balls even in the cool weather, I made it to the top. I found a typical temple and not much else. The view of metro Fuzhou was fuzzy and gray. Even if the air had been clear, it wouldn't have looked much different than any other concrete jungle on Earth. I wandered around the White Pagoda temple complex and came upon a statue of the Buddha, and then it hit me. I couldn't parse my feelings in the moment. I said out loud, "That's a lot of climbing to see a fucking statue."

I felt triumphant and heartbroken at the same time. Here I was, going places, doing and seeing things that seemed impossible to me less than a year ago. While I should have been raising my arms above my head in a sort of Sylvester Stallone-as-Rocky Balboa victory pose, I was empty.

Later in the afternoon, I opened the first of two bottles of red wine. Around 10:00 p.m., I took a taxi to Jazz and Blues Club and regretted it straight away. Something was off, worse than the previous night. The vibe. The attitude. I didn't see any other foreigners and I didn't feel good being there.

Without Miranda or other familiar faces, Fuzhou seemed like a waste of time. And, in fact, the *Lonely Planet China* book even said that, in so many words, on page 543.

There was something enigmatic about that last day in Fuzhou. The weather cleared a bit. At least the rain stopped.

Following a late morning sauna house visit, I went down to a neighborhood with cobblestone streets and bought a few cans of Pearl River Beer from a mom-and-pop market. There was a restaurant next door to the market where a man was wiping down the tables in front, so I asked him if I could sit and drink the beer. "Sure, go ahead," he said and offered me a cigarette. I smoked and drank for a while, browsing the pictures on my new camera's memory card and deleting the unnecessary items.

Throughout my travels in Asia, I had a routine of saving all my camera shots to my laptop at the end of the night. But somehow, that didn't happen after my first night at the Jazz and Blues Club. I realized that I didn't have any pictures of Miranda. I deeply regretted losing the camera on the previous trip. *How could I have been so stupid? I should have gone back to Nana's birthday party and retrieved the camera.* The unsaved photos were the ones I wanted. I came all this way to reclaim those photos. Everything about Fuzhou reminded me of lost and squandered opportunity.

I could have hit the bus station and gone somewhere else for a few days, but I couldn't move. It's not like I loved the girl, but I came all this way to see her, and it didn't happen for whatever reason. I was mad at myself for having *expectations*. I felt bad that Miranda blew me off, but I didn't blame her. *Something* happened beyond our control.

Meanwhile, I wandered from the restaurant and went to a secluded little park next to a canal where I got high the day before. Young children were playing down the alley. The colors at the park were the same as I'd imagined them, but not quite. The setting was the same, but the sun hit the horizon from a different angle. I almost started weeping.

On the ferry ride back to Matsu, cruising down the Min River, I was badgered by nagging questions. *How did people 500 years ago make their way across the imposing mountain terrain of Fujian Province?* Standing on the rear deck of the ferry boat, I looked out on the alternately ragged and lush riverside and wondered, "How the fuck did people make their way here?" I considered Marco Polo and the great explorers of history. *Where did they keep the drinking water? Where did they shit? How did they wipe their asses?* The questions were never-ending.

Having come to Asia the way every buck-toothed Nebraskan villager comes to Las Vegas and sits down at a Blackjack table for the first time, I was fuckin' happy to be there. I didn't know the rules and probably wouldn't win anything. But luck, above everything else, has no master and doesn't discriminate. I believe the universe favors the blind risk-taker more than any other of its children. And everybody loses, here and there, from time to time. *I lost, that's all.* I hoped I wouldn't have to get used to it.

China has a vast recorded history, and their only secret, from what I could see, was persistence. These may be remembered as China's New Golden Years. For the first time in a long time, maybe ever, the Chinese people (not only the government bureaucrats) had money and a certain amount of personal autonomy (which, ironically, wouldn't last).

I'm not making a judgment, just an observation. As Jesus once said, and if he didn't, he probably should have, "I don't make the laws, Saul. I just interpret them." I certainly didn't begrudge the average Chinese of their newfound capitalist wealth. In fact, I was happy for them. If I had been raised in the shadows of Mao Zedong and the Cultural Revolution, I think I'd be barking and yapping and pissing on the floor, too. Now, I will say this: I'd only seen just a thumbnail sketch of the outright cannibalism of their beloved environment and natural resources. Up and down the Min River, entire mountainsides have been chiseled away, looking like half-eaten sandwiches. Driving along the Beijing-Fuzhou Highway, 100 kilometers from the nearest big city, ugly factory villages belch and chain-smoke filth into the sky. Now I know where all my "Made in China" T-shirts come from.

I spent the first 40 years of my life appraising "mountains worth climbing." China, as a destination, was nothing more than something to see. It was no different than Mt. Everest or the Eiffel Tower or the bush of the Australian Outback. Everywhere I went in Asia, I was asked, "Why?" *Why are you here? Why do you want to see this?* Real people don't climb Mt. Everest "because it's there" any more than I went to China "because it's there." That's a stupid answer to a dumber question, but I appreciate the concept of defining achievement by your own standards. Do you know what people do once they get to the top of Mt. Everest? A Tibetan Sherpa would say, "They figure out how to get down."

12

Along for the Ride

After Celeste left Knowledge Press in the fall of 2008, we started hanging out as friends. I had no intention of "dating" her or even trying to get her into bed. She was too young and immature, and I was too old and greasy for any type of serious relationship. The last thing I wanted to do was mess up her life.

We saw each other once or twice a week, strictly platonic friends, usually going out for dinner or taking her dog for a walk in the park on Sundays. She already found a new job at an aviation museum, and she was pursuing her dream of winning a spot in a work exchange program at Disney World in Orlando, Florida. We held hands occasionally, but it wasn't sexual.

For several months, I was the big brother she never had, not a suitor. I liked her bubbly, carefree personality, and I needed more of that in my life. And she was a bright woman who could speak (and read) Japanese and French in addition to Mandarin, Taiwanese, and English. Above all, it was nothing serious. I was encouraging and supportive, helping her with the application for the Disney World gig.

Just before I left for the Christmas trip to Fuzhou, we went for a walk to enjoy the lights in Daan Park. I can't say that "I don't know how it happened" because I saw it coming, but we wound up kissing for the first time. The next day, I told her that it couldn't happen again.

"Why? Didn't you like it?"

"Of course I did. But...I'm too old for you. It would never work out if we took it any further."

"You're just being a big stupid bear (*da benxiong*). I don't care how old you are. What difference does it make?"

A *lot*. It makes a lot of difference, darlin'.

I tried to avoid Celeste when I returned from Fuzhou, but she was persistent, and I was…weak. We saw each other a few times before the upcoming Chinese New Year and, eventually, wound up sleeping together. Where it would go from there, who could say? I didn't have a good feeling about it, but I went along for the ride.

The cram school hosted a monthly series of speech contests for the students, held on the second Saturday morning of the month. For the first six months, Felix asked me to help "judge" the contests. The gig paid an extra 60 bucks, and I didn't mind the variety. It was something to do, and it was over before noon. When the contest ended, I'd pop over to check on Carter Dietz and the conversation class. The problem was arriving on time (8:00 a.m.) because I was usually blackout drunk every Friday night. Five alarms weren't enough to roust me from a blackout.

The contests took place in the cram school's main auditorium, and I sat on a panel of three judges just off to the right of the stage, where I'd pretend to take notes during the speeches. Note-taking was pointless because the best speeches were always so much better than the rest. I just wrote down the names of the "winners." The two-minute speeches came in three categories and divided by age group, so there were a total of 12 competitions and winners. Some categories had only one contestant; others had 20 contestants. Judges had to sit through a minimum of 60 speeches.

The first time I went down there, I was vaguely excited because I thought I'd be judging the contest, as in, submitting my winners, and that would be the end of it. Felix said they needed me because I was the final arbiter of good English. It was a minor ego boost.

When it came time to hold deliberations, I shared my winners and the other two judges (teachers from the ZYEA branch in Taichung) immediately scowled and said, "Oh no, no, no, no. *Those* kids can't win.

We want *these* kids to win." They submitted an alternate slate of winners based on popularity and the teacher associated with their class. The whole system was rigged from the get-go. I smacked myself on the forehead. *Of course, it figures.*

The second week of January, I showed up 15 minutes late to the speech contest after an all-night drinking binge and hadn't even gone to bed yet. The alcohol was coming off me like an aura. Constantly on the verge of nodding off, I could barely keep myself together. The other judges were smirking and making snide comments. It was so bad that Lonesome Carl pulled me aside during a break and asked if I was drinking because people in the audience could smell the booze. I assured him that I was not, in fact, drinking, but I might have been overserved the night before.

This prompted an interaction that may have led to Stephan's departure from the cram school and the company. When the contest was over, Lonesome Carl insisted that he take me to lunch so we could "talk about what happened up there today." *Fuck off, Carl. We both know what happened up there.* We went out for hot pot, and Carl started talking about Crazy Tooth and how much he wanted to strangle her. She was messing with his numbers and making him look bad. Felix was coming down hard on his ass.

I casually mentioned that Stephan said he dated Crazy Tooth (Peggy) when she first started at ZYEA. Years ago.

Lonesome Carl went off. "That bitch is a liar! *I fuckin' knew it!*"

I begged him not to say anything about it to Felix. Carl promised to keep the secret.

Monday morning, one of the managers from the cram school came to see Felix. I didn't like this guy. He was a tall, middle-aged dude with an oversized head on a skinny frame, and he was never nice to me, so I called him Mr. Pez. He told Felix what Lonesome Carl told him about Crazy Tooth (in Mandarin, but I heard my name and listened closely).

Felix rolled his head over toward me and said, "Is this true? Did Stephan date Peggy?"

"That's just what I *heard*, boss. I don't know what happened. It was a long time ago."

Felix and Mr. Pez conspired to trick Peggy into admitting it, while I walked out of the office and got Carl on the phone.

"Dude, what the fuck? You promised not to say anything."

"I didn't say a word to the Old Man."

"Yeah, but what's-his-name is down here in the office, and he just spit it out. I know what you did. *You* didn't tell Felix. You had Mr. Pez do it. That sucks, man. I thought you were my friend."

"I *swear* that I did not mention your name. You have nothing to do with it. I swear to God."

"Well, you just lied to God, Carl, cuz that dude said, 'Your boy Charlie told Carl that Stephan and Peggy were dating.'"

"*He did not!*"

"He did fucking too, Carl! Do you think I'm stupid?"

"I *promise* this will not come back to you."

"If Felix thinks I can't be trusted... Dude. *I can't have it.*"

"Felix isn't worried about you. Trust me, OK? I promise. This will not come back to haunt you."

"Your promise means shit to me, Carl," and I hung up.

The whole thing blew over in a couple of days, and true to Lonesome Carl's prediction, Felix wasn't worried about how or when I knew anything. He said I was a "good friend" for not ratting on Stephan. "When life is a sea of trouble, only a good friend is there at your side." But what became of it was the end for Stephan. Peggy never felt any repercussions because she was pregnant with her Taiwanese boyfriend's child and went on maternity leave at the end of the month.

Maybe a week later, Stephan called me and said, "They're trying to get rid of me, man."

"What? Who is?"

"The cram school. They want me out of there."

"Impossible. If that were true, I would have heard something about it."

Stephan had been *persona non grata* in the company for a while. Daisy said his constant complaining about lack of promotion for his classes was getting on the Captain's nerves. Stephan's excuses for missing certain classes were unacceptable. To top it off, he got busted by the government for falsifying his work information on the ARC that Felix sponsored. It cost Felix and ZYEA a shitload of money and invited additional government scrutiny. I didn't know how or when they would get rid of Stephan; I just knew it was gonna happen. The fact that he dated Crazy Tooth may have been another reason to cut him loose.

"Listen, man," Stephan groaned. "I'm telling you. They want me out."

"How do you know?"

"How do I know? *I'll tell you how I know*. They just jacked up the price of tuition for my Non-Stop English class by four hundred percent!"

"They did not. NSE is Felix's baby. He'd never sabotage NSE."

"They did. Four hundred percent."

"How much was the class originally?"

"Fifteen thousand Taiwan per quarter. They raised it to forty-five thousand. None of my students are going to pay that for the class. They're all dropping out."

"Let me see what I can dig up on this price increase, OK?"

"Nah, man. Fuck it. I'm done."

A few days later, Captain Felix rolled into the office and asked, "Have you talked to Stephan recently?"

"I heard you're getting rid of him"

Felix scowled. "He's only down at the school to get laid. He's not a serious teacher. He's a cancer in the company." Felix mentioned Black Betty and some other chicks that Stephan had (allegedly) "violated," and how the students didn't like him, and his class numbers were shrinking, etc.

"So, how did you find out about Black Betty?"

"It wasn't a big secret."

Stephan's main gig was managing a different cram school (under the table). Without Zhang Yi English Academy sponsoring his ARC, he had to leave Taiwan for a little while.

As you might imagine, the cultural misunderstandings, the social *faux pas*, and the emotional uncertainties of my future made life interesting, but it generated the kind of personal insecurity I wouldn't wish on my worst enemy. At the end of the day, brushing aside all the amusements, I learned a valuable lesson. Communication makes the difference in our lives.

Above all, how Stephan got squeezed out of the company was very telling about the Taiwanese work environment. In many cases, when they wanted to get rid of you, they didn't simply give you the boot, they made life intolerable until you got the hint and left on your own accord. Or they tripled the price of your classes, knowing you wouldn't have a single student sign up, and hence, there'd be no class for you to teach.

13

Guangzhou

Following my return from the second Fuzhou trip, Chinese New Year (Year of the Ox) was around the corner, and everybody was feeling the pressure to get shit done before the holiday. Captain Felix and Daisy, once again, had the same concern: *What are you going to do for the 10-day holiday?* The insinuation being that I couldn't stay alone in Taipei. And, of course, Felix said the airfare was on the house, and he'd throw in some pocket money and whatnot.

The problem with traveling in Asia during the Lunar New Year is a billion people are trying to move around at once. Anybody who hasn't booked their flight or train tickets in October of the previous year might as well stay wherever they are or prepare for sticker shock. Flights to certain destinations can be scarce, super expensive, or non-existent.

During the second week of January, we were sitting in the office, and Felix said, "Have you decided where you want to go for Chinese New Year?"

I mentioned Guangzhou, and Captain Felix was suspicious. "Why do you want to go there?"

Guangzhou was, at the time, the black market capital of illegal narcotics in China. Drugs of all types could be freely purchased on one street, in one specific neighborhood, sold by one nationality of people, and tacitly endorsed by the local government. According to my sources, Jianshe Sixth Road (*Jianshe ma lu*) in central Guangzhou was the closest thing to an open-air drug market in Asia.

Put yourself in my shoes for a minute. Single, 40-year-old swinging bachelor, doing well for himself, sexually, in Asia. That part of life was sewn up tight. To be honest, I was bored of hookers and chasing after untenable situations with women. Dating Celeste was more of a looming problem than anything else. And sure, *it was awesome.* I knew some dudes who would've killed to trade places with me. But it was all getting, I daresay, kind of banal. Drugs seemed to be the next logical progression to upscale the experience.

I didn't want to lie to Felix, but I couldn't be honest, obviously. So I told him that I studied Cantonese in college, which was true. I took three semesters of Cantonese at City College of San Francisco. And I made up another excuse about wanting to see some historical sites, like the first Islamic Mosque in China, which is, in fact, in Guangzhou.

Felix said, "I don't think it's safe for you to spend ten days in Guangzhou."

"Oh, I'll fly to Hong Kong, and I'll spend a couple of days there, and then I'll take the train to Guangzhou,"

Felix eyed me and didn't respond.

"Seriously," I said. "I'll be fine. Don't worry about me."

"I was born in Guangzhou," Felix said. "Maybe one day, we could visit my birthplace."

"Hell, yeah! Let's do it!"

Never a man to linger on a moment in time, Felix moved on to more pressing issues.

This was my first Chinese New Year, and I was getting all kinds of advice from local and foreign contacts. Without coaching or prompting from Stephan or Daisy or the Captain—or anybody else who weighed in on my plans—I realized the actual Lunar New Year—the day *after* Chinese New Year's Eve—would be a great time to fly. I bought a round-trip ticket to Hong Kong and scored a seat on the high-speed rail to Guangzhou, my ultimate but questionable destination.

★✱★

Meher Baba said that God is an ocean without boundaries. One drop in, one drop out.

Borders are strange, compelling, definitive, and yet, merely lines in the sand. Tonight, the tide will come and wipe them away. Tomorrow, we begin the process of drawing the lines again. We grasp the Alfred Korzybski stuff about the "map is not the territory," so borders, though generally invisible, have barriers that never end. Within these borders we find more borders, some much easier to transmute than others. People become the borders.

Guangzhou is 600 km southwest of Taipei, but it might as well be the next town over. The only non-geographic differences between Guangzhou and Taipei is dialect and perceived ethnicity. It would take an experienced eye to tell the difference between the business districts of either city. Separated by open water, a boundary of sorts, they are sister cities, next-door neighbors, and kissing cousins. Appearance and function aside, Taipei and Guangzhou are worlds apart.

I left for Hong Kong on the first morning of the Lunar New Year. Both airports were almost empty. The flight was maybe half full. I reserved a hotel room at the most reasonable option, the Hong Kong Y.W.C.A. Hotel in Central on Robinson Hill, avoiding the tourist spectacle of Kowloon. Above all, the hotel was within striking distance of Lan Kwai Fong—the nightlife area of Central—and recommended by *Lonely Planet*.

Hong Kong is... It's easy to get around and a miracle of modern engineering. The skyscrapers built into mountainsides make it worth the trip. It's one of the big cities everyone should see at least once, if you get the chance. I've never been so impressed by the human urge to pile as much shit on top of other shit as possible. Aside from its stunning, gravity-defying infrastructure, the "tourist Hong Kong" is no different than New York. I got the same sense of awe and wonder at the Statue of Liberty as I did the Central–Mid-Levels escalator or standing at the Avenue of Stars and looking out across Victoria Harbor. These amazing feats of architectural and civil engineering are something humanity should be proud of. I don't deny them. The problem is: after you see the sights, you must check in with the people.

Most of the local folks you meet on the tourist circuit are just doing their jobs. They have to be nice to you, and their aroma of obligatory friendliness is palatable. And again, I get that. I've been there. What's troubling about Hong Kong is that once you meet the real people, the real Hong Kong, they're kind of rude and stuck-up. They remind me of how people from New York make such a goddamn point of saying they're from Manhattan or Brooklyn or Astoria, and everybody else is like, "Who the fuck cares?"

While Hong Kong is an overwhelmingly international city, the former British colony was, in 2008, still very British. If it weren't 75 percent Chinese, half of whom speak English with a British accent, you'd swear you were in some alternate reality of London Town. Double-decker lorries driving on the left side of the road. Elevators are called "lifts." Locals have a pint at the pub. I concede that Benny Hill, the Sex Pistols, and 12 years of American History classes have shaped my concept of British society. I love British rock music and I have no problem with the United Kingdom or the people of Britain, Scotland, Wales, and Northern Ireland. That doesn't mean I have to like Hong Kong.

That night, I rode the Central–Mid-Levels escalator up to Conduit Road and walked back down, stopping for beers along the way. Around midnight, I hit the main drag of Lan Kwai Fong and couldn't shake the "Spring Break" feeling. Like I had *no business* being there. I saw more than one expat wearing a pink Polo with an upturned collar.

Early the next morning, I took the MTR to Tsim Sha Sui East and walked to Hong Hom Station, collected the train ticket, and boarded the high-speed train for a leisurely two-hour ride. It was cold and the skies were gray, but I was excited to arrive in Guangzhou. Everything went smoothly, and I vaguely remember the taxi ride from the train station to the hotel.

I booked a room at Guangdong Victory Hotel on Shamian Island, a sandbank at the southern end of Guangzhou city proper. The island had several hotels, a youth hostel, two dozen restaurants, and tourist shops selling curios and souvenirs and whatnot. It was not so much of an island as an oasis. The island was divided into two concessions given to France and the United Kingdom by the Qing Dynasty. At this point, it was a relic of the colonial European period, with quiet pedestrian avenues pillared by shady trees and lined by historical buildings with pedigree displayed on bronze plaques.

The routine kicked in. Unplug the phone, unpack, shower, turn on the TV, kick back for a few minutes, and let the moment linger. Get up, get dressed, and get out. Look for Bar Street or places mentioned in guidebooks.

It was late afternoon when I took the subway across the river to Baitan Bar Street (aka Bai'etan River View) for reconnaissance. Bar Street (*jiuba jie*) is just what it says: a street lined with various but usually identical bars. For the most part, it's the same bar on repeat, each with a different name or theme; the same god-awful throbbing of techno, the same lukewarm Tsingtao Beer, the same skimpily clad 20-year-old girls behind the bar. Thankfully, there is little or no pretense on *jiuba jie*. There are neon lights and sharply dressed hawkers trying to rope you into their establishments. All the dirty shit happens behind the curtain. But it's not about glamour or prestige or even camaraderie or fun. Bar Street is all about separating you from your cash. A "typical" Chinese bar street won't get kicking until midnight.

Baitan Bar Street wasn't happening, so I got back on the subway, headed for the Martyr's Shrine area, looking for a pub called Elephant & Castle. The pub had been described as "trusty and comforting" to "creepy and dangerous," both of which worked for me. Online reviews said E&C had been there a long time and it was popular with expats.

Eventually, I found Elephant & Castle. The off-duty Guangzhou cop at the door waved me in without question. Once inside, it was standard dive bar atmosphere: smoky, low lights. A rugby match on a single TV above the well.

A group of black guys were gathered at the far end of the bar. They were Nigerian, and I was expecting to see them. I sat about a third of the way into the bar and ordered a Carlsberg from the bartender, a predictably attractive young woman. A few seats away, middle-aged white guy with salt-and-pepper hair was hunched over his Guinness. To his right was a large-framed, bearded, grizzly-looking white dude who radiated an outlaw vibe.

There was an enclosed room with a pool table in the back and a courtyard beyond that. A mixed group of black and white guys were playing a game of pool and sharing a massive joint. The smell was pungently obvious. Every so often, I could hear snatches of their conversation. It took tremendous willpower not to march into the back room and introduce myself, but I remained patient. *These things take time.*

The bartender came over. "Where are you from?"

"Taiwan..." *Dammit, don't say that.*

"Taiwan is..."

"I know, China."

"What do you do in Taiwan?"

"I'm a writer."

The salt-and-pepper guy turned to me and said, "So yer an American then, yeah?"

"I am."

"Right, well. We don't see as many Yanks as we used to." I detected an Australian accent with British grammar.

"Oh, I see..." I replied, staring at the TV.

"Who do you favor? Which side do you support?"

"You mean in this rugby game? Man, I don't even understand the rules, let alone who is who."

He held out his hand. "I'm Brian. And you are?"

The introduction was interrupted by two white guys entering the bar in mid-conversation or mid-argument, hard to say which, and they headed straight for the back of the bar. They greeted the Nigerian guys like regular buddies and got down to playing pool.

For the next hour, Brian and I took turns buying the round and playing *What's Your Story?* The conversation was intelligent, if not, lucid. Brian's story: the director of an art academy in Guangzhou. Originally from Australia, he went to university in the U.K., and he was married to an Argentinean woman. They had three children, all of whom were waiting for him in Buenos Aries. Brian said "mate" and "brilliant" the way I say "dude" and "awesome." He seemed harmless, if not a bit of a narcissist. Occasionally, I interjected to ask about the guys in the back. I wanted to know what was *up.*

"Don't mess with that lot," Brian said. "Very shady."

He was considerably more demonstrative every time I brought it up. Finally, I just said, "Do you get high?"

"I don't."

Out of nowhere, the grizzly-looking guy wedged himself into the conversation by coming up behind us and asking, "So, what do you fellas know about chainsaws?"

Not a bad conversation starter.

Timothy T. Butler was, among other things, five-time World Champion Lumberjack, talent agent, producer, chainsaw artist, and "humorous birthday party clown" from Oregon. That's not a joke. Said so right on the business card. And Tim T. Butler was a nuisance who wouldn't stop talking.

Brian was visibly perturbed by Mr. Butler's presence. At one point, Brian grabbed my shoulder in show of restraint, shaking his head vigorously until the bartender came over and told Butler to knock it off.

"There's a place I fancy across the bridge," Brian said. "If you like young girls, you're welcome to join me."

I scoffed. "What do you mean by young?"

"Legal, of course," he made a 180-degree scan of the bar, "and it's better than this depressing shithole."

When Brian said 'across the bridge,' I thought he was talking about going to another part of the city, perhaps separated by a river. He was talking about the pedestrian bridge that crossed the busy Huanshe East Road. And when he said young girls, I was hoping he meant, at the very minimum, age of consent girls (i.e., legal in China). Shocking but true: China's legal age of consent for male-female consensual sex is 14 years old. However, girls under the age of 18 are still considered minors and, by law, not allowed in places where alcohol is served. And I was certain that it was not a good idea for a foreigner to take a 17-year-old back to his crib. It might not be wrong, but it isn't right.

The pedestrian bridge is a 20-meter span across the six-lane avenue. In the dark of a winter evening, it's a perfect place for drug dealers and pimps to post up, leaning against the railing, waiting for clientele. We passed a handful of dealers and pimps before we wound up in an underground place called the Gipsy Club, a generic Chinese nightclub with loud music and lots of young women. Brian ordered two beers from the bartender, who gave me the stink-eye. There was no one in the joint except for us and the girls.

"We're a bit early, mate," Brian said. "Most nights, it gets moving around twenty-three hundred or so." I was annoyed that he used military time.

A few girls came over and exchanged giggly chatter with Brian. They couldn't have been 18 years old, wearing training bras and braces on their teeth. I squirmed.

"Which one do you fancy?" he asked.

"I dunno."

"You don't have to decide now. It's not that kind of place."

"I don't know how the game works."

"You take her back to the hotel and give her a proper fucking, d'ya know what I mean?"

"That's ambiguous at best."

"If one of the girls likes you, which is quite possible, she'll be on about it."

"You mean she'll let me know?"

"Right."

"These chicks look really, really young, Brian."

He smiled and said, "They are. That's the appeal, mate."

There were at least a dozen women, girls, females—lounging in the booths, pecking away at cell phones, painting their nails, basically doing nothing but sitting around waiting for the night to get started, applying makeup, and primping each other. The longer I looked, the more I realized that these girls were 18 and older. Nevertheless, it still made my skin crawl just a bit. Instead of an "all right" mood, the vibe was "all wrong."

From the moment I decided to visit Guangzhou, I vowed to avoid hookers. *No chasing tail on this junket. I'm on a different mission.* No matter what, I'm going home alone. No chicks. Period. This was all about the drugs. I wanted to leave the bar right then and there, but I stayed for the experience, nothing more.

Brian was right about the hour and the method. Groups of men began arriving and filling the seats. About two beers later, one of the girls appeared next to me. I don't remember her name, but her face was caked with cosmetics. I'm not a fan of those fake eyelashes. Same with manicures. I don't care about your fingernails. Anyway, I offered to buy the girl a drink. She accepted but said she didn't drink.

Brian got up to excuse himself from the bar. I said I was leaving, too, and he said, "Ah, nah, mate. Have a bit of a look at the floorshow, right? It's brilliant. Hang in there, mate." With another hand on my shoulder, he said something about an early day and catch you tomorrow at Elephant & Castle, round eight, you said? Don't be late.

Feeling on my own, I stopped trying to communicate with the girl and she left. I suddenly got the feeling that every Chinese guy in the bar was staring at me, and as I looked around, *just about every Chinese guy in the bar was staring at me* or had just been staring at me and now looked away to avoid eye contact. I drank my beer and gazed absently at the liquor bottles for a few minutes. The bartender waved me off when I motioned to settle my tab. Brian paid.

Beating it out the front door into the frosty air, I made a beeline for the pedestrian bridge and loitered around the south exit until a black guy approached and said, "What you need, mon?"

"What you got?"

"Hash tonight, brother." He spoke in a deep, velvety, mesmerizing tone. "It's the good stuff. Golden brown. Get you very, very high." *This dude should be a voice-over artist.*

"Can I just get a gram?"

"For one gram, I can do fifty yuan. But if you buy five, one-fifty for the whole thing."

"Just one tonight. Is that OK?"

"Of course." He reached into his jacket and produced an Altoids tin loaded with hash in pre-packaged weights.

After we made the deal, the dealer said, "You new in town? I haven't seen you before."

"On vacation."

"Ah, Guangzhou is excellent for vacation."

"By the way, you ever move other substances?"

"Anything you need, mon," he said, sort of anxiously looking around. "I'll be here tomorrow night. Same time, same place."

"Good to know," I said, shaking his huge, calloused hand.

The next morning, I woke up early and went down to the restaurant in the lobby. I drank two cups of coffee and checked my email. To my surprise, the minimart across the street sold rolling papers. Back in my room, I took two Marlboro cigarettes and shook out the tobacco onto a tea tray. After thoroughly blending the tobacco and hash, I used a folded business card to fill the rolling paper and the blunt end of a pen cap to pack the mixture tightly. Forty-five minutes later, it was the best-looking joint I had ever rolled in my life. I left it to dry on the tea tray while I soaked myself in yet another hot, steamy shower.

I smoked half the joint and got so high that I was afraid to leave the room. Two hours passed. "Yo, chief," I said to myself, "you need to back off this shit. Take it easy. We don't want to be cooped up in the room for eight days."

It was 10:30 a.m. when I started walking from Shamian Island to a part of the old walled city to see an exotic animal market. I knew the basic premise of this market was horrific, but I wasn't ready for emaciated puppies, kittens, and birds in cages—nothing that you might call exotic, like lemurs or Komodo dragons. In a way, I was relieved not to see feline monkeys or lizards. Until I reached the furthest outskirts of the market and found...well, you know. The exotic shit. And I learned from a turtle vendor that the market virtually shuts down during the lunar holiday, and they were freelancers selling their animals on borrowed time. The Real Deal wouldn't be on display until mid-February. I was disgusted with myself for being there.

I spent the rest of the afternoon at Yuexiu Park, where I walked half a mile uphill to an eight-story temple and climbed yet another set of stairs to get to the top. I just didn't understand the temples on hilltops. Still don't. Why make it so difficult to worship? I kind of like the old Catholic idea that you can just roll up off the sidewalk, and the doors are never locked. At any rate, I found a secluded spot and smoked the rest of the hash. Jesus, I was high.

Back at the hotel, I had dinner in the Chinese restaurant before heading upstairs to shower and dress for the evening. Housekeeping had been in my room while I was gone. They replenished my towels, plugged the phone line back into the wall, and left a little heart-shaped chocolate perched on the pillow. I drank the three beers in the minibar, watching CNN, and called room service. Three minutes later: knock-knock. More beer. The service in that hotel was the best I'd ever seen anywhere.

At 7:45 p.m., I jumped in a taxi and arrived at Elephant & Castle right on time. The bartender said, "Your friend just left."

"He did?" I looked at my cell phone. It was 8:01 p.m. "That's strange. Did he say if he was coming back?"

"Maybe in an hour. Probably not. Try Gipsy Club."

"No... I'll have a Carlsberg, please."

The same group of guys were playing pool in the back room. I studied them for a little while and drank the beer. One of the white guys came up to the bar. "Hey, Trixie. Is Lola working tonight or what? *We need drinks back there!*" He shot me a weird look. *Trixie*, I mused.

"Lola comes in at eight," Trixie said.

"It's ten after eight."

"She will come." Trixie quickly tilted her chin up. "What do you want?"

"Gimme two Tsingtao and a Hennessey for the Prince."

"OK. I bring it back to you."

The guy noticed I was staring and turned to me. "Hey," he said. "I don't usually do this, but you're staring at me, and you're white, so let's get it over with. I'm Steve."

"Nice to meet you, Steve. I'm Charlie."

"Are you new in town?" He sucked on the upper rack of his teeth, and for a second, I thought he had dentures. "I thought I saw you in here last night, talking to that Aussie pedophile, what's his name?"

"Brian."

"Yeah, that cunt. You're not with him, are you?"

"Oh no, no, no, no, no... I'm just... Just visiting. Waiting to meet a friend."

"Whatever." He nodded and made a 180-degree scan of the room in the space just above my head. "A friend? Here? Not likely. But anyway, welcome to Guangzhou."

"I was wondering. What are you guys playing back there? It looks like cut-throat, but it's not cut-throat."

"Killer."

"Killer? Never heard of it."

"That's cuz we invented it. You want to play?"

"Sure. But I suck at pool."

"It's not about that," Steve said. "Come on back when you're ready. I'll introduce you to the crew."

I finished the beer and motioned to Trixie that I was going back to the pool table. Again, there was a heavy, pungent aroma of marijuana and/or hash in the air.

"Gentlemen," Steve announced. "This is Charlie. Fresh blood."

The other white guy came forward and said, "Hey, I'm Monty. Steve's a real prick, isn't he?" Monty laughed and put his hand on my shoulder like a frat brother to an esteemed pledge.

Monty pointed to a Chinese guy. "That's Albert." He pointed at two very tall Nigerians. "That's Malik and Jerome. They're *brothers*." Monty started laughing, referring to the 'brothers' remark. Malik and Jerome nodded and smiled. Finally, Monty nodded toward a Nigerian guy in an all-white suit, sitting off to the side of the pool table. "And that's the Prince. No shit. He's a real fucking Prince! He calls the shots in here."

I nodded at everybody because it didn't seem like handshakes were appropriate for the venue. Steve handed me a pool cue and said, "No pun intended by Monty, but here's how we play killer." I missed my first shot badly. I handed the cue back to Steve, shrugged, and looked for a good place to stand and watch.

The Prince had a silver tray in his lap. On the tray were several different piles of tobacco, weed, and hash, as well as rolling papers and a small pair of scissors. While the rest of us played the game, the Prince worked meticulously on a finger-sized joint. When he was finished, Malik came and removed the tray. The Prince put the joint to his lips, and Jerome came forward with a lighter. He took two huge puffs, admired his craftmanship, and said, "Charlie, come. You're our guest this evening. I insist." Malik put an empty chair next to the Prince. I hesitated for a moment.

"Go on," Steve said. "It's a rite of passage if you're going to hang."

I sat down next to the Prince, and he passed me the joint. I took a big draw and handed it to Jerome.

"So, Charlie," the Prince said. "Where are you from?"

"San Francisco."

"Ah, yes, I know it well. My father owns a building there. The Grosvenor Hotel on Pine Street."

"Really?" I was staring at his long, bony fingers and even longer, polished fingernails.

"What brings you to Guangzhou, Charlie? Certainly, it's not the weather."

"I'm here on vacation. I live in Taiwan. I'm here for the New Year holiday."

"Taiwan? Hmm. Yes. Many hard feelings about Taiwan in China."

"You're not fuckin' kidding." I immediately felt stupid for using profanity in front of royalty.

"What do you do in Taiwan, Charlie?"

"I'm a writer for an educational publishing company. We do textbooks and stuff."

"You are not an English teacher?"

"No, sir."

"Monty and Steve are English teachers. Most foreigners in Asia teach *something*, but not you. Why is this?"

"I got lucky and found a writing job."

"I think it is more than that."

I bit down on my tongue for a second before saying, "Do you mind if I ask what you do in Guangzhou?"

"Of course, I do not mind," the Prince said. "My father does business with the local government. I assist him with his business dealings and such." The joint made the rounds, and Jerome handed it back to the Prince. "If there is anything you need while you're in Guangzhou, please do not hesitate to ask. We are friends." He leveled his eyes. "Yes?"

The correct answer to *that* question is, "Yes, we are friends."

The game of killer had come to a halt—it was my shot. Monty called out, "Come on, Charlie. We're fucking waiting on you!" I looked at the Prince and he approved with a slight wave of his hand. I grabbed the pool cue from Monty, took and badly missed the shot. Albert was up next. I leaned against the wall farthest from the Prince. The game continued and Lola showed up to deliver our drinks. Monty and Steve carried the room with their non-stop banter, and I kept quiet and out of the way.

Half an hour later, the mood of the room changed dramatically. A thick, leather-clad Nigerian walked in, followed by a flinty-eyed Chinese policeman. Trailing behind them were two hookers in matching pink dresses. The leather guy approached the Prince, who remained seated, and they spoke in French. The cop stood nearby; the hookers held hands by the door. Jerome, Malik, and Albert formed a semi-circle behind the Prince.

Steve said, "OK, boys. Court is now in session. Let's take a breather while I take care of business." He set the pool cue in the middle of the table. Monty approached me and said, while giggling, "This might take a while. Let's chill out." The Prince, Steve, and the leather guy moved to a secluded table in another part of the bar. The cop walked to the front of the bar and sat down at a small table. The hookers in pink stood by the door and stared at me. Jerome, Malik, and Albert disappeared.

"Lola!" Monty cried out. "Lola, we need drinks! Where is that minx?" He produced half a joint and sparked it up. "God, it's so hard to find good help."

Monty appeared to be in his late 40s, dressed in pick-up-game attire, with bushy brown hair and eyebrows arched in upside-down U-shapes that gave him the permanent expression of amusement. He spoke with a distinct Northern California accent, so it was no surprise when he said he was born in Vallejo and grew up in the Richmond District. Monty was always laughing or telling a joke or making a joke out of something you said. Nothing could be taken too seriously with Monty.

"So, um," I said. "What was all that about?"

"Ah," Monty said. "Just regular business."

"The Chinese guy sitting by the door. He's a cop, right?"

"Oh yeah. He's a cop. The owner brought him in for security." Monty handed me the joint.

"So...it doesn't matter that we're getting high in here?"

"Not at all."

"What's with the gangster in black leather?

"Listen," Morty said. "Man, I'm sorry. I forgot that you don't know Guangzhou. It's like this..."

According to Monty, it all started back with the Opium Wars. Exactly how the Nigerians wound up running the drug trade in Guangzhou, he couldn't be sure, but it involves close ties (read: corruption) between Nigerian royalty and the Guangdong provincial government all the way down to beat cops on Huanshe East Road. To hear Monty tell it, Guangzhou was the most corrupt place in China, and we were sitting in the most corrupt bar in Guangzhou.

Lola arrived. "Lola, baby!" Monty cried. "Have you given any more thought to what I asked you last night?"

"I don't want to marry you, Monty," Lola said.

"Why not?" he guffawed.

"You're a pig, and your wife would be jealous."

Monty rolled his head toward me and said in a mock whisper, "I'm not married." Out of the corner of my eye, I saw the Prince and the black leather guy leave through the front door. The hookers in pink were long gone. Steve returned with a satisfied look on his face.

Monty asked, "How'd it go?"

"It's the shit, man."

"Better than last time?" Steve dropped a small package in Monty's lap.

"Oh, good God!" Monty cried, waving a soap bar brick of brown tar under my nose.

"Suppose I was interested in purchasing a small quantity of that?" I asked.

"Break him off a piece, Monty," Steve said.

Monty gave me a thumbnail-sized chunk.

"How much do I owe you?"

"Forget it," Steve said. "Enjoy."

The conversation was lively, and the game was always contentious, even if I routinely lost and had to re-rack the balls. Monty said they met every night at some point between 6:00 and 8:00 p.m. for Happy Hour and I was welcome to join them (for the duration of my visit, like an invitation to hang).

I could see myself hanging out with these guys—sort of a boy's club, which I prefer to co-ed socialization when drinking to get drunk and doing drugs to get high. I can say stupid things to women after seven beers, which may turn into regrettable actions when I get high.

It was past midnight when I stumbled out of the bar.

In the morning, I stayed in bed until the maid knocked for the third time. Again, I pressed the DO NOT DISTURB button conveniently located in rollover distance above the nightstand and forced myself into a hot shower. I finally made it down to the lobby for coffee just before noon.

The weather was soup-foggy and wet-cold. I was hardly motivated to walk around all day. I loitered in the café for 20 minutes before returning to my room to get high.

Again, it only took a couple of hits before I was really fucking high. Anxious high. Paranoid high. Disturbingly high. I snuffed out the remaining half-joint and left it resting in an ashtray. Struck by a sudden urge to vacate the room, I put on my jacket, grabbed my camera, and took the elevator up to the "rooftop garden" featured in the hotel brochure. It was nothing special. The sky was overcast and dreary. There wasn't much to see except the generic Guangzhou skyline. I took a few pictures and went back to my room.

Much to my dismay, the maid had been back to clean the room, leaving another set of fluffy towels, a dry terrycloth bathrobe, and making the bed. She also emptied the ashtray. The thoughts running through my head were variations of the ultimate "What if?" *What if* the maid recognized the smell or the shape of the joint? *What if* she reported it to the manager? *What if* she was on the phone with the police right now?

It took me a few minutes to calm down. I decided the best thing to do was to stay out of the room for the rest of the day. I grabbed most of my things, except toiletries and a few T-shirts, stuffed them in my pack, and left the hotel. For the first hour, I gave myself a historical walking tour of Shamian Island. Then, I went across the river toward the Beijing Road marketplace. I ate lunch at a hot pot restaurant, where I was inundated with food items I didn't order or recognize. I was slowly coming down off the high.

Around 4:30 p.m., my throat felt scratchy. I bought a lukewarm can of Pearl River Lager from a mom-and-pop and shot-gunned it on the spot. And then another. The shop owner watched me with a mix of wonder and suspicion. I was neither amused nor concerned. I had all but dismissed the maid-joint incident. My only thought was that if the Chinese authorities wanted to find me, they would *find me*. I was free to swallow the sights and the sounds and the experience of traveling alone in China. I reached a mental and emotional plateau. I *loved* walking in China because every step brought a new experience or sensation. I saw myself as the ultimate alien—as if I was truly on another planet, at the very least, in an alternate reality. No matter where I wandered, chances were excellent that I'd see it for the first time. *That's a lot of climbing to see a statue?* No, you didn't come all this way just to see the statue, you came to see everything leading up to it. And everything looks different on the way down, too.

It was sundown when I came across the mosque I read about in *Lonely Planet China*, The Mosque Dedicated to The Prophet. I vaguely remembered the author saying something about 'smooth minarets' and 'non-Muslims are not allowed' and the compound was heavily guarded. I didn't see anybody with guns. I didn't see anybody except a recycling scavenger rifling through the garbage cans across the street. I stood outside the gate and took pictures of the minaret pitched against the twilight sky.

I walked in through the front gate of the mosque. The place was deserted. Well, almost deserted. I wandered around the compound for five minutes and didn't hear or see anyone. There were several empty little rooms set around a central courtyard. I took pictures without using the flash and crept around in the darkness.

Crossing the courtyard to the entrance of the prayer room, I saw massive chandeliers and Arabic script painted on the walls. Royal blue carpet on the floors. Outside was a sign that read: "Entrance to Muslim Only." Many pairs of slippers were lined up just outside the threshold. Inside and to the left, one solitary man was bent over, deep in prayer. I stood and watched for a minute. My heart raced. The man did not sense my presence as far as I know. He raised his upper body every so often but for the most part, stayed in the prone position. Suddenly spooked by a distant sound, I got the hell out of there as fast as I could without breaking into a sprint.

Twenty minutes later, I was at Elephant & Castle, having a beer with Steve at the bar. Steve was from Baltimore, in his mid 40s, divorced, and had been teaching English in China since "me and the old lady parted ways."

Steve was cantankerous in the league of "a cactus is prickly." You had to be careful what you said to him because he could escalate in a heartbeat. That's probably why I liked him. The best thing about Steve was he took ownership of his personality. Of course. I like that in a drinking-slash-drug buddy. You know you can trust this guy with your drug money, but you wouldn't let him within three meters of your girlfriend. I got the impression he was channeling Jack Nicholson in *Carnal Knowledge*, tempered with a dose of circa-1975 Ted Bundy.

I told Steve about my carelessness with the joint in the hotel room.

"You don't have to worry about that," he said. And then he slipped me a small plastic baggie with a gram of brown tar. "Don't say anything. Just take it and enjoy."

Monty showed up. Then Albert. Then the Prince, Jerome, Malik, and a "cousin" named Dexter who just arrived in Guangzhou from Jamaica. We were clustered around the bar making introductions and greetings when the Chinese cop came in and posted up at the door.

The Prince moved to the pool table and we all followed. I was in trouble with Dexter from the moment we met. He was on me like bad breath. Dread-locked and fluent in English, Dexter went out of his way to tell me he was from "Jamaica, mon" and repeatedly pressed a handwritten phone number on a blank business card in my hand. "Now you have my number, mon," Dexter said. "Call me for whatever you want."

"Thanks, Dexter," I said, handing him the three extra cards. "I only need one card."

I was eliminated from the first game of killer after two shots. I stood and watched, cringing. Dexter was a nightmare. He wouldn't leave me alone. Both Monty and Steve tried to diffuse the situation by asking Dexter about Jamaica, but it was hopeless. He would answer their questions directly to *me*. When he wasn't taking his shot in the game of killer, Dexter was in my face. *Do you want to buy some weed? Do you want a Chinese hooker? Why don't you want some weed? Why don't you want a Chinese hooker?* Every question led to another.

At one point, I made eye contact with the Prince. ***Help me.*** He blinked slowly and deliberately and looked in the other direction. After two more games of killer—which I lost on purpose so I had to re-rack the balls, and thus, avoid Dexter for two minutes—I had more than enough. And fuck it, I was flush with hash again. I could return to the hotel room and get high in peace. Dexter started getting a bit more antagonistic, putting a finger on my sternum, talking about some weird "imperialist American" bullshit, and I prepared to exit.

Monty handed me a joint. "Here, Charlie," he said with sympathy. "I don't understand why this dickhead is bothering you. Sorry, I tried."

I took the deepest pull my lungs could muster and went into the men's room. Dexter followed me and posted up at the next urinal, talking non-stop about living in Libya and how he hated the mercenary American government, and George Bush is Satan, and he said, "I can understand why Bin Laden blew up the World Trade Center, do you know what I mean, mon?"

"No, I honestly don't," I said, zipping up my fly. And then I walked out of the bathroom, made a left instead of a right, headed for the front door, hailed a taxi, and went back to Shamian Island.

I stayed away from Elephant & Castle for a few nights, instead cruising around other bars and sights in town. Having the hash made everything so fun and vibrant. There were several interesting experiences and incidents, but nothing special. Certainly, nothing like the characters at Elephant & Castle.

One morning I was having coffee in the hotel lobby, checking my email and reading the news. I received a Facebook friend request from my old friend and bandmate in Chicago, Jason Weisman. We fell out of touch several years ago, not with bad blood, but distance and time. Jase and I hadn't seen each other in nearly a decade. A few minutes after approving his friend request, he popped up on Messenger, and we had a long and lively chat.

At first, Jase didn't believe that I was in China, so I sent him a photo.

"Holy shit, Charlie! You're really in China. That's fuckin' insane!"

Moments like this didn't happen often, but I felt a small twinge of satisfaction with my life choices. And it was great to reconnect with Jason. I missed him.

The final night in Guangzhou, it was me, Monty, Steve, and Albert at Elephant & Castle. I showed up around 6:30 p.m. The Nigerians—and Dexter, thank God—were nowhere in sight. Monty said they had business in Hong Kong and wouldn't be back until next week. It had the makings of a very relaxed evening. At some point, Steve and I got into a discussion about drugs, specifically which drugs we liked and which ones we didn't. Steve, not surprisingly, tended toward the amphetamine side of the scale, while I preferred opiates.

"Can you even *get* cocaine in Guangzhou?" I asked.

"You can get anything you want in Guangzhou."

"From the Nigerians?"

"The Prince doesn't like to move that shit in here. He only moves hash to foreigners. If you want the harder stuff, you have to go down to Jianshe Sixth Road and get it from the street dealers. They're all under his control, so they're totally safe."

"Where the hell is Jianshe Sixth Road?"

Steve scoffed and gave me a puzzled look. "What?"

"I've never heard of that street."

"Yes, you have."

Of course, I knew all about Jianshe Sixth Road. I was just waiting for someone like Steve to willingly take me down there and show me the ropes.

"Come on, I'll show you," Steve said. "Grab your coat."

"Now? I don't..."

Steve was already heading for the door. I grabbed my jacket and followed. We left the bar and took a dozen steps toward the pedestrian bridge. Steve stopped and pointed at the T-intersection of Huanshe East Road and Jianshe Sixth Road. "There it is."

"Oh," I said. "I was up and down that street several times this afternoon. I never saw any dealers there." This was true. I even ate lunch at the McDonald's.

"That's because you were there during the day. They only come out at night." It sounded more like an indictment than a rebuttal.

Jianshe Sixth Road was sometimes known as the foreigner street (*laowai jie*) because many businesses were Western-oriented. In addition to McDonald's, there was Pizza Hut, Subway, KFC, Cold Stone Creamery, Starbucks, a variety of Italian restaurants, and a wall-to-wall gauntlet of shops geared toward both upscale consumers and low-brow locals. The gargantuan four-star Garden Hotel dominated the southeastern corner of Jianshe and Huanshe East Road.

During the day, Jianshe looks like any other street. In fact, this district was quite nice and civilized. At night, the west side of the street transformed into an open-air drug and prostitution market. The drug dealers prowled the sidewalks while the hookers stood in the alcoves of shops that had closed for the evening.

Steve and I crossed the pedestrian bridge and started down Jianshe. Within seconds, the same deep-throated Nigerian dealer from the other night met us in front of KFC. Steve knew him on a first-name basis. "This is Irving," Steve said. "Anything you want, he can get."

"What are you looking for tonight?" Irving asked, looking away, barely acknowledging my presence. Steve wandered off and started talking to a hooker nearby.

"Oh, I'm not really—I don't—oh well, what do you have?"

"I've got cocaine, crack, hash, weed, heroin, ketamine..."

"Brown Sugar?"

"Of course." I had to love the Nigerian accent. "I've got the Brown Sugar. You are a wise man."

"And give me five grams of the hash, too."

"Ah," Irving said, "big spender. I'll cut you a very good deal."

There were three types of heroin available on the black market in Guangzhou *at this time*. Black tar heroin is made for injecting and smoking. I never used black tar because I don't do needles, and smoking black tar (aka chasing the dragon) can be a little messy if you don't know what you're doing—and I don't. The odor of black tar is unpleasant, too. Heroin No. 4, which is known as "China White", is made for snorting and injecting. Both black tar and No. 4 require some additional chemical reaction to make them suitable for injection. China White easily dissolves in heated water. Snorting China White made me nauseous, and you really have no way of knowing how pure it is and what it's been cut with. I called it "China Yellow" and I only did it a few times. The final type is Heroin No. 3, a brown powder and primarily for smoking, known as "Brown Sugar" and has the lowest potency of the three—20 to 30 percent. China White, on the other hand, depending upon how many times it's been cut by middlemen, is 80 to 90 percent pure, and generally speaking, what accounts for the majority of overdoses.

"How much do you want?"

"Just enough for tonight."

"One-fifty yuan, plus the hash, give me three hundred."

Irving reached into the inside pocket of his jacket and produced a tiny ziplocked bag. The dope was brown and crumbly and perfect for rolling with tobacco, and enough for at least two days. I was returning to Taipei the next night, so there was no way in hell I could or would want to finish it all. The best thing about No. 3 is that it doesn't get you too high, so you don't come down too hard, and it's easy to smoke. You can pad the landing by drinking or smoking hash when you feel it start to fade. At least, that's the way it worked for me. Two days of smoking low-potency heroin is not going to turn you into a frothing addict. You might vaguely miss it for a few days—hardly what can be considered withdrawal—but it's a void that can be filled with a couple of bottles of wine.

"This will treat you very well," Irving said. I handed over the money and took possession of the dope. Irving disappeared over the pedestrian bridge.

Steve returned, "Well, how'd it go?"

"Fine. Got what I wanted."

"Great. Let's get back to Elephant & Castle. It's fucking freezing out here."

"Do you know that girl?"

"Know her? Ha. Let's just say we've met."

Back at the bar, we were joined by a new foreigner, Calvin, a short, pudgy Australian dude in his mid 30s who resembled the Little Caesar's "Pizza! Pizza!" cartoon character. Both Steve and Monty were slightly dismissive of Calvin's presence. I don't know what happened to Albert. He was gone. Now that I think of it, Albert and I never had any communication other than handing off the pool cue or circulating a joint.

Steve made no mention of our little escapade down to Jianshe Sixth Road. I toyed with the idea of rolling a joint with the dope, but I was already high enough from the hash and figured it would be best to keep quiet.

Calvin commanded my attention with a bewildering story about his Chinese mother-in-law chasing him out of the house with a meat cleaver. Steve and Monty, having heard the story, tuned out and resumed playing pool, leaving me the sole member of Calvin's audience. He ended the story by saying, "I'll knock that bitch out if she isn't careful. D' you know what I mean?"

"No, actually, I don't know what you mean," I said.

Calvin cocked his head. "Huh?"

"I know what you mean, but *I don't know what you mean.* If you're talking about physically assaulting your mother-in-law, which sounds like a terrible idea, then yes, I understand what you mean. But seeing as how you just told me she threatened you with a knife, and you ran all the way here, I can't make the connection." I repeatedly pointed my index fingers together. "What you're saying doesn't correspond with your actions. Are you speaking figuratively or literally? Just how are you going to knock this woman out? With your charisma?"

"Huh," Calvin said, now cocking his head in the direction of Monty and Steve. "Where did you say you found this guy?"

"We didn't find him," Monty chuckled. "He found us."

The heroin was burning a hole in my pocket. When Happy Hour ended at 8:00 p.m., I bid farewell to the crew and said I'd see them tomorrow, same time, same place. I didn't mention it was my last night in town because I didn't think anybody would miss me anyway. *What difference did it make?* I taxied back to the hotel and got to work rolling a joint.

I smoked cautiously at first—two hits, before snuffing it out. Good choice. The dope was considerably stronger than the shit I used to get in San Francisco. The main goal was to function while high. It's a waste of time to nod out in a hotel room. Back home, I liked to get high and wander the neighborhood at night. I loved how it distorted familiar surroundings with an auratic glow of newness.

It was still early, around 10:00 p.m. when I walked into a well-known spot on Shamian called Lucy's, more of a restaurant than a bar, but it had an outdoor patio with umbrella tables and plenty of Chinese kids employed to ferry the drinks. I had the whole patio to myself. It was good to sit out there and not hear anybody talk about anything. It was Guangzhou in quiet mode.

One thought demanded a recursive loop. *I know what you mean but I don't know what you mean.* Fresh in my mind from the episode with Calvin, I traced it back to the "proper fucking" comment made by Brian

209

at the Gipsy Club. I knew what he meant, but *I didn't*. There was a huge contextual gap between what I was asking and how he answered. The Prince said his father did business in Guangzhou, which leaves a lot to the imagination. I understood what he was saying, but I didn't truly understand. The episodes with Dexter and Calvin. The hilltop temple in Yuexiu Park. *I get it, but I don't get it.* Juxtaposed by Chinglish public signage that seemed nonsensical but made sense. The sign in the bathroom at Lucy's says, "Be particular about social moralities and no relieving of nature everywhere." *Be a civilized human being and don't piss on the floor.* And I mused over the "Request Not Accept Crossing Photo Catch Taking" at the Gipsy Club. *No cameras from this point forward.*

Doing drugs in a foreign country is not necessarily right but it's only wrong if I got caught, which seemed unlikely in a place like Guangzhou. The cut and dried, black and white applies only to questions that can be answered with yes or no. Most of the area out here is gray, a continual swirl of *yin* and *yang*.

I believe in ghosts but remain skeptical when it comes to borders and the duality of life. You are either here or there and once you cross the border to *there*, you're right back at being *here*. My perceptions of language fail to elucidate the "truth" of my experience. My understanding of reality is not what's truly going on. The world *can* change in one day; all the borders and boundaries can be swept away with a good swift kick. And we're back to Korzybski and the maps versus the territories.

All this was coursing through my mind on the patio at Lucy's. I smoked the second half of the joint, drank four or five beers, and sat out there alone until one of the kids came and said they were closing. I paid the bill, finished my beer, and handed the glass to the kid. Then I remained seated until they turned off the lights. It was as good as things get. That's the truth.

14

The End of the Beginning

"I don't think I can hang out with you anymore," Carter Dietz said when I told him about the Guangzhou experience. We were drinking at a beer bar in Ximendeng behind the Red Theater.

"Carter, what? This has nothing to do with you and—this—Taiwan and Taipei and whatever. What's the problem?"

"Do you *not* understand how dangerous that shit is?"

Carter was neither a prude nor a stranger to substance abuse; he just didn't like the implications. If I was willing to take these kinds of risks on a goddamn whim or because I'm too weak to control my habits, then I was a liability. Carter didn't want to be associated with liabilities, and who could blame him? But I wasn't trying to impress him or convert him to my way of thinking. *I was just telling the story. I needed to tell someone.*

"Most of all," Carter said, "I don't want to hear about you locked up in Guangdong, because, frankly, dude, I'm not about to bail you out or visit you." He kicked the leg of my chair and leaned back, moving away from me. Carter was a good kid. I knew he meant well.

"That's fine," I said. "I wouldn't call you to bail me out of anywhere. I'm older than you, obviously. I know what the fuck I'm doing. And second, you don't have any money, either. So, get off your high horse. I just want to talk about it. I'm not trying to sell you anything."

Carter counted his fingers—1, 2, 3—and said, "I can count on one hand the number of people who would have the balls to smuggle drugs into Taiwan, and I'm scared, no, terrified, of all three. You scare me, bro. You make me nervous. I know you're a good guy, but, come on, there's gotta be a limit. There's gotta be a place where you say, 'Oh hell no, I'm not going to cross international borders with a bunch of heroin.' I mean, dude, *who the fuck does heroin?* And any number of cops could be on us right now. Do I want to be associated with some wrecking ball expat who's going to wind up in jail? No! I don't want any part of it!"

"Nobody is asking you to be a part of it, man, I'm just telling you what happened. I have—one, two, maybe three friends, besides you, with whom I could even talk about it. And it wasn't a bunch of heroin—I brought five grams of hash and a tiny bit of heroin. But—but—never mind. I'm not trying to suck you into the vortex of my life, Carter, I'm just giving you a window seat."

"I prefer to sit on the aisle." He folded his arms across his chest.

"OK, I won't talk about it again. Ever. Let's just forget it." I didn't want to lose Carter as a friend, no matter what.

Carter smiled and said, "By all means, Charlie, I mean, I love you, man. You saved me from Global International. But come on, man. Do you even care what happens to you? And I'm not—I fucking swear—I'm not going down with you."

"How could you go down with me? Seriously? Dude..."

From that moment forward, I never talked about drugs with Carter, even though we stayed friends for a very long time.

The relationship with Celeste was doomed from the start and I didn't mind giving it away for the same reason. *Of course,* it was doomed. When I left for Guangzhou, we had a tentative agreement about monogamy: *I promised not to pick up any hookers.* So, I returned to Taipei with sort of a pride. It was a time in life when I conquered my demons of self-discipline and kept my word of honor.

Shortly after my return, Celeste learned that she was chosen for the internship-slash-work exchange program at Disney, and she'd be leaving in April, roughly a month away. I was thrilled for her. In a way, it was a perfect way out for me. I could let her go, free and easy. No remorse, no disappointment. No harm, no foul. I cared for her like an older brother to a younger sister, not a lover.

Celeste said she didn't see the internship as an obstacle to maintaining our relationship. "Lots of people have long-distance relationships," she reasoned, "and it's only six months. I'll be back before you know it."

It's funny to hear how people screw up their lives and lose jobs and relationships by posting stupid shit on social networking sites like Facebook until it happens to you or someone you know. Then it's not so funny anymore. I checked Facebook every time I checked my email, but I was not what you might call an avid user of the site. So, it made sense that I only *once* clicked on Celeste's profile or photos. I already knew what was going on with her. Or so I thought.

While I was in Guangzhou, Celeste went on a four-day trip to Kenting in southern Taiwan, during which time she met a guy and they "had a good time together," as she put it. She vehemently denied anything happened sexually between them and said they were just friends.

That's where we left it until the week before Celeste was due to leave for Disney World. Frankly, I didn't care one way or the other. But the first sign of something fishy was a message from a mutual Facebook friend posted on Celeste's profile, which somehow showed up on *my profile* and mentioned the guy she met in Kenting: a geeky European named Pavlik.

Shortly thereafter, I got a private message from the mutual friend, Nancy, that read: **"Have you seen these?"** and a link to a photo buried deep in one of Celeste's photo albums that frequently went 150 shots deep. Celeste was very aware of the fact I never looked at photo albums. This selection of shots was in the 124-of-133 range. The first was her looking quite chummy with the guy, his arm around her shoulder, standing in front of a palm tree. The next featured them at dinner, again, quite the couple. Here, he's holding her like a fireman carrying a dead child. The next one looked like they were kissing.

I called Celeste and said, "Just be honest and tell me what happened. I'm not mad at you." But she denied, denied, denied. Fair enough.

Another message came from Nancy. It read: **"...and these?"** with a link to a photo album on the geeky European guy's profile entitled "Pavlik's Latest Asian Konquest, featuring Celeste." Not necessarily porn-level, but I can imagine it went there.

Again, another call to Celeste and she denied everything. *Fine, I believe you. Focus on getting ready for Disney.*

Now, I must explain this Nancy chick and her motivation to contact me. I barely knew Nancy, having met her once at Celeste's KTV birthday party near Xinyi-Warner. Nancy and I didn't even have a regular conversation. We became Facebook friends only as a tangential afterthought. So, why would she want to rat on Celeste? It *had to be* between the women. In fact, Nancy was on that trip to Kenting, and she was in the running for Mr. Stud Pavlik's attention. Celeste won out. Nancy was a sore loser.

Now, my suspicions aroused, I clicked again on Celeste's profile and found a seemingly innocent post from one of her friends in Japan, dating back a few weeks. It read (in Japanese): "Are you OK? Let me know how the test turns out." Celeste responded to the message in Chinese characters. And it occurred to me that she never mentioned a test or any kind of problem. I copied the Chinese text of Celeste's response, pasted it in a translator, and...it said, "I went to the doctor. Not pregnant."

Celeste fought the ensuing interrogation every step of the way. It dragged out for a full week. The math didn't add up. If Celeste thought I got her pregnant, she would have told me. And we always used condoms. Therefore, I couldn't have been "the father." She denied, denied, denied. I went back to her Facebook profile and took a good look at her photos. Turns out, I was either blind or incredibly naïve. There were shots of Celeste and Pavlik together all over the place.

Celeste finally broke down and admitted everything including the fact that they "used condoms except for one time." She begged me not to break up with her.

"You don't want a long-distance boyfriend while you're at Disney," I said. "You should fly—be free. There are no strings attached to us. Just go, have fun."

"But what about when I get back? Will you be my boyfriend again?"

"Am I your boyfriend now? Was I your boyfriend when you were fucking that Euro guy in Kenting?"

Celeste caught her breath. "Is there any chance you'll ever want to see me again?"

"I doubt it, but who knows?"

It was tough. I felt stupid yet absolved. Those are hard-to-reconcile feelings. If you've been unfaithful to former girlfriends, you might cut current girlfriends a little bit of slack. To me, an occasional indiscretion—a dalliance, if you will—was not grounds for dumping someone. But Celeste continued to lie about it after she got caught. Getting caught is one thing, but I couldn't abide her refusal to admit the truth. And I know how hard it is to fess up. I would never trust Celeste. I didn't want her as a girlfriend and vice versa. I knew that I would probably feel sad for a little while. I knew what had to be done.

Celeste left for Florida, ironically, on my 41st birthday—it was a Saturday and the first anniversary of my arrival in Taipei. I declined to see her off at the airport with her family. Instead, I spent the weekend on the rooftop, getting sloppy drunk and high, listening to my jams. Had myself a good cry. It wasn't mournful crying—it was cathartic. And it was the first time I'd cried since being reunited with Mao-mao. So much had happened since then. All the emotions passed through me, and I let them run their course.

Monday morning, when Captain Felix walked into the office, I said, "Hey, when are you going to take me to that secret island? You know—paradise for men, hell for women?"

Felix smiled and peered over his aviator glasses. "When do you want to leave?"

"Whenever you're ready."

About the Author

Christian Adams, author of *The Lazy Bastard Guide to Mandarin*, lives in the Philippines with his family. He is also an independent musician and the sole proprietor of Black Sunshine Media.

xtianadams.wordpress.com
blacksunshinemedia.com

www.ingramcontent.com/pod-product-compliance
Lightning Source LLC
Chambersburg PA
CBHW051616120626
46551CB00014B/1818